Alfred Schutz

ON PHENOMENOLOGY

AND SOCIAL RELATIONS

THE HERITAGE OF SOCIOLOGY

A Series Edited by Morris Janowitz

Alfred Schutz

ON PHENOMENOLOGY
AND SOCIAL RELATIONS

Selected Writings

Edited and with an Introduction by

HELMUT R. WAGNER

THE UNIVERSITY OF CHICAGO PRESS

CHICAGO AND LONDON

Standard Book Number (Clothbound) 0–226–74152–4
(Paperbound) 0–226–74153–2
Library of Congress Catalog Card Number: 73–102072

THE UNIVERSITY OF CHICAGO PRESS, CHICAGO 60637
THE UNIVERSITY OF CHICAGO PRESS, LTD., LONDON

Printed in the United States of America

Contents

v

Acknowledgments

As EDITOR of this volume, I wish to express my sincere appreciation of the help and support I have received during the various stages of its preparation. In the first place, I owe thanks to Professor Morris Janowitz for suggesting the inclusion of a volume on Alfred Schutz into the series The Heritage of Sociology and for entrusting me with the task of putting it together. The Committee on Faculty Research of The Colleges of the Seneca greatly facilitated my preparatory work, in 1968, by a Summer Grant. The execution of this project, however, would have been impossible without the continuing support of Mrs. Ilse Schutz. Welcoming the planned publication of a selection of her husband's writings by the University of Chicago Press, she fostered my editorial efforts with valuable advice, with relevant information, and by making available to me various unpublished manuscripts of Alfred Schutz. Most of all, she took an active hand in the long and painful process of disentangling the international copyright complications which held up the production of this volume for a considerable period. For all this, I am deeply indebted to her.

HELMUT R. WAGNER

Introduction

THE PHENOMENOLOGICAL APPROACH
TO SOCIOLOGY

I. *The Work of Alfred Schutz*

TOWARD A SYNTHESIS OF SOCIOLOGY AND PHENOMENOLOGY
The writings of Alfred Schutz constitute the framework of a sociology based on phenomenological considerations. Schutz was not the first thinker to attempt such a synthesis, but he was the first to do it systematically and comprehensively. He brought to this task a thorough acquaintance with the philosophy of Edmund Husserl, a philosophy which represented a radical departure from previous ways of philosophizing. He confronted this philosophy not with sociology as a whole but with a sociological approach which, in its own ways, marked a similarly radical beginning: Max Weber's sociology of action and understanding.

Schutz's first and most fundamental work, published in 1932, was called *Der sinnhafte Aufbau der sozialen Welt*, "the meaningful construction of social reality." It would have merited the subtitle "Husserl and Weber." The work of these two men formed the cornerstones of Schutz's thinking. Further stimulation came from many sources. Prominent among these, in Schutz's earlier period, was the work of Henri Bergson, William James, and Max Scheler; and in his later period that of John R. Dewey, George Herbert Mead, Charles Horton Cooley, and William I. Thomas.

Schutz stood simultaneously in the camps of philosophy and sociology. But he did not develop a "philosophical sociology" as a field within a larger system of sociology as, for instance, Georg

1

Simmel and Max Scheler had done before him. Rather, he transcended these attempts in his lifelong efforts to create the foundations for a complete and self-sufficient system of sociological thought and procedure.

BIOGRAPHICAL NOTE   Alfred Schutz was born in Vienna in 1899, and died in New York in 1959. He served in the Austrian-Hungarian Army during the First World War, and studied law and the social sciences in Vienna. His most distinguished teachers were Hans Kelsen (law), Ludwig von Mises (economics), Friedrich von Wieser and Othmar Spann (sociology). During his study years, he became deeply interested in the work of Max Weber and of Edmund Husserl. After publication of *Der sinnhafte Aufbau der sozialen Welt,* he became personally acquainted with Edmund Husserl, whom he visited repeatedly. The correspondence between the two men ceased only with Husserl's death. Husserl invited him to become his assistant at the University of Freiburg, an offer which Schutz declined reluctantly, due to other obligations.

In 1938, in the face of Hitler's impending occupation of Austria, Schutz emigrated to Paris. A year later, he arrived in the United States, where he joined Alvin Johnson's University in Exile, later renamed the graduate faculty of the New School for Social Research. Except during the very last years of his life, Schutz divided his activities between his academic endeavors and a demanding full-time business position. During his New York years, he enjoyed contacts with such students of Husserl as Dorion Cairns, Aron Gurwitsch, Marvin Farber, and Felix Kaufman, and with such representatives of the German sociological tradition as Carl Mayer, Albert Salomon, and Kurt Wolff. Together with Marvin Farber, he established the International Phenomenological Society, and he joined the editorial board of the journal, *Philosophy and Phenomenological Research* at its inception in 1941. He contributed various articles to this journal as well as to *Social Research,* edited by Alvin Johnson at the New School, and to other journals and symposia. An untimely death interrupted his preparations for a definitive, systematic representation of what he considered to be the structures of the world of everyday life and the prevailing system of relevance in it.

SCHUTZ'S WRITINGS   *Der sinnhafte Aufbau der sozialen Welt,* recently translated under the title *The Phenomenology of the Social World,* was the only study Schutz published while still living in Europe. In the United States he started his writing career, appropriately, with the essay "Phenomenology and the Social Sciences." In all, he published thirty-two titles, most of them originally in English, and a few in French, German, or Spanish. Four more essays were published posthumously. Between 1962 and 1966, three volumes of *Collected Papers* appeared, containing the bulk of his writings since 1940.[1]

One essay by Schutz had not been published in full at the time of the preparation of this volume. Written in 1940 under the title "Parsons' Theory of Social Action," it was a critical review of Talcott Parsons' *The Structure of Social Action.* After various discussions and an exchange of letters with Parsons, Schutz decided to abstain from publishing the essay, but its concluding part appeared a year after his death under the title "The Social World and the Theory of Social Action."

Professor Thomas Luckmann of the University of Frankfort has prepared an edition of Schutz's final work on the basis of Schutz's own elaborate outlines, notes, and written instructions. It bears the title *Die Strukturen der Lebenswelt.* A large segment of this study, which was given its final form by Schutz himself, is called "The Problem of Relevance."

CONTENT AND FORM OF SCHUTZ'S WORK   As a thinker, Schutz was possessed by a single purpose, that of laying the foundations of a phenomenological sociology. In their substance, his writings form an interrelated whole. His first publication all but completely delineated his lifelong concerns; it contained the basic themes and posed the problems for most of his later writings. The latter are essentially elaborations, occasional modifications,

[1]   A complete bibliography of Schutz's writings is contained at the end of this volume.

further clarifications, and extensions of his original position. This internal consistency is the more remarkable since the foundations of Schutz's work were laid in the academic-intellectual culture of the German-Austrian area before World War II, and were reaffirmed during and after a process of personal acculturation to everyday life, business activities, and academic pursuits in the United States.

In form, Schutz's American writings consist of essays independent of each other. Some are systematic and go straight to the core of the author's concerns; some contain empirical demonstrations of selected phenomenological conceptions; some juxtapose the ideas of other writers with Schutz's own considerations; and some are explications of the philosophical foundations of his work. The lack of external coherence of this body of writings is rooted in the very conditions under which Schutz worked. His demanding managerial position allowed him to be a philosopher only in his spare time. This factor alone explains the piecemeal character of his American writings. The shortcomings of this procedure, which he chose as the only alternative to complete silence, were aggravated by the fact that he could not write for one specific audience. On various occasions, he faced audiences of established phenomenologists, of philosophers in general, of a broader intellectual public, of college faculties distributed over various disciplines, of social scientists in general, and of sociologists in particular. Schutz could never assume that his individual lectures and papers had a cumulative effect on anyone but a small circle of like-minded scholars and students. Thus, he could not avoid the various repetitions which are found in the body of his papers. Since most of his audiences were not familiar with the fundamentals of phenomenology, Schutz felt compelled to summarize them before speaking to any specific topic. As a whole, his collected essays convey the impression that he was constantly engaged in the propagation of the phenomenological approach. Only in this manner could he hope to be heard without being grossly misunderstood.

GUIDING POINTS FOR THE SELECTIONS   The aim of this volume is to offer a *systematic representation* of Schutz's thoughts insofar as they are relevant to sociology. Coherent sequences have been selected from his book *The Phenomenology of the Social World* and from about twenty of his essays. These sequences have been topically arranged and combined, regardless of source, to reduce repetitions to a minimum, to bring together scattered treatments of specific topics, and to represent the whole range of the author's thoughts.[2]

Not included are Schutz's technical papers on phenomenology proper and his critical expositions of a number of essentially philosophical writings by men like Max Scheler, Jean-Paul Sartre, and others. Selections from *Der sinnhafte Aufbau der sozialen Welt* have been rendered in the translation by George Walsh and Friedrich Lehnert; selections from essays have been taken from the original publications.

II. *Points of Departure*

THE PHENOMENOLOGICAL BASELINE   In his first study, Schutz confronted Max Weber with Edmund Husserl. Since it would be hard to understand Schutz without knowing something of these two men, their positions will be briefly discussed.

Husserl's ultimate goal was the creation of a presuppositionless philosophy. Its irreducible starting point is given in the experiences of the conscious human being who lives and acts in a "world" which he apperceives and interprets, and which makes sense to him. He deals with this world in the intellectually spontaneous yet active mode of intentionality: There is no phase or aspect of human consciousness which appears in and by itself; consciousness is always consciousness of something. The forms of consciousness are tied to the content of experiences. Experience is attention "directed" upon objects, whether real or imagined, material or ideal; and all such objects are "intended." This is an "immanent process of all experience"; the object is apperceptionally constructed in the synthesis of different "perspectives" in which the object is actually seen or remembered later in typified fashion.

---

[2]   The complete text of most of Schutz's essays can be conveniently found in the three volumes of his *Collected Papers*. See the bibliography.

That this is so can be grasped reflectively; and phenomenology issues from such reflection. Its first step is the elimination of all preconceived notions concerning the ultimate nature of those objects and that reality with which human consciousness is concerned. Husserl insisted on an initial "suspension of belief" in the "outer world," either as it is naïvely seen by an individual in everyday life, or as it is sophisticatedly interpreted by philosophers or scientists. The "reality" of this outer world is neither confirmed nor denied; rather, it is "bracketed" in an act of "phenomenological reduction." What is left after the elimination of all ontological assumptions are the given processes of human consciousness and their "intended objects." The latter, now, are no longer understood as objects in the outer world but as "unities" of "sense" or "meaning" in the "inner world" of the conscious individual. Psychological reduction, then, preserves the whole "world" of human experience as a world of apperceptive "appearances" of objects in the human mind and their concomitant intended meanings. This central concern with subjective experience is twofold: it pays attention to the conscious processes of experiencing itself, to the "noetic"; and it deals with that which is the object of experience, the "noematic."

Husserl did not confine phenomenological reduction to the empirical-psychological level. Results obtained on this level are subjected to a second process of reduction; they are "purged of every empirical and psycho-physical element." By disregarding the "factual side of the phenomena," the "eidos" of the a priori forms of experience is discovered. With it, "eidetic phenomenology" is constituted: "The phenomenological reduction reveals the phenomena of actual internal experience; the eidetic reduction, the essential forms constraining psychical experience."

Finally, Husserl added the ultimate level of a "transcendental phenomenology," bracketing not only the outer world but also individual consciousness. Thereby, he hoped to come "face to face at last with the ultimate structure of consciousness." However, we need not concern ourselves here with this attempt. Its relevance for the phenomenological sociology of Schutz is remote. In reverse, the significance of Husserl's phenomenological psychology for this sociology cannot be exaggerated.

Husserl's phenomenological psychology extends beyond the boundaries of the individual consciousness. It is concerned with intersubjectivity as well as with subjectivity. Thus, he suggested that "a similar 'bracketing' of objective, and description what then 'appears' (noema in noesis), can be performed upon the 'life' of another self which we represent to ourselves, the 'reductive' method can be extended from one's own self-experience to one's experience of other selves." He even spoke of an "intersubjective reduction" of a "common consciousness" to "that which unites individual consciousnesses in the "phenomenological unity of the social life." Lest he be misapprehended, he stressed that "the 'intersubjective,' phenomenologically reduced and concretely apprehended, is seen to be a 'society' of 'persons,' who share a conscious life." Our consciousness of other selves "offers us more than a reduplication of what we find in our self-consciousness, for it establishes the difference between 'own' and 'other' which we experience, and presents us with the characteristics of the 'social life.' " Thus, a further task accrues: "revealing the intentions of which the 'social life' consists." The phenomenologist must not only examine "the self's experience of itself," but also "its derivative experience of other selves and of society."

What Husserl indicated here was nothing but the task which Alfred Schutz had set himself when he attempted to find a phenomenological foundation for that "sociology of action and understanding" which Max Weber had promulgated in the last decades of his life.[3]

THE SOCIOLOGICAL BASELINE   Weber had outlined his particular approach in a set of paradigmatic statements, published in their final form only after his death.[4] He started by defining soci-

[3]   For Husserl's own exposition of his philosophy, see his article "Phenomenology" in *Encyclopaedia Britannica*, 14th ed., vol. 17 (Chicago Edition, 1946), pp. 699–702. The passages quoted above are from the article.

[4]   *Wirtschaft und Gesellschaft*, 3d ed. (Tuebingen: J. C. B. Mohr, 1947), pt. 1, chap. 1, "Soziologische Grundbegriffe," pp. 1–30. We decided to work from the German original rather than the Henderson-Parsons or other available translations, none of which are free of occasional shifts or meaning.

ology as "a science which attempts to understand social action interpretatively and, thereby, to explain it causally in its course and effects." Action is human conduct which may consist of physically tangible activities, of activities of the mind, of deliberately refraining from acting, or of intentionally tolerating actions of others. In each case, however, human conduct is considered action only when and insofar as the acting person attaches a meaning to it and gives it a direction which, in turn, can be understood as meaningful. Such intended and intentional conduct becomes social if it is directed upon the conduct of others. This, in a nutshell, is Weber's conception of subjective meaning as a crucial criterion of human action. It was because of this conception that Schutz saw in Weber's theory of action a bridge which would allow him to pass from the realm of phenomenology to that of sociology.

Weber insisted that sociology is, or at least should be, centrally concerned with the subjective meaning of social conduct. But he used the term *subjective meaning* in more than one way: he designated by it the meaning which the actor himself ascribes to his conduct as well as the meaning sociology imputes on the conduct of an observed actor. In the latter case, he again envisaged two possibilities: either the sociologist tries to find what would be a typical average of the meaning numerous persons ascribe to the same type of action; or he constructs an extreme, or ideal, type of such conduct, showing its characteristics under "pure" conditions. Essentially, any ideal type of action is based on the assumption of strictly rational conduct on the part of the ideal-typical actor. Weber was predominantly concerned with "rational action" not because he assumed that it was the most frequent type of human conduct, but because it was that type which is most accessible to outside analysis. However, he allowed for two additional types: traditional conduct, following the lines of custom; and nonrational behavior, actually a residual category which he failed to analyze properly.

Weber's famous concept of *Verstehen*, or understanding, is closely connected with his theory of subjectively meaningful conduct, designating in fact nothing but the grasping of the subjectively intended meaning of such conduct by somebody else, notably a sociologist. Understanding may be empathic or rational. As sociologist, however, he was primarily concerned with rational understanding. Such understanding may issue from the direct observation of an actor and thus constitute "actual understanding." Or it may be based on the underlying motivations for the observed action; in this case, it is "explanatory understanding." A motive is nothing but a "context of meaning" which appears as the "reason" for human conduct first of all to the actor himself, and secondarily to the observing sociologist. In paying attention to motives, the sociologist is involved in motivational interpretation.

There are two senses in which, according to Weber, sociologists may speak of the validity of findings related to subjective meaning and motivation. The motivational interpretation of an action is "meaningfully evident" but not causally certain. However, it becomes "causally adequate" when the sociologist convinces himself of the existence of a chance that a certain succession of meaningful behavior, when enacted by numerous persons at various times, will always or frequently occur in the same fashion. No causal laws of human conduct can be established; a sociologist deals at best with "typical chances" that certain factual constellations, accessible to observation, will lead to certain courses of social action.

In agreement with this postulate, Weber defined a social relationship as the conduct of several persons who, according to a given context of meaning, direct themselves toward and orient themselves upon each other; it exists "completely and exclusively" in the chance that social action takes place in a predictable meaningful fashion.

CRITICAL SYNTHESIS   Schutz had been quick to realize the significance of the approaches of both Husserl and Weber, and never wavered in his conviction that each of them had posed the crucial questions in his field. Nevertheless, he subjected each of their specific conceptions and solutions to long and painstaking scrutiny, thereby showing the ingenuity and importance of some, the need for revision and extension of others, and the insufficiency of still others.[5]

Thus, after long years of intensive study of the latest publications of Husserl, Schutz came to the conclusion that Husserl's repeated attempts at solving "the problem of intersubjectivity" on the level of transcendental phenomenology had ended in failure. Furthermore, he came to the conclusion that Husserl "was not conversant with the concrete problems of the social sciences," a fact which hampered him greatly when dealing with social relations and social groups.[6] As sociologist, Schutz was well equipped not only to spot such shortcomings but to overcome them, and to develop some of Husserl's rudimentary concepts into foundation stones of a sociological theory of the social world. In the course of this endeavor, he made various significant contributions, notably, his treatment of the phenomena of typification in the spheres of everyday life. Last but not least, he cut through the Gordian knot of the problem of intersubjectivity, disposing of it in a way which was as ingenious as it was simple.

Dealing with Weber thoroughly and, in a sense, definitively in his first study, Schutz recognized the brilliance as well as the shortcomings of the German sociologist's fundamental yet overcondensed theory of social action. Weber had never pursued his general methodological and theoretical problems further than the actual requirements of his own substantive work demanded. Thus, he operated with tacit assumptions which themselves called for systematic investigation, and he made various of his key terms do multiple duty without analyzing the differences in their application to different levels of sociological reasoning.

Schutz's critique of Weber did not result in the refutation of any of the latter's basic postulates. Rather, it amounted to clarifications, to the exposure of hidden meanings, to the development of individual concepts beyond the point at which Weber had

---

[5]   Weber's theory of action was expressed in a paradigmatic sketch offering a bare minimum; Husserl's conceptions were painstakingly developed in detailed, highly technical analysis without always leading to definite conclusions.

[6]   See item 1959c of Bibliography, p. 88.

broken off his analysis, and to the establishment of the different meanings some concepts assumed when used in different contexts. In this sense, Schutz simply developed Weberian conceptions in the direction indicated by Weber himself. Yet, by adding insights gained from phenomenological psychology, Schutz's analyses of such concepts as subjectively meaningful action, observational and motivational understanding, subjective and objective interpretation, themselves became relevant contributions to that interpretative sociology which has its roots in Weber's work but has grown largely beyond him.[7]

In terms of its most fundamental points of departure, the work of Schutz may be considered a synthesis of Husserl and Weber. But this synthesis was accomplished in long processes of selection, adaptation, and modification of relevant components of the theories of both, resulting not in a simple recombination of these components, but in their transformation into the building stones of a self-sufficient phenomenological-sociological theory.

III. *The Framework of Schutz's Phenomenological Sociology*

The selections included in the present volume should speak for themselves. Yet, they are only parts of longer essays or chapters, and the materials occurring under a common heading may stem from different sources. They do not always provide their own introduction; neither are individual selections necessarily linked to each other by explicit transitions. To assist the reader, the following survey of Schutz's basic thought closely follows the order in which the materials from Schutz's writings are themselves presented in this volume.

THE SCOPE OF SCHUTZ'S THINKING   In content, Schutz's ideas and conceptions may be subsumed under five central topics: the phenomenological foundations for the kind of sociology he envisaged (part I of this volume); the structure and functioning of

[7]   Schutz's critical appraisal of Weber is found in *The Phenomenology of the Social World*, especially in chapters 1, 4, and 5.

human consciousness and its social ramifications (parts II and III); the structure and functioning of the social world as a set of mental constructs and their dual roots in individual experience and pre-given patterns of social relationships (part IV; the characteristics of different realms of human experience (part V); and the theoretical-conceptual as well as methodological foundations of a phenomenologically oriented sociology (part VI).

The following scheme outlines these topics and their major subthemes in the form and sequence used in this volume.

I. *Phenomenological Foundations*
   1. Exposition and appraisal of a broad range of Husserl's phenomenological conceptions, notably those of relevance for the social sciences.
   2. Exposition and development of the conception of the Life-World, a conception which is central to the phenomenological approach to sociology.

II. *The Cognitive Setting of the Life-World*
   3. Discussion of subjective experience in daily life and the interpretation of the world which springs from it.
   4. Analysis of the socially given means of orientation and interpretation at the disposal of the individual in everyday life.
   5. Investigation of the factors which make for selective attention to aspects of the environment experienced, and the ensuing spheres and systems of relevance, prominently including the processes of typification and the application of type concepts.

III. *Acting in the Life-World*
   6. Development of a subjective theory of human action, dealing with action as a process anchored in the motivational functions of "reasons" and "goals," and guided by anticipations in form of planning and projecting.
   7. Clarification of the problems of volition, choice, freedom, and determinism within the context of human action.

IV. *The World of Social Relationships*

8. Analysis of interactional relationships issuing from intersubjective processes as expressed in We-relations.

9. Investigation of the intersubjective processes of face-to-face communication among fellow men under special consideration of the linguistic forms of these processes.

10. Exposition of the characteristics of indirect social relationships among anonymous contemporaries, and the social linkages between contemporaries and their predecessors on the one hand, and their successors on the other.

11. Treatment of the problems of the social distribution of knowledge.

V. *Realms of Experience*

12. Development of William James's conception of multiple universes and realities into a comprehensive theory of multiple provinces of meaning, focusing on the juxtaposition of the paramount reality of daily life to the provinces of meaning of dreams and phantasies on the one hand, and those of scientific cognition on the other.

VI. *The Province of Sociology*

13. Exposition of the roots of sociological reasoning and sociological methodology in the world of everyday life. Development of basic methodological procedures for sociologists, centering on the formation of concepts in general, on procedures of typification in particular, and the combination of both in the construction of ideal types.

14. Application of the phenomenological approach to specific sociological topics and areas of inquiry.

(i) PHENOMENOLOGICAL FOUNDATIONS Phenomenology is concerned with that cognitive reality which is embodied in the processes of subjective human experiences. In setting up the corresponding frames of reference of his philosophy, Husserl developed a considerable number of concepts. Most of them present difficulties to the reader who is not steeped in the highly unconventional ways of phenomenological reasoning. Schutz, therefore, was concerned with a careful explanation of those of Husserl's concepts which were relevant for his own studies. The opening group of selections[8] consists of a general appraisal of the significance of Husserl for sociology, followed by Schutz's rendering of the sociologically crucial phenomenological concepts of consciousness, experience, meaning, conduct, "attention to life," and "acting in the outer world."

In this context, Husserl does not figure as the sole creator of the fundamental building blocks of phenomenology; Henri Bergson and William James occur as independent contributors. As early as 1889, Bergson published his first investigations into the nature of the experience of time: the durée, or "inner time," of subjective experience in contrast to the "outer time," or "cosmic time," measured by clocks. James, one year later, contributed his no less fundamental explorations of the "stream of consciousness," the flow of thoughts, notions, and inner expressions together with their associational and emotional "fringes" or "halos"; the actual process of experiencing consciousness which is as remote from the precision of a syllogistic proposition as is Bergson's durée from the ticking of a metronome.[9]

Since experience is always experience *of* something, we turn from experiencing to the content of experience.[10] According to Husserl, all direct experiences of humans are experiences in and of their "life-world"; they constitute it, they are oriented toward it, they are tested in it. The life-world, simply, is the whole sphere of everyday experiences, orientations, and actions through which individuals pursue their interests and affairs by manipulating ob-

---

[8]   See chap. 1, this volume.

[9]   Henri Bergson's *Essai sur les données immédiates de la conscience* was published in 1889. William James's volumes *The Principles of Psychology* followed in 1890, containing the chapter "The Stream of Thought." Edmund Husserl's first truly phenomenological study, the second volume of his *Logische Untersuchungen*, came out in 1901. These three studies, eventually, gained equal importance for the development of a phenomenological approach to the field of sociology.

[10]   See chap. 2, this volume.

jects, dealing with people, conceiving plans, and carrying them out.

Schutz focused on this life-world from various angles. First, he analyzed the "natural attitude" with the help of which man operates in the life-world: a stance taken in recognition of the hard facts, the conditions for his actions as encountered in the objects around him, the will and intentions of others with whom he has to cooperate or otherwise deal with, the impositions of customs and the prohibitions of law, and so on. This stance is essentially pragmatic, prevalently utilitarian, and meant to be "realistic."

Second, Schutz dealt with the dominant factors which circumscribe the conduct of any particular individual in the life-world. At any moment of his practical life, a man finds himself not simply in a specific situation which contains the limitations, the conditions, and the opportunities for his pursuits; this situation is an episode in his ongoing life. He stands in it as a person having gone through the long chain of his prior life experiences. Both the content and the sequence of these experiences is unique to him. [At any time,] the individual finds himself in a "biographically determined situation." Thus, subjectively, no two persons could possibly experience the same situation in the same way. Most of all, each has entered this present situation with his own purposes and objectives in mind, and appraises it accordingly; and these purposes and the concomitant appraisals are rooted in his past, in his unique life history.

Third, Schutz dealt with the means by which an individual orients himself in life situations, his "store of experience" and his "stock of knowledge on hand." He cannot interpret his experiences and observations, he cannot define the situation in which he finds himself, and he cannot make any plans for even the next minutes without consulting his own stock of knowledge. Schutz showed that this stock is structured in various ways. In any particular situation, some of its elements are very relevant, others more marginal, and still others irrelevant. On the other hand, certain items in this stock of knowledge may be precise and distinct, others vague and obscure. As a whole, an individual's stock of knowledge is by no

means coherent and free from contraditions. As long as incoherent and contradictory elements are not brought to bear on the
same situation, the individual may remain blissfully unaware of
them. The same pragmatic bent prevents the individual, as long as
he remains in the natural attitude, to seek systematic and logically
clear knowledge about anything beyond the requirements of his
practical operations and plans, which, frequently, assume routine
character.

(ii) THE COGNITIVE SETTING OF THE LIFE-WORLD   According to phenomenological theory, each individual constructs
his own "world." But he does this with the help of building blocks
and methods offered to him by others: the life-world is a social
world which, in turn, is prestructured for the individual. Thus, we
proceed to Schutz's analysis of this interplay between an individual's efforts to comprehend the social world around him and
the cognitive prestructurization of this world itself.[11]

The individual takes the social world around him as much for
granted as the existence and use or avoidance of natural objects
or animals found in his natural environment. This world, then, is
given to him. Given to him, with it, are the interpretations of the
manifold phenomena, relationships, and so forth, of the social
world, as developed by the cultural "in-group." These interpretations, taken as a whole, form the "relative natural conception of
the world," which, in turn, is based on a "central myth."[12] This
world view contains not only the broad interpretation of the place
of the community among other human communities and in the
realms of nature, cosmos, and the supernatural, but also the
many customs and norms regulating human conduct, plus the
many recipes for practical behavior in social as well as technical

[11]   See chap. 3, this volume.
[12]   Schutz borrowed the first of these terms from William Graham
Sumner, and the third one from Robert M. MacIver. The second one comes
from the German philosopher, Max Scheler, who spoke of the *relative-
natürliche Weltanschauung*, a term roughly equivalent to the "ethos" or
"world view" of American anthropologists. In his translation of the term,
Schutz used the terms "conception of the world" and "aspect of the world"
alternatively. In this introduction, the first version is used throughout.

matters. Yet, where sociologists like Sumner and Durkheim saw this whole cultural superstructure as a deterministic and coercive mechanism, Schutz emphasized the subjective meaning of a person's membership in his community. This meaning springs from the efforts of an individual to achieve a definition of his own place, his general role within the community and, especially, within the various subgroups to which he belongs. Thereby, Schutz showed that even the socially most stereotyped cultural ideas only exist in the minds of individuals who absorb them, interpret them on the basis of their own life situation, and give them a personal tinge which the reporting anthropologists so often ignore.

The question, then, is how the manifold private interpretations of the components of the relative natural conception of the world, in any cultural community, combine into a common world view. Schutz emphasized that such a unity of outlook depends, first of all, on the belief of the members of the community that they share their views about the world. Second, it depends on their using the same standardized expressions and formulations when applying or explaining those views. In this sense, as Schutz expressed it, the in-group arrives at, and maintains, a collective self-interpretation, representing a common, inside view of the community. The members of any neighboring cultural community, having their own relative natural conception of the world, view the first community strictly from the outside. Their own community, in turn, occurs in the outside view of their counterparts. Thus, the outside view of other communities becomes part of the relative natural conception of the world of any in-group.

Again, Schutz brought these considerations back to the level of subjective meaning. In his revealing study "The Stranger,"[13] he analyzed the problems of orientation and adaptation which befall a person who, having been raised in one cultural community, is transferred to another one. He comes with a fixed (outside) picture of the host community and finds that it does not prevent his becoming disoriented, while his old notions of the conduct of everyday affairs prove to be largely useless. Thus, he is forced first

[13]   *American Journal of Sociology* 49 (1944):499–507.

to become an observer of the ways of life of the host community, and second to reconstruct, piece by piece, at least those sets of rules for practical conduct without which everyday life would be impossible for him. His reception by members of the host community, in turn, reflects his attempts at adaptation from the outside. On the one hand, his position is considered one of uninvolvement. On the other hand, his acceptance of routine behavior is felt to be void of the underlying "spirit" of the native community. Therefore, he remains the man who cannot be trusted; his loyalty to the in-group remains in doubt.

Of specific sociological relevance, in this context, is the following observation. If detachment is characteristic of "the stranger," he becomes the one who, as observer, is able to offer an "objective" view of the host community: there is no objective meaning of group membership outside of that established by a person who views the cultural community from the outside.

To this point, the selections from Schutz's writings have amply indicated that the individual, in his orientations within the lifeworld, is prodded and guided by instructions, exhortations, and interpretations offered by others to him. If he constructs his own view of the world around him, he does so with the help of the raw materials offered to him in this constant exposure to follow men. Both the exposure to these cultural materials and their selective and interpretative acceptance of them, presupposes a common language as a means of communication between persons as well as an instrument of cognition for the individual.[14]

In his treatment of language as a universal culture medium, Schutz was mainly interested in the vernacular, the actual everyday language of people within their groups and communities. He treated it not in terms of its mere technical aspects but in its broader meaning contents. On the one hand, its terms, phrases, and syntactic forms, in themselves, amount to a kind of preinterpretation of the world named in these terms, characterized by these phrases, and described with the help of its grammatical and syntactic forms. On the other hand, these terms, phrases, and forms

[14]   See chap. 4, this volume.

are endowed with particular meanings, and they are surrounded by associational and emotional fringes. Some of these additional and superimposed meanings are essentially private, particular to one person or a small circle of intimates; others are typical of specific groups and strata, occupations or age and sex groups; and still others belong to the linguistic community as a whole, yet cannot be learned by the foreigner from a dictionary or grammar book.

Among categories pertinent to the problems of expression and communication, Schutz, using the spade work done by Husserl, dealt specifically with the concepts of mark, indication, sign, and symbol. It is typical for the concrete forms of any of these categories, that they must appear in some physical form: they must be things to be seen, sounds to be heard, or other objects of perception by man's senses. Yet, it is also typical of them that the physical form they take in any particular case is more or less accidental. Every specific mark, sign, etc., takes on a physical appearance, but none of these appearances in itself is a mark, sign, etc. Their physical appearance is merely a potential vehicle of meaning. Whatever shape it takes, a physical appearance becomes a mark or sign solely by virtue of the meaning some human, or group of humans, attaches to it. There are no marks or signs as such, but only marks or signs for somebody.

The selections on this topic do not include Schutz's discussion of symbols, which presupposes considerations to be offered in a later context. The other three categories, in Schutz's writings, assume the following specific characteristics.

Marks are subjective, personal reminders, used by individuals in order to simplify their return to a task previously abandoned, or to remind themselves of something. Marks should be distinguished from indications, which are objects, facts, or events not set up as signs but whose presence is taken by someone to indicate other objects, facts, or events otherwise not noticeable. The indicated event may be considered to be simultaneous with the appearance of the indication, like fire and smoke; it may precede the indication, like footprints in the snow; or it may follow it, as rain follows a halo around the moon. Signs, by contrast, are either artifacts that are made or used by someone in order to communicate some idea to somebody else, or expressive actions serving the same purpose. A sign, then, points back to some expressive and communicative intention of its user, and it points forward to somebody "reading" the sign and getting its message. When artifacts serve as sign vehicles, such as direction signs or pieces of printed or written communication, an indeterminate time-span may separate the actual giving of the sign and its reception. By contrast, when expressive and communicative actions serve as vehicles, intention and realization of communication become simultaneous. In each case, however, the recognition of the sign as sign and its correct, that is, its intended meaning, depends on the use of the same objective sign system by both parties. Thus, a direction sign gains meaning from the geographical context comprising, at the minimum, both the place at which the sign is located and the place to which it points. Similarly, the words in verbal messages gain their meaning from the linguistic system which form their objective matrix.

The use, definition, and discussion of the concepts of marks, indications, signs, and symbols has been beset by ambiguities. In his contribution to the Fourteenth Symposium in Science, Philosophy, and Religion, in 1954, Schutz exposed this confusion and offered a remarkable clarification of the issues.[15] Most important, he separated the concept of sign from that of symbol, terms which are frequently used synonymously, as Schutz himself had used them in 1932.[16] Now he showed that it is imperative to make a terminological distinction where there is a factually relevant difference. Symbols, according to him, are signs of a second order, or signs of signs, as we shall show later. Schutz's clarifications, by the way, make it clear that the application of the term, symbolic, in the "symbolic interaction" label for the social psychology of George Herbert Mead, is an unfortunate choice. This is not because it means the use of the term "symbol" where Schutz would use the term "sign," but because it ignores the distinction between

---

[15]   The contributions and discussions of this conference were published in the following year. See item 1955*b* in the Bibliography.
[16]   See 1967, pp. 118ff.

two substantively distinct categories of expressive and communicative vehicles of meaning. This, again, would be of minor consequence were it not for the fact that Mead himself dealt not only
with ordinary communication but also with problems of artistic
expression and thereby advanced from the sphere of signs to that
of genuine symbolism.[17]

The selections from Schutz's writings found in the last part of
the section on the cognitive setting of the life-world return from
the general characteristics of vehicles of expression and communication to some pertinent aspects of their actual use, a use which
is always selective.[18] What, in any given situation, is formulated,
communicated, and understood, is only a fraction of what could
be noticed. Not everything present in a situation is relevant to the
persons involved in it. In fact, some of the factors in a situation
impose themselves upon the actors and thus constitute imposed
relevances. Others are singled out by the individual as important
to him now; these assume volitional relevance.[19]

During the very last years of his life, Schutz devoted considerable time and effort to the further exploration of the "problems of
relevance," going far beyond his earlier treatment of this problem.[20] Aside from the distinction between imposed and volitional
relevances, highly important in itself, he analyzed three distinct
kinds of relevances: motivational, thematic, and interpretational.

---

[17] For Mead's position, see George Herbert Mead, *Mind, Self, and
Society* (Chicago: The University of Chicago Press, 1934), pp. 147–49,
passim. The author of the present introduction hopes to demonstrate his
point in a critical study of the basic resemblances and differences in the
theories of Mead and Schutz.

[18] See chap. 5, this volume.

[19] In an as yet unpublished manuscript, *Die Strukturen der Lebenswelt*, Schutz spoke of *"auferlegte Relevanz"* and *"freiwillige Relevanz."*
The literally correct rendering of the second adjective would be "voluntary," but we consider "volitional" a term that comes closer to the intended
meaning of the phrase.

[20] In a posthumously published essay (1966a), Schutz offered a
highly condensed representation of the final version of his conception of
relevance. An extended treatment of the problem is contained in the book-
length manuscripts which, at the time this introduction was written, were
still awaiting publication.

Since it was not possible to include in this volume a sufficiently condensed statement on these matters by Schutz himself, a short characterization of these three kinds of relevance is offered here.

Motivational relevance is governed by a person's interest, prevailing at a particular time in a specific situation. Accordingly, he singles out the elements present in the situation which serve to define the situation for him in the light of his purposes on hand. This motivational relevance is imposed insofar as he has to pay attention to certain situational elements in order to come to terms with them; or it springs from the spontaneity of his volitional life: he feels free, that is, unhampered, to define the situation in accordance with his plans and intentions. Motivational relevance of either kind works satisfactorily only in situations whose general features and ingredients are sufficiently familiar.

If this is not the case, the situation cannot be defined in a pragmatic fashion, that is, by way of the recombination of sufficiently known elements. Thus, the motivational tendency toward action must be suspended, at least temporarily. The situation has become problematic. Now, the individual must concern himself with the recognition of the problem he has on his hands. He must turn from a potential actor into a potential problem solver. To do this, he must define what the problem is. It has gained central relevance for him; it has become the theme of his cognitive efforts. Therefore, Schutz designated the relevance of the problem as thematic relevance. Of course, what elements in which situation produce a problem for a specific individual, depends on his pre-given interests. The unknown or problematic in a situation becomes relevant only insofar as it blocks the forming of a definition of the situation in accordance with the person's present intentions and plans. Thus, instead of proceeding with his plans, he must concentrate on cognitive, investigative activities. Solving the problem has gained priority over the original project.

The third kind of relevance, called interpretational by Schutz, occurs as an extension of the second one. The recognition of the problem itself, its formulation as a problem on hand, necessitates further interpretation. A new interpretation, however, can only be accomplished by putting the problem itself in the larger context of the frustrated actor's knowledge, which, he surmises, has a bearing on the understanding of the problem. If the theme of the problem can be sufficiently explained by the routine knowledge at his disposal, interpretation occurs quickly, and action can be resumed. However, if the person in question cannot come up with a routine solution of the problem, he must make deliberate efforts to arrive at its satisfactory interpretation before he can even move, in additional deliberate efforts, toward its actual solution. Whatever he singles out as potentially important for these efforts, falls into the domain of interpretational relevance.

Our selections from earlier writings of Schutz contain these distinctions in rudimentary form. Thus, he spoke of imposed and of intrinsic relevances, the latter being the "outcome of our chosen interests" and resulting from a free decision to solve a problem, and so forth. The term, then, is close to that of volitional relevance. In addition, we discover hints at motivational, thematic, and interpretational relevances. But, in their substance, the selections offered pick up the topic of relevance with the analyses of other differentiations. Speaking of the realm of everyday life, Schutz argued that any specific interest, leading to the establishment of a problem, brings about a sorting-out of one's given knowledge into various zones or regions of decreasing relevance. There is a zone of immediate, primary relevance, comprising elements of knowledge which have to be clearly understood in order to allow a person to master the developing situation. This is the region of the know-how, of techniques and skills in the broader sense. A second zone is mediately connected with the first, for instance, because it furnishes ready-made tools or other help for the attainment of the projected goal: I must know what tools are available, but I do not have to know how they are produced. And I must know what expert to consult, without having the expert's knowledge. A third zone of relevance comprises regions which, "for the time being," have no connection with the prime concerns. Schutz called them relatively irrelevant; they may, however, become mediately relevant later. Finally, Schutz spoke of a zone of absolute irrelevance, knowledge which we are convinced neither has nor ever will gain any relevance for the problem on hand. Schutz stressed that these zones are not closed regions but rather diversified, odd-shaped configurations.

Moving into the realm of sociological analysis proper, Schutz paid attention to social systems of relevance, that is, relevances which in any cultural community are part of the social heritage. They are taught to the young generation as such. Given its cultural hierarchy of values, any social and cultural group establishes its own "domains of relevance." These domains constitute a particular hierarchical order. As a rule, they are heterogeneous: the criteria for what constitutes achievement in one domain are not necessarily identical with those of another domain. If, for instance, technical achievements and religious concerns form two different domains of relevance, we surmise that engineering skills are irrelevant for religious achievements, and vice versa. This holds regardless of whether the domain of technical or that of religious relevance is recognized as the more important one. In the first case, technical principles would dominate the relative natural conception of the world of the community; in the second case, religious ones. The individual with all his personal problems and his actual relevances, of course, is found acting in a social world which has already provided these broad domains of relevance, and he will orient himself upon them.

This treatment of the problem complex of relevances, within which men find their bearing in the world of everyday life, leads us to the consideration of additional means which make this world cognitively manageable. Its myriads of phenomena, each of them a unique occurrence, are sorted out into a limited number of classes: similar phenomena are considered the same, called by the same name, and considered alike in important characteristics. The world is a typified world, said Schutz, and he dealt extensively with its typifications. The corresponding selections provide access to this topic via the discussion of the typification of objects, animals, and so forth. This is followed by a short elucidation of the role played by language in typification. It shows that even mere naming constitutes typification. Then comes another short statement that nobody could possibly account for any of his experiences without resorting to typifications.

Individual typifications have social implications. Schutz pointed out that various of the pet terms of sociologists, such as system, role, institution, etc., refer back to typifications made and used by individuals. Yet, in reverse, most of these typifications are socially preestablished. In a final selection, Schutz referred to the close tie between typification and relevance: men would be unable to recognize what is relevant and what belongs to which domains of relevance, were it not for their acquaintance with "the socially approved system of typifications and relevances." Taken together, these passages should demonstrate the way in which Schutz mediated between the primary sphere of immediate human experience and the derived spheres of preestablished cultural interpretations, be it in form of the given linguistic system, be it in form of prescribed hierarchies of relevances.

Schutz benefited greatly from William I. Thomas's famous conception of the definition of the situation. Following Thomas, he used it both in order to describe an individual's idiosyncratic attempts at orienting himself in untypical situations and his acceptance of the culturally preestablished definition of typical situations. On the other hand, Schutz's theory of relevance provides a set of motivational underpinnings for Thomas's dictum; it invites its expansion in a direction which promises to open up new possibilities for its social-psychological application.

(iii) ACTING IN THE LIFE-WORLD   So far, we have concentrated on Schutz's dealing with the cognitive aspects of the life-world. We are now able to focus on his treatment of active and dynamic aspects of this world of everyday life.[21] The next group of selections, then, is concerned with the problems of human action, including those of motivation in general, and of specific planning. Initially, Schutz's definition of three key terms is given: *conduct*, a term reserved for actually or potentially meaningful active experiences in general; *action*, a term designating conduct which has been "devised in advance"; and *working*, a term referring to action which has been planned in order to bring about

[21]   See chap. 6, this volume.

a change in the outer state of affairs with the help of bodily movements.

Proceeding to the subjective driving forces behind human action, we encounter Schutz's theory of motivation. Here, we are indebted to him for a highly relevant contribution: the exposition of the two-pronged character of motivation. On the one hand, men act from goal-directed motives, which reach out into the future. Schutz called them "in-order-to motives." On the other hand, men have, and are concerned with, "reasons" for their actions. These reasons are anchored in past experiences, in the personality a man has developed during his life. Schutz named them "because motives." He insisted that the subjective meaning of motives must be clearly distinguished from their objective meaning. In the ongoing experience of carrying out an action according to his preconceived plan, the actor directly experiences his in-order-to motives. Therefore, they are essentially subjective. By contrast, when acting, he is not aware of his "because motives." He can grasp them only in retrospect, in an act of reflection, which may but does not necessarily occur after the act has been finished. On the other hand, even an observer may be able to reconstruct an actor's "because motives" from the accomplished act. Therefore, argued Schutz, this kind of motive is essentially objective.

From here, the selections proceed to Schutz's treatment of "conscious" conduct in contrast to "nonconscious" behavior. An action, as conscious conduct, is distinguished from all other conduct, primarily by the existence of a guideline for it, the "project" of the action, its operational plan. The project, said Schutz with John R. Dewey, is a "dramatic rehearsal of future action"; an imagining or phantasying of the planned action as already finished. Projects, of course, are based on various degrees of knowledge of the factors involved; they may be rather precise and detailed, or they may exist in the form of a relatively vague outline. In any case, they are different from the actual result of the action: the execution of an action always adds to or modifies the project.

Insofar as action is based on conscious planning, it has frequently been called rational. The next selections show Schutz following up the equivocations of the term *rational action*. In view of the existing ambiguities, he considered Weber's concept of rational action an ideal not attainable in everyday-life conduct. Of course, he did not deny that men make rational choices in terms of their relevant knowledge on hand. Yet, he preferred to call everyday action characterized by such choices reasonable rather than rational, making allowances for the unavoidable shortcomings of practical knowledge. No individual, probably, is ever to have knowledge of all actually and potentially relevant factors in those situations in which he "works" toward the realization of his plans.

Planning is anticipation of future events. Typifications play a role in all anticipations. Basing himself on Husserl, Schutz explained that they depend on two typical "idealizations"; that of "and so forth and so on": what happened in the past can and will recur in the future; and that of "I can do it again": I can repeat my actions. With these idealizations, men express their confidence in the basic structure of the life world: it remains unchanged, it can be relied on in future conduct. This is so even though any experience has its "horizon of indeterminacy," making absolute certainty impossible. Going beyond Husserl, Schutz explained the remaining uncertainty in terms of two factors. First, anticipations are necessarily based on typical expectations in typical contexts. Actual conduct, however, at best approaches these typicalities; it makes for deviation of results from anticipations. Second, during the execution of a project, the actor's system of relevance itself undergoes changes. Consequently, he sees the finished result, in retrospect, in a different light from that in which he saw its imagined result at the outset. Foresight differs from hindsight.

In three of the last four final selections of the present section, Schutz specified the character of projecting. It is not simply fancying or phantasying of a future state of affairs. Rather, it is "motivated phantasying." As such, it is guided by pragmatic considerations: the phantasy is of practical, realizable nature, and it occurs with the intention of actually carrying out the project. Motivated phantasying, in addition, occurs in the larger context of a person's long-range goals and interests. Any concrete project is but a small segment in the individual's hierachy of plans: plans for the hour, for the day, for longer periods, and for life; but also plans for leisure, for subsistence, and so forth.

The presentation of Schutz's theory of action, motivation, and projecting would be incomplete without offering his position on the question of free will and determinism in human conduct.[22] Like all exponents of interpretative sociology, he considered man a being who, in principle, is free to decide on the course of his actions, or to decide to refrain from acting. This holds, most of all, for those actions which are considered voluntary, that is, which belong to the spheres of volitional rather than imposed relevances. The meaning of such actions springs just from "the freedom to behave one way rather than another." Of course, the action itself is irreversible. Once completed, it is "closed and determinate."

Yet even in the realm of imposed relevances, man's actions are not completely predetermined. Even in the most coercive situation a man can decide not to act as ordered, if he is willing to accept the consequences of disobedience.[23]

According to widespread opinion, freedom of choice implies the existence of at least two possibilities, and the actor decides to accept one or the other. On the basis of Bergson's early investigations, developed further by Husserl, Schutz demonstrated that this is not necessarily so. Rather, choices occur in step-by-step processes. On each level, immediate, small-scale alternatives are considered and either chosen or rejected. Later decisions of this kind may lead back to earlier steps, bringing about their revision. Thus, it may be added, the freedom of choice turns out to be the freedom to construct any project, before its enactment, in such a loosely coherent process, a process composed of whole chains of partial decisions. In certain cases, this process may be characterized by a considerable wavering between small-scale alternatives. Yet in retrospect, this same process would occur, to the actor, as a unitary act of choice between two large-scale alternatives. Or, to use Husserl's terms, the polythetic process of the construction of a project, once completed, turns into a synthetic act of choice.

[22]   See chap. 7, this volume.
[23]   This follows directly from Weber's conception of human action, which includes the alternative of not acting, and especially from his characterization of the coercive relationship of domination: ". . . it cannot mean anything but the chance of having an order obeyed" (Max Weber, *Wirtschaft und Gesellschaft*, p. 29).

Another group of selections shows Schutz's concern with the experience "of doubt, of questioning, of choosing and deciding, in short, of deliberation." Without having come to doubt the adequacy or correctness of some elements of his everyday knowledge, a person would not involve himself in deliberation and choice. In his discussion of choice, Schutz started with ideas formulated by John R. Dewey, even though he could not accept the latter's conceptions of habit and stimuli as the basic ingredients of human conduct. Instead, he introduced Husserl's distinction between problematic and open possibilities. The first kind arises from a predicament of experience: external phenomena, which come to the attention of an individual, may be experienced in ambiguous forms. Thus, doubtful situations arise for the individual; situations apparently containing mutually exclusive tendencies, each of them equally plausible. As a consequence, if a person faces such an ambiguous situation, he will oscillate between possibilities and counterpossibilities. His indecision will last until he finds additional evidence in favor of one or the other alternative, or else his own interests and motivations push him in one rather than the other direction. By contrast, open possibilities are not ambiguous but merely indeterminate. For instance, I may assume that the back of an object is of the same color as the front; but, as long as I do not or cannot check this, my assumption is nothing but an "empty anticipation." It lacks substantive corroboration.

Two further selections deal with the subjective processes involved in "choosing among objects" and in "choosing among projects." Such choices occur within the larger processes of defining situations. By selective definition, we may say, some of the manifold open possibilities contained in a situation are converted into problematic ones. That is, they are singled out for attention and treated as a problem to which a tentative answer has to be found. The difference between choices among objects and choices among projects is simply the following: objects are externally given and, in this sense, belong to the sphere of imposed relevances; projects, however, are of the potential actor's own making; thus, they are controlled by volitional relevances.

A final selection in the present section focuses on the "weight" an individual may assign to each item in a set of multiple possibilities. Such weighting, of course, depends on his given interests, both momentary and long-range ones. It decides not only which of a number of alternative immediate goals is to be preferred, but also which of possible alternative courses of action leading to the same goal may be adopted.

The selections combined under the heading of "Acting in the Life World," deal with motivation, "rationality," planning and projecting, freedom of choice, and deliberation. Doubtless, the reader of this section will realize that all of these conceptions apply to human action in general, be it individual or social. According to Weber, as confirmed by Schutz, both types of action refer to actions of single persons. The difference between them rests solely in the object of the action in question. Individual action is directed upon nonsocial objects, be they things of nature, artifacts, or ideas. Social action occurs when, according to the intention of the actor, action is directed upon other persons, who are seen by him as conscious human beings. It itself, then, remains one-directional.

(iv) THE WORLD OF SOCIAL RELATIONSHIPS   Schutz's considerations of both the cognitive and the active aspects of everyday life in terms of individual experiences have already shown that the orientations and the conduct of individuals in the life world are greatly influenced by preexisting linguistic forms and cultural orientations, not to speak of the existence of other human beings. Schutz, of course, proceeded from a preliminary individualistic perspective to the direct analysis of social relationships.[24] Social interaction involves the social action of at least two people who orient themselves upon each other. And living in the world of everyday life, in general, means living in an interactional involvement with many persons, being entangled in complex networks of social relationships.

The phenomenologically most basic problem, here, is that of intersubjectivity. Husserl himself had realized that the answer to this problem was crucial for his whole philosophy. However, his

[24]   See chap. 8, this volume.

repeated and highly penetrating attempts at solving it on the ultimate level of his transcendental phenomenology were found to have been unsuccessful. Schutz, after a painstaking analysis, decided that Husserl's line of attack on the problem was misplaced. He suggested that intersubjectivity should be treated as a "fundamental ontological category of human existence," a precondition of all immediate human experience in the life-world,[25] to be accepted as something which is unquestionably given with the apperception of other individuals in their physical appearance.

In the life-world, Schutz started his argument, intersubjectivity is no problem. The individual takes the existence of others for granted. He perceives their bodies and their bodily movements, including the speech sounds they produce; all these are directly presented to him. Simultaneously, and spontaneously, he endows the sensory configuration of the other before him with psychological life. He takes it for granted that this life exists within or "behind" the observed movements; the observed movements are spontaneously associated with and taken to be expressive of it. In the individual's experience of others, perception and assumption are fused into one. The sensory experience of a person by another, then, is at once endowed with consciousness, feeling, and the like, all similar in kind to one's own consciousness and feeling. In the technical terms of phenomenology, the given presentation of the other's physical appearance is necessarily paired with the sensorily not given appresentation (see Glossary) of his human nature.

Schutz took care to explain that immediate experiences of others arise in a "communicative common environment," a situational environment which two (or more) persons share who are able to communicate with one another. Although experienced from different subjective vantage points, this (interactive) environment is filled with objects and events apperceived by both. Consequently, the interactive and communicative relationship between them allows for mutual understanding and consent: what happens in the common situation is experienced simultaneously and in com-

25   See Schutz's essay "The Problem of Transcendental Intersubjectivity in Husserl" *Collected Papers* III:82.

mon. Of course, the situation is elliptical: it has two subjective foci. Each of the persons in it lives through his own experience of the situation, of which the other is a part. But he not only experiences himself in the situation, he experiences the experiencing of the situation by the other. This is the experience of the "We." Schutz condensd his description of the phenomena connected with this We-experience into the "general thesis of the alter ego": "The alter ego . . . is that stream of consciousness whose activities I can seize in their presence by my own simultaneous activities." Schutz emphasized that this general thesis constitutes a fundamental frame of reference for both phenomenological psychology and sociology.

The cognitively most conspicuous feature of intersubjectivity, of course, is mutual understanding. The next selections offer Schutz's analysis of this concept. At the outset, he dealt with the ambiguities connected with the common use of the term, understanding. He ferreted out three ways in which it may be said that the action of someone is "understood" when he has no intention to communicate with others; and five ways when he uses linguistic signs with communicative intent. Yet "the only strict meaning of the term" refers to grasping what is going on in the other's mind. Only in this case, asserted Schutz, may we speak of "genuine subjective understanding." Such understanding may be achieved by imaginarily putting oneself in the place of the other. Thereby, the Thou becomes "the other I." During the process of one's actual involvement in a communicative common environment with somebody, the other I occurs in immediate vivid experience. While this touches on empathy, it goes beyond it because the other is experienced as a being of its own, not a reflection of the experiencing person's self. Empathy is reduced to a minimum when understanding another person is attempted reflectively in retrospect. This, according to Schutz, is the only course open to a person who deals with the conduct of another who has no intention to enter into a communicative relationship with him. An understanding of him, under this condition, can only occur in form of the imputation of a subjective meaning to the course of action observed.

Proceeding further, Schutz asked the question, what is actually understood when we speak of subjective understanding? He argued that such understanding does not necessitate sympathetic introspection; neither does it demand a grasping of the complexities of another individual's total personality. But in all circumstances it must be understanding of the other's motivations: Subjective understanding is motivational understanding. Its extent may be limited to the actual requirements of given concrete interests in others within specific situations. At a minimum, that is, in the case of purely factual dealings, one merely looks for the typical motives of typical actors, thereby moving out of the sphere of genuine subjective understanding into that of predefined conceptions. At the maximum, that is, in the closest personal relationships, mutual subjective understanding will reach deeply into the inner lives of the persons concerned. Subjective understanding, then, ranges from the nearly complete typification of motives to the highest degrees of human intimacy.

As Schutz showed further, the dynamic pattern of mutual understanding is that of the "reciprocity of motives." A social actor, in directing himself to another person, expects to bring about a certain action by that person. The desired and expected reaction of the other, then, is the in-order-to motive of the first actor.[26] If the other understands this intention and responds, the in-order-to motive of the initiator of the interaction becomes his because motive. While at first answering because a question was asked, however, the second actor may in turn address the first one out of a now awakened interest of his own. Having thus established an in-order-to motive for himself, he provides a because motive for the first person.

Schutz complemented the thesis of the reciprocity of motives with that of the reciprocity of perspectives. The latter, we may say, functions as the general framework of the former. As mentioned before, the communicative common environment is elliptical: one situation, two subjective perspectives. Each of the persons involved, however, deals with this characteristic of the situation by reasoning that, were he in the other's place, he would experience the common situation from the other's perspective, and vice

[26]   This is strongly reminiscent of Mead's conception of "calling out the response of the other."

versa. Furthermore, he assumes that the relevances connected with their common or complementary purposes relegate the coexisting individual differences in the two perspectives into the domain of relative irrelevance.

According to Schutz, simultaneous involvement in a communicative common environment constitutes an at least temporary We-relationship. Alternately, he specified this involvement as face-to-face situation. Thereby, he took a leaf from the writings of Charles Horton Cooley, even though he did not follow the latter in restricting the term *We-relationship* to intimate face-to-face contacts.[27] In the next set of selections, Schutz attended to the development of Thou-orientations and the emergence of We-relations. In its "pure" form, a Thou-orientation springs from the grasping of the existence of the other person in face-to-face interaction; it manifests itself in an intentional turning toward the other as a living and conscious human being. If the Thou-orientation of one person is reciprocated by the other, if both turn intentionally toward each other, a We-relationship results and is experienced as such. It is expressed in their mutual awareness of each other, and it constitutes a usually sympathetic participation in each other's lives, even if only for a limited period. Additional selections, fitting the same context, deal with the complex processes of conversation in We-relationships, and with the manifold forms of directly experiencing others in face-to-face situations, as opposed to the reflective awareness of the We-experience in retrospect.

Face-to-face involvement with others is the dominant form of social encounters. But, occasionally, anyone may find himself in everyday situations in which he does not actively participate: he finds himself in the role of an observer. Schutz's treatment of observation in everyday life is added here as an aspect of his analysis of the life world, which gains additional importance for the later discussion of the observational method in sociology.

[27] We are touching here upon what may be one limitation embodied in the phenomenological approach as developed thus far: its strong rationalistic bent. Schutz, for instance, considered the polar distinction between primary and secondary relationships conceptually expendable.

A person who accepts the role of observer remains outside the on-going interaction which constitutes the we-relationship on hand. More particularly, his orientation toward the observed actors is one-sided. He is separated from the direct experience of reciprocal intentions and motivations, which is characteristically theirs. Therefore, he can but indirectly interpret their motives. He may, for instance, in phantasy transpose himself into the roles of the interacting partners, and think of motives he himself would have were he in their places. But, also, he may merely resort to pre-established typifications, viewing the observed persons as typical actors in typical situations. Finally, he may analyze the observed acts, trying thereby to infer what motives would satisfactorily account for them. If the observer is a genuine observer, he remains detached, takes no sides, has no stake in the outcome of the ongoing interactive process.[28] Thus, he must be considered objective by definition. Because for Schutz, the objective point of view is simply the point of view, the perspective, of the uninvolved observer.

The discussion of interaction would be incomplete without a discussion of intercommunication.[29] The next group of selections deals with Schutz's considerations of the ways in which men make themselves understood by each other with the help of verbal exchanges.[30] Thoughts are expressed by combinations of words. Words, in order to be communicated, require a vehicle for their transmission from one person to the other: sounds that can be heard, gestures that can be seen, written messages that can be read. These vehicles are signs; they are endowed with meanings by the person producing them. In order to serve their communicative purpose, however, they must be received by another person, as carriers of the meaning intended by the giver of the sign. Inter-

28   This attitude is in sharp contrast to that of another kind of apparent observer: the spectator at an athletic contest. He, as a rule, is a partisan, roots for "his" team or "his" man, and is not an observer at all, but a vicarious participant in the action going on in the stadium.

29   The term *intercommunication* may sound redundant. However, we insist on its use in order to indicate clearly that what Schutz meant by communication was a two-way street, a genuine exchange, and not the one-directional outpourings of the mass-communication media.

30   See chap. 9, this volume.

communication results when a response is forthcoming in the same fashion, and an exchange develops.

While all communication depends on the use of vehicles, the use of particular vehicles may be relatively irrelevant. This is most obviously so when the content of the communicated ideas tends to be rational and factual. Such thoughts easily can be correctly transmitted in various (modern European) languages; in each language the message may be spoken, written, or printed; and any number of available alphabets may be used. In intercommunication, as mentioned before, the user of the sign preinterprets it in terms of the expected interpretation by the person addressed. This, of course, presupposes the utilization of an interpretational scheme which is known to all the persons involved; it includes sets of common abstractions, standardizations, and typifications, both those that belong to the formal body of the language and those that are particular to specific linguistic subcommunities.

Schutz paid particular attention to the intersubjective characteristics of direct intercommunication, those occurring in the "vivid presence" of face-to-race relations. The selections on this topic close with samples of Schutz's discussion of gestural expression, visual expression, and musical communication. The analysis of the latter is a most original and exciting part of Schutz's analysis of intercommunication. He, himself an accomplished musical performer, derived from this specific analysis the general concept of a "mutual tuning-in relationship between the communicator and the addressee" in all other forms of intercommunication.

Like Cooley, Schutz saw in face-to-face relations the prototype of all social relations. Yet, he paid full attention to the realities of modern life in which many links between men are of mere indirect character.[31] The ensuing relationships are derived and indirect. In such relationships, the other person is felt only as a remote originator of some act accomplished possibly far away and long ago, such as the writing of a book I am now reading. Practically, relationships of this kind are of an unending variety.

All direct relationships are situational affairs, and turn into

---

[31]   See chap. 10, this volume.

indirect relationships when the face-to-face involvement ends. The transition from the direct to an indirect experience of others may be gradual: a parting friend fades out rather than disappears in a flash.

As Schutz discussed further, indirect relationships fall into extended continuum patterns of growing anonymity. They range from the region of persons I have encountered and may encounter again to that of artifacts which merely bear witness of the one-time existence of their entirely unknown makers.

Schutz called persons with whom we have, had had, or will have, face-to-face interchanges, our fellow men. Fellow men are within our direct experience: present, past, or potential. Persons who coexist with us in time but do not enter in any direct relationship with us, are called contemporaries. Insofar as we deal with them, we do so in an "indirect We-relationship." We acquire knowledge of specific contemporaries in various ways: we remember somebody we have met in the past; somebody describes another person to us; in the extreme case, we infer the existence of others merely from cultural objects. If we orient ourselves upon remote or even anonymous contemporaries, we display what Schutz called a They-orientation.

In many cases, such as the utilization of commercial products, "they" remain completely in the background. If we think about them at all, it is only in terms of general types: automotive engineers, automobile workers, and the like. Thus, as Schutz said, "when I am They-oriented, I have 'types' for partners." The They-relationship, then, consists of mutual albeit rather general and possibly completely anonymous apprehension of remotely connected "partners."

Schutz designated the total (potential and actual) sphere of They-relationships as the "world of contemporaries." This world is complemented by the "world of predecessors" and possibly that of successors. Indirect relationships are not necessarily tied to contemporaneity. The author of the book I am reading now may have died long ago; the object I am concerned with at the moment may have been made by an unknown person in a past century. Both belong to the world of my predecessors. In reverse, I may anticipate a world of successors. Thus, a person making a will may not only assume that his immediate heirs will outlive him, but he may decide what part of his estate is to be given on to the as yet unborn children or even grandchildren of his heirs.

The world of predecessors, of course, is completely determined. It consists of irrevocable facts which have influenced our present. The world of successors, by contrast, is "nonhistorical and absolutely free." Its anticipation is speculation, not prediction: the future does not unfold according to immutable historical Law.

With the discussion of indirect social relationships, we have entered the spheres of macrosociology, that is, of the societal "system" of the distribution of labor and functions, the cohesion and maintenance of the whole in and through myriads of actions and interactions of myriads of individuals. Schutz dealt with this complex of sociological analysis essentially from the cognitive angle. Therefore, he was greatly concerned with the problems of the social differentiations of knowledge which is part of the structural differentiation of society. A group of selections pertinent to this topic forms the final part of the section on social relationships.[32]

If we reject the notion that a social system is a self-contained giant mechanism in which individuals serve as mechanical parts, the question arises: How do the subjective decisions and actions of individuals, and their differentiated but always limited and partial relationships with one another result in "society" with its, relatively speaking, quite astonishingly high degree of cohesion and order? From the starting point of phenomenology, the answer must be sought in the intentions and orientations of these individuals, guided by their knowledge of those spheres of social life which are relevant for their own existence. Since nobody can possibly know all, it becomes a matter of the agreement and combination of the highly partial, very segmented, and often vague knowledge of individuals. This, in a word, is what Schutz called the social distribution of knowledge.

Even within smaller social units, members differ in their knowledge of the life spheres of the group. What they share with others

[32]   See chap. 11, this volume.

is part of the group's "world within common reach." This world, strictly speaking, is a zone of overlapping relevances, leaving out part of each individual's total world within reach. But, what is within common reach presupposes a minimum of agreement on the part of the individuals concerned. However, this "common" knowledge will not have to be identical in thoroughness and detail: it may range from the pragmatically limited common-sense knowledge of the "man in the street" to the knowledge of the expert. In certain matters, the "well-informed citizen" occupies an intermediary position between the two. What Schutz said about zones of relevances applies here in a new way: each man, in terms of his whole life situation, approaches expertness in some area or other; but he is and remains the "man in the street" in many others; finally, he may strive for additional enlightenment in a few.

The two sections "Acting in the Life-World," and "The World of Social Relationships," comprise the bulk of these selections from Schutz's writings. They contain Schutz's sociologically most relevant considerations. Together, they offer simultaneously an approach to and an interpretational framework for the establishment and treatment of the subject matter of a sociology proceeding from phenomenological considerations. The two terminal sections deal with (1) the relationship in which sociology itself stands to its subject matter, the life-world; and (2) the theoretical and methodological instruments and procedures of a sociology thus determined.

(v) REALMS OF EXPERIENCE The strength of the phenomenological approach lies in its point of departure: the experience of the world of everyday life. In making this world the basic subject matter of sociology, Schutz did not deny the existence of other realms of human experience; he merely asserted its inescapable ascendancy over them. Sociological analysis itself transcends everyday-life experience. It is a metasocial endeavor which is rooted in experiences within the life-world yet transcends it in a particular fashion.

Sociology and, for that matter, any scientific or rational-logical approach to phenomena of common human experience, constitutes but one way of transcending the "realities" of the life world. There are many others. For this reason, Schutz was concerned with the general aspects of the transcendence of everyday experience.[33] On the one hand, he considered some of the means and instrumentalities by which it is achieved and explained. On the other hand, from his analysis of some specific realms of transcendence, he derived the basic characteristics of all nonpragmatic realms of experience, and established their general linkage to the world of everyday life.

By transcendence, Schutz did not mean metaphysical concerns, but experiences reaching beyond and lying outside of the total meaning context of the life-world. The experience of transcendence is part of everyday life. Man accepts as unquestionably true that the world existed before he was born, and will continue to exist after his death. He is convinced of the existence of a physical universe in its quasi timelessness and its expansion toward an outer limit, possibly infinity. Above all, however, he accepts the social world as a whole, including the large regions forever beyond his grasp and experience; and he accepts its historicity, its extensions into both the past and the future. He often copes with such transcendences by constructing, or accepting, ordered systems of interpretation of the meaning complex in question—"nature," "society," and so forth. These interpretative "systems" are themselves meaning complexes of a transcendental order; they assume the characteristics of "realities" of their own. Reference to such realities demands the use of appresentational signs of a higher order. Schutz reserved the term, symbol, for the designation of such signs.

In this, he followed the suggestions of the German existential philosopher Karl Jaspers.[34] What meaning attaches to the Jaspers-Schutz conception of symbol? An ordinary sign, in the sense of our earlier definition,[35] is a bipolar term of reference, consisting of the term which names the thing or event, etc., and the thing which it names: the name evokes the idea of the thing; the thing or event

[33]   See chap. 12, this volume.
[34]   Jaspers, *Philosophie* (Berlin: Julius Springer, 1932), vol 3, chap. 4.
[35]   See subsection ii above.

evokes the name. The name itself is an object or event in the outer world: a sound combination, a written word, or whatever, referring to another object or event in the outer world. In matters transcendental, however, the "thing" meant is not located in the spheres of the experienced reality of the life world. The name-thing pair now refers to a third member, namely, the idea meant by the symbol. Or, as Schutz said, a symbol is the sign of a sign.

Realms of symbolism may be of an unending variety, ranging from religious symbolism to the metalinguistic symbolism of rationally constructed and strictly logical systems, such as those of mathematics. In between, we find the realms of dream interpretation, of poetry, and many others. Schutz illustrated the symbolic interrelation between man and cosmos by the Chinese Yang and Yin principle, that between the sacred and profane by Greek mythology, that between men and Society by political symbolism, that between artistic expression and content by poetry, and that between the phenomena of nature and the "ideally isolated systems" of science by the corresponding metalinguistic devices.[36] It is characteristic of these and other possible realms of symbolism that they refer to experiences and ideas which are not ostensibly evident and therefore cannot be grasped, explained, or exposed by the appresentational name-thing combination of the sign; they require a more complex scheme of expression.

The initial selections offer a more extensive exposition of the Jaspers-Schutz conception of symbol, and they illustrate the connection between universal areas of symbolization rooted in existential human conditions, and the cultural varieties of their expression. This is followed by another set of selections, dealing with a variety of realms of experience. William James was the first to offer a penetrating treatment of the "various orders of reality" within which man lives, the "many worlds" or "sub-universes" of human experiences.[37] Schutz accepted these fruitful suggestions,

[36]   Factually, Schutz based himself on the works of Marcel Granet, Bruno Snell, Eric Voegelin, T. S. Eliot, and Goethe, plus Philipp G. Frank and Herman Weyl. See 1955*b*, pp. 180–83, 190–93.

[37]   James, *The Principles of Psychology* (New York: Holt, 1890) vol. 2, chap. 21, "The Perception of Reality," pp. 283–324.

replaced James's terms with the more appropriate one, "finite provinces of meaning," and carried the analysis further into the realms of social experience. He agreed with James that, for the *experiencing* individual, each of these provinces of meaning appears as unquestionably real yet is incompatible with the others. James had argued that, on the whole and in the long run, the various sub-universes of reality are subjugated to the "paramount reality of sensations." Schutz added that the "multiple realities" of nonpragmatic experiences are inferior to the "paramount reality of everyday life" and, in a sense, remain dependent on it. Thus, the world of dreams is very intermittent and extremely variegated; with his awakening, man returns to a much more continuous, coherent, and enduring world of daily life. In general, the hard facts and realities of the life-world tend to assert themselves over against, and penetrate into, the realms of daydreams, art, and so on. Yet, as long as the experience lasts, its peculiar "style" dominates: dreams, daydreams, and the like, suspend the laws, causalities, contingencies of everyday life, and we never challenge this suspension while dreaming, etc. The province of scientific reasoning, too, has its own characteristic style. In contrast to the realms of phantasy and free-floating imagination, "pure science" at least aims at knowledge for its own sake, operates with its own brand of rationality. It consists of purposive yet nonpragmatic intellectual action, follows systematically established plans, and subjects itself to rigid rules of logic and procedure.

In a still unpublished study, *Die Strukturen der Lebenswelt,* Schutz expanded the discussion of the dependency of other realms of meaning on the paramount reality of everyday life. While the immersion in a nonparamount realm of reality is total and the return to the paramount reality of everyday life constitutes a "leap" accompanied by a "shock" of varying intensity, any expression of the experience itself must resort to symbolic means. And these means are objects and events in the sphere of everyday life. For instance, the creative activities of artists occur technically in this sphere. He who paints uses canvases, colors, brushes, etc.; he who writes novels or articles must use paper and writing implements. Thus, a kind of simultaneity of two realms of meaning occurs.

What is to be achieved in the artistic or philosophic-scientific realm must be technically executed with the means available in the life world. As long as the creative or rational-intellectual activity goes on, the "accent of reality" is put on it, and the reality of the life world is hardly noticed. Yet, it makes itself felt: while the writer works, his body gets slowly tired and hungry. Eventually, the physical states of his body intrude into his consciousness; he will stop and rest, or eat. Or he is interrupted suddenly: the ink in his fountain pen has run out; the typewriter ribbon gets entangled; he has used the last sheet of paper; somebody bursts into the room with a lot of flourish and noise. These realities of the life world assert their imposed relevances, and push him out of the realm of his nonpragmatic pursuits. Thus, he must step back into the life-world.

In this way, other provinces of reality remain within the reach of the paramount reality of everyday life, are liable to interference, and cannot be completely separated from the life-world. Schutz's analysis of the working of the social sciences, as will be shown later, demonstrates that this applies to them as well. However, as fields of ongoing activities, they are not only of the dualistic character described; they are linked to the life world in still other ways.

(vi) THE PROVINCE OF SOCIOLOGY   The last group of selections covers Schutz's view of sociology as a province of meaning dominated by the philosophic-scientific style of thinking and governed by the quest of knowledge about matters social.[38]

Following Max Weber, Schutz was an exponent of interpretative sociology.[39] In the first of these selections, Schutz addresses himself to the question, Why should the subjective point of view be preferred in the social sciences? Dealing with the positivist-behaviorist schools of thought who reject this view, he made it

[38]   See chap. 13, this volume.
[39]   The term *interpretative sociology* was introduced by the late Howard Becker in order to characterize collectively the various sociological orientations which called for a subjective interpretation of social phenomena. (Some writers, including the translators of Schutz's *The Phenomenology of the Social World*, prefer the form *interpretive sociology*.)

clear that, not for all but for quite a few problem areas of sociology, two questions will have to be answered: (1) What does this social world mean for me the observer? and (2) What does this social world mean for the observed actor within his world and what did he mean by his acting within it?

Schutz made clear that he accepted the idea of a set of general methodological principles valid for the natural as well as the social sciences. But he argued that the logical positivists were not at all justified in their claim that only specifically natural-science procedures constitute scientific methods. He saw the sociological undertaking as an "exploration of the general principles according to which man in daily life organizes his experiences, and especially those of the social world." In elaboration of this, he suggested ways by which to utilize the method of *understanding* within the framework of a subjective sociological approach. The understanding of the observed social actors' meanings and motives provides the raw material for sociologists. The latter have to construct their objective concepts on the basis of the typifications used by these actors in their everyday affairs.

The consideration of specific methodological considerations of Schutz starts with his description of the "disinterested attitude of the scientific observer," a crucial part of the style of scientific investigation. This is followed by a treatment of the formation of sociological constructs according to rules of sociological relevance, most of all the postulates of logical consistency, subjective interpretation, adequacy, and rationality. A discussion of the reasons for, and the functions of, the adaptation of models of rational action in sociology follows.

Models of action are to be complemented by ideal types of human conduct. One of two classes of such types comprises (1) the pregiven objective meaning contexts of action; (2) the resulting products of action; (3) the courses of action themselves; and (4) real or ideal objects insofar as they are results of human action. These are "course-of-action types," and include types of results and products of finished courses of action. A second class of types of human conduct comprises ideal types of actors, or personal ideal types. Both types are closely related. But, for certain purposes, course-of-action types can be constructed and used independent of social actors. Personal ideal types, on their part, remain tied to corresponding course-of-action types.

Schutz described personal ideal types as puppets who have been created by sociologists; they are endowed only with those characteristics he wants to investigate. The puppets are activated by thought experiment. Any pure form of motivation can be studied in this fashion. In addition, Schutz suggested the creation of habitual ideal types, in which personal motivation is replaced by culturally standardized behavior patterns. Finally, he paid attention to ideal types of collectives, of languages, and of cultural objects in general. Thus, parallel to his treatment of social relationships among contemporaries, he drew the lines of his typology from the micro- to the macrosociological level.

The overwhelming concerns of Schutz were theoretical and methodological. Yet he brought aspects of his theory to bear on literary criticism, music interpretation, political theory, sociology of knowledge, sociological inquiry, and social problems.[40] It is difficult to categorize these essays. Professor Arvid Brodersen (Oslo), the editor of the second volume of Schutz's *Collected Papers*, assembled them under the label, "Applied Theory." Brodersen pointed out that this term may be misread as could, we may add, the term "empirical studies." He meant it to designate "the use of theory for a more adequate interpretation of social reality" and an "application of philosophical thought to the interpretation of society.[41] This description is adequate, but it should be added that the essays under consideration vary tremendously among themselves with regard to their closeness to empirical con-

---

[40]   See the following items in the Bibliography: 1955a, 1951b and 1956a, 1952, 1946, 1944 and 1945a, 1957a.

[41]   "Editor's Note," *Collected Papers* II:ix. The second part of this volume contains all the essays listed above in footnote 40, plus two items. One is a very short piece, "Some Equivocations in the Notion of Responsibility," and the other an essay called "Tiresias, or Our Knowledge of Future Events" (1959). This contribution seems to be misplaced. It contains basic explorations of the characteristics of prediction in everyday life and, as such, would belong to the exposition of the cognitive structure of the life-world itself.

cerns (the term "empiral" taken in the broadest sense). All of them, however, exemplify sound procedure. While they employ frames of reference constructed from parts of Schutz's social-phenomenological theory, they simultaneously test theoretical assumptions and yield insights which, in turn, lead to the critical refinement and extension of theory.

The very last group of selections[42] stems from two sources. One source is the essay "Equality and the Meaning Structure of the Social World." Written in 1957, it reflects Schutz's concern with the problems of racial equality in the United States. Essentially, it deals with the meanings attached to the slogans and objectives of practical efforts to solve the prime social problem of the country, and with the possibilities and limitations of the solutions sought. The other is the earlier essay "The Homecomer," a fascinating elucidation of the problems facing the soldier coming home from the war. Doubtless, Schutz was guided here by his own experiences in Austria after World War I; but the soldiers of World War II who returned to the United States found themselves in a basically similar situation. The essay demonstrates the possibility of a phenomenological social psychology addressing itself to types of fundamental human experiences under varying conditions.[43]

(vii) SOCIOLOGY MAKES SENSE   Unlike some of the leading figures of modern sociological theory, such as Pitirim Sorokin or Talcott Parsons, Schutz did not develop a coherent substantive theoretical system. He subscribed to Weber's view that, in principle, the processes of social life and of history are inexhaustible. But he was essentially preoccupied with the intellectual "problems" —in the genuine philosophical sense—which arise from and in sociological activities and which, most significantly, loom behind the unquestioned assumptions with which the great majority of sociologists operate.

To a considerable degree, then, Schutz's contributions concern

[42]   See chap. 14, this volume.
[43]   The recent work of a few American social psychologists, such as Harold Garfinkel, bears some relation to Schutz's theory, and opens up broader empirical possibilities for the whole approach.

the fundamentals of the discipline and thus reach deeply into the metasociological realm.[44] Yet, he did not consider himself a specialist in metasociology. His preoccupation with fundamentals led him directly into the areas of sociological methodology. Finally, he involved himself in substantive investigations, mainly of theoretical but also of empirical character. His life work, then, comprises basic contributions in these three divisions of the province of the social sciences: metasociology, methodology, and substantive sociology.

His overwhelming metasociological interest focused on the establishment, delineation, and interpretation of the subject matter of sociology. Thirty-five years before him, Durkheim had posed the crucial question, What is a social fact? Inspired by both Husserl and Weber, Schutz reformulated this question: What is the social reality with which sociologists concern themselves? Like Durkheim, he sought the answer in the spheres of human consciousness, in the mind of man. Unlike Durkheim, he did not treat the facts of this reality as "things" of coercive character. Instead, he understood this reality as one which men construct for themselves from their intersubjective experiences. Of course, linguistic typifications and cultural norms, definitions, and the like enter the individual's image of the social world, serve as a most important kind of building stones for it, and lend it sufficient coherence and uniformity to make mutual understanding and thus meaningful interaction possible. However, the collective elements in human orientations neither eliminate individual spontaneity and volition nor even prevent idiosyncratic interpretations of cultural typifications and

---

44   The term *metasociology* has been given various connotations. It means, within the context of the present exposition, a systematic concern with questions that are logically prior to sociology, for instance those of preexisting subjective interests and value-orientations that motivate a person (a) to consider sociology a worthwhile undertaking in which he should engage himself, and (b) to select specific areas, topics, and problems for his sociological work. These subjective concerns were foremost in the mind of Max Weber when he developed his conception of a "value-free" sociology. Schutz focused upon a related yet distinctly separate area of incisive metasociological decisions: the delineation of the subject matter of sociology.

definitions. This conception of social reality offers the most radical and most consistent justification of sociology as an intellectual discipline sui generis; with it, the definite base line of all social phenomena has been reached.

Schutz's methodological conceptions follow from his definition of the subject matter of sociology. While sociology constitutes a specific province of meaning set apart from the world of daily life most of all by its particular cognitive style, the activities which constitute its operations, ranging from observation to conceptualization and typification, are themselves modeled after processes which occur in the realms of immediate experiences within this life-world.

The foremost substantive contributions of Schutz are theoretical in nature and consist essentially of conceptual frames and typological devices developed in the analysis of fundamental processes occurring in the life-world. These include, among others, his treatment of motivation and projecting and the resulting refinement of the Weberian model of social action and interaction; his exploration of the processes of typification within various settings of social relationships and the concomitant linguistic forms of their expression and stabilization; the linkage between stereotypes of social actors and role theory; his groundwork for a sociology of knowledge which starts with the common-sense knowledge of the world of everyday life and the cognitive processes in which it is established and applied, and which opens up such unexplored fields of investigation as that of the social distribution of knowledge. Several of Schutz's papers are of direct empirical significance. In them, he applied various social-phenomenological conceptions to a wide range of specific topics. Thereby, he showed that these conceptions shed an entirely new light on various kinds of more or less well-known social phenomena and experience. Simultaneously, he tested aspects of his theory by confronting them with facts. And finally, these confrontations contributed to the refinement of the concepts themselves.

In the past, these contributions have been largely ignored or else relegated to the lunatic or at best irrelevant fringes of the sociological discipline. But Schutz was not a sectarian. Most important, he appraised the results of his own investigations with that reservation which is inherent in any genuine scientific attitude. To him, they were merely "valid until further notice." He repeatedly told his students that, while he was certain to have posed the right questions, he was not sure to have found the correct answers. He considered himself a sociologist within a broad sociological tradition, both European and American, and with a place among contemporary sociologists.

Thus, he never denied his theoretical debt to Max Weber and the earlier exponents of the German *Geisteswissenschaften*. Likewise, he paid homage to Georg Simmel, in spite of the latter's neo-Kantian foundations; and to Emile Durkheim and his students, their positivist bent notwithstanding. Of the British functionalists, Bronislaw Malinowski interested him greatly. None of these social scientists were phenomenologists and some were indifferent to the subjective approach itself.

Schutz's intellectual ties with past and contemporary American thinkers were similarly broad. As shown, he accepted various contributions offered by such dissimilar men as William James, John R. Dewey, George H. Mead, William G. Sumner, Charles H. Cooley, and William I. Thomas. His first theoretical undertaking after his arrival in the United States was a searching inquiry into the foundations of Talcott Parsons' study *The Structure of Social Action*. Later he entered into exchanges with men like Robert M. MacIver, Howard Becker, and Edward Shils. If he did not come to grips with the work of such sociologists as Robert E. Park, Florian Znaniecki, and Pitirim A. Sorokin, it was not through sectarian conceit but because of his heavy professional obligations outside the academic field.

The present selections from the writings of Schutz are offered in the spirit in which he wrote them: not as the foundation stones of a particularistic system but as contributions to a well-established although not universal sociological tradition. This is the tradition which expressed in various ways, takes as its point of departure the social actors who constitute society, rather than the social systems and institutions which are the products of their activities. Without negating macro-sociological concerns, Schutz extended Weber's approach further into the social-psychological realm. It is prevalently in this realm that his work could become important for the exponents of the recently revitalized subjective approaches in American sociology and social psychology, symbolic-interactional theory among them. It is hoped that the present volume will foster critical discussion and further investigation of the basic issues posed by Schutz. His work stands before us not as a finished body of theory but as the restless effort of an exceptional mind. It constitutes a challenge.

I. Phenomenological Foundations

1

PHENOMENOLOGICAL BASELINE

Focus on Phenomenology

So FAR, social scientists have not found an adequate approach to the phenomenological movement initiated by the basic writings of Edmund Husserl in the first three decades of our century. In certain quarters the phenomenologist is held to be a kind of crystal gazer, a metaphysician or ontologist in the deprecatory sense of the words, at any rate a fellow who spurns all the empirical facts and the more or less established scientific methods devised to collect and interpret them. Others, who are better informed, feel that phenomenology may have a certain significance for the social sciences, but they regard the phenomenologists as an esoteric group whose language is not understandable to an outsider and is not worth bothering with. A third group has formed a vague and mostly erroneous idea of what phenomenology means, on the basis of some of the slogans used by authors who merely pretend to be phenomenologists, without using Husserl's method (such as Theodor Litt), or used by phenomenologists (such as Max Scheler) in non-phenomenological writings dealing with subject matters of the social sciences. . . .

An attempt to reduce the work of a great philosopher to a few basic propositions understandable to an audience not familiar with his thought is, as a rule, a hopeless undertaking. And in regard to Husserl's phenomenology there are also several special difficulties. The published part of his philosophy, characterized by a condensed presentation and highly technical language, is of a rather

Reprinted from the following items in the Bibliography: 1945*b*, 77–79, 95–97; 1941, 443–46; 1967, 45–47, 51–53, 53–57; 1945*c*, 537–38, 539–41.

fragmentary character. He found it essential to start again and again with his inquiry into the basic foundation not only of philosophy itself but also of all scientific thinking. His aim was to show the implicit presuppositions upon which any science of the world of natural and social things, and even the current philosophy, are based. His ideal was to be a "beginner" in philosophy, in the truest sense of the word. Only by laborious analyses, by fearless consistency and by a radical change in our habits of thinking can we hope to reveal the sphere of a "first philosophy" which complies with the requirements of a "rigorous science" worthy of the name.

It is true that many sciences are commonly called rigorous sciences, the term referring usually to the possibility of presenting the scientific content in mathematical form. This is not the meaning in which Husserl used the term. . . . It was his conviction that name of the so-called rigorous sciences, which use mathematical language with such efficiency, can lead toward an understanding of our experiences of the world—a world the existence of which they uncritically presuppose, and which they pretend to measure by yardsticks and pointers on the scale of their instruments. All empirical sciences refer to the world as pre-given; but they and their instruments are themselves elements of this world. Only a philosophical doubt cast upon the implicit presuppositions of all our habitual thinking—scientific or not—can guarantee the "exactitude" not only of such a philosophical attempt itself but of all the sciences dealing directly or indirectly with our experiences of the world. . . .

This outline of Husserl's general aim may explain the great difficulties encountered by a beginning student of phenomenology who attempts to attach to this philosophy one of the customary textbook labels, such as idealism, realism, empiricism. None of these school-classifications can be adequately applied to a philosophy that puts them all in question. Phenomenology, searching for a real beginning of all philosophical thinking, hopes when fully developed to end where all the traditional philosophies start. Its place is beyond—or better, before—all distinctions between realism and idealism.

In addition, these introductory remarks may help to remove a widespread misunderstanding of the nature of phenomenology—the belief that phenomenology is anti-scientific, not based upon analysis and description but originating in a kind of uncontrollable intuition or metaphysical revelation. Even many serious students of philosophy have been induced to classify phenomenology as metaphysics, because of its admitted refusal to accept uncritically the givenness of sensory perceptions, of biological data, of society and environment, as the unquestionable point of departure for philosophical investigation. Moreover, Husserl's use of certain unfortunate terms, such as *Wesensschau,* has prevented many from acknowledging phenomenology as a method of philosophical thinking.

For a method it is, and one as "scientific" as any.

Phenomenology and Social Sciences

A few final remarks may briefly suggest where the importance of phenomenology lies for the social sciences. It must be clearly stated that the relation of phenomenology to the social sciences cannot be demonstrated by analyzing concrete problems of sociology or economics, such as social adjustment or theory of international trade, with phenomenological methods. It is my conviction, however, that future studies of the methods of the social sciences and their fundamental notions will of necessity lead to issues belonging to the domain of phenomenological research.[1]

To give just one example, all social sciences take the intersubjectivity of thought and action for granted. That fellowmen exist, that men act upon men, that communication by symbols and signs is possible, that social groups and institutions, legal and economic systems and the like are integral elements of our life-world, that this life-world has its own history and its special relationship to time and space—all these are notions that are explicitly or implicitly fundamental for the work of all social scientists. The latter have developed certain methodological devices—schemes of reference,

---

[1]   See A. Schütz, "Phenomenology and the Social Sciences," in *Philosophical Essays in Memory of Edmund Husserl,* ed. Marvin Farber (Cambridge, Mass., 1940), pp. 164–86.

typologies, statistical methods—in order to deal with the phenomena suggested by these terms. But the phenomena themselves are merely taken for granted. Man is simply conceived as a social being, language and other systems of communication exist, the conscious life of the other is accessible to me—in short, I can understand the other and his acts and he can understand me and my doings. And the same holds good for the so-called social and cultural objects created by men. They are taken for granted, and they have their specific meaning and way of existence.

But how does it happen that mutual understanding and communication are possible at all? How is it possible that man accomplishes meaningful acts, purposively or habitually, that he is guided by ends to be attained and motivated by certain experiences? Do not the concepts of meaning, of motives, of ends, of acts, refer to a certain structure of consciousness, a certain arrangement of all the experiences in inner time, a certain type of sedimentation? And does not interpretation of the other's meaning and of the meaning of his acts and the results of these acts presuppose a self-interpretation of the observer or partner? How can I, in my attitude as a man among other men or as a social scientist, find an approach to all this if not by recourse to a stock of pre-interpreted experiences built up by sedimentation within my own conscious life? And how can methods for interpreting the social interrelationship be warranted if they are not based upon a careful description of the underlying assumptions and their implications?

These questions cannot be answered by the methods of the social sciences. They require a philosophical analysis. And phenomenology—not only what Husserl called phenomenological philosophy but even phenomenological psychology—has not only opened an avenue of approach for such an analysis but has in addition started the analysis itself.

Consciousness

Discussing the methods of investigation open to psychologists[2] James points out that all people unhesitatingly believe that

[2]   *Principles*, vol. 1, p. 185.

they feel themselves thinking and that they distinguish the mental state as an inward activity from all the objects with which it may cognitively deal. "I regard," he says, "this belief as the most fundamental of all the Postulates of Psychology, and shall discard all curious inquiries about its certainty as too metaphysical for the scope of this book." "That we have cogitations of some sort is the 'inconcessum' in a world most of whose other facts have at some time tottered in the breath of philosophical doubt."

First of all, this basic position is the common platform from which both James' psychological research and Husserl's phenomenological meditation begin. The first indubitable fact to start from is the existence of a personal consciousness; the personal self rather than the thought has to be treated as the immediate datum in psychology and the universal conscious fact is not: "Feelings and thoughts exist" but, "I think" and "I feel." Within each personal consciousness thought is sensibly continuous and changing, and as such, comparable to a river or a stream. "Stream of thought," "stream of experiences or cogitations," "stream of personal conscious life," these terms both philosophers use for characterizing the essence of inner personal life. For both the unity of consciousness consists in its through-and-through connectedness. It is, says James, but our abstract conceptual thought that isolates and arbitrarily fixes certain portions of this stream of consciousness.[3] . . .

For Husserl the personal life of consciousness as an indubitable fact leads to the apprehension of and theoretical inquiry into the "realm of pure consciousness in its own self-contained Being." Let us examine this position more closely. From the beginning Husserl's problem was a twofold one: first, to establish an *a priori psychological* discipline able to provide the only secure basis on which a strong empirical psychology can be built; secondly, to establish a universal *philosophy*, starting from an absolute "principium" of knowledge in the genuine sense of this term. We are chiefly interested in the first.

Husserl starts with the explanation of the characteristics of psychological experience. While just living along, we live *in* our experiences, and, concentrated as we are upon their objects, we do not have in view the "acts of subjective experience" themselves. In order to reveal these acts of experience as such we must modify the naïve attitude in which we are oriented towards objects and we must turn ourselves, in a specific act of "reflection," towards our own experiences. . . .

Husserl's next step is to reveal the insight into the "intentionality" of consciousness. Our cogitations have the basic character of being "consciousness of" something. What appears in reflection as phenomenon is the intentional object, which I have a thought of, perception of, fear of, etc. Every experience is, thus, not only characterized by the fact *that* it is a consciousness, but it is simultaneously determined by the intentional object *whereof* it is a consciousness.[4] Types and forms of this intentionality can be described. This description can be performed on two different levels: first, within the natural attitude—and all that has been stated so far refers to this level; secondly, within the sphere of phenomenological reduction. This basic concept of Husserl's theory needs further explanation.

In our everyday life, or, as Husserl says, "from the natural standpoint," we accept as unquestionable the world of facts which surrounds us as existent out there. To be sure, we might throw doubt upon any *datum* of that world out there, we might even distrust as many of our experiences of this world as we wish; the naïve belief in the existence of *some* outer world, this "general thesis of the natural standpoint," will imperturbably subsist. But by a radical effort of our mind we can alter this attitude, not by transforming our naïve belief in the outer world into a disbelief, not by replacing our conviction in its existence by the contrary, but by suspending belief. We just make up our mind to refrain from any judgment concerning spatiotemporal existence, or in technical language, we set the existence of the world "out of action," we "bracket" our belief in it. But using this particular "epoché" we not only "bracket" all the common-sense judgments

4   E. Husserl, Ideas: *General Introduction to Pure Phenomenology*, tr. Boyce Gibson, § 36.

of our daily life about the world out there, but also all the propositions of the natural sciences which likewise deal with the realities of this world from the natural standpoint.

What remains of the whole world after this bracketing? Neither more nor less than the concrete fulness and entirety of the stream of our experience containing all our perceptions, our reflections, in short, our cogitations. And as these cogitations continue to be intentional ones, their correlative "intentional objects" persist also within the brackets. But by no means are they to be identified with the posited objects. They are just "appearances," phenomena, and, as such, rather "unities" or "senses" ("meanings"). The method of phenomenological reduction, therefore, makes accessible the stream of consciousness in itself as a realm of its own in its absolute uniqueness of nature. We can experience it and describe its inner structure. This is the task of phenomenological psychology. . . .

The transcendental reduction is important for phenomenological descriptive psychology not only because it reveals the stream of consciousness and its features in their purity, but, above all, because some very important structures of consciousness can be made visible only within this reduced sphere. Since to each empirical determination within the phenomenological reduction there necessarily corresponds a parallel feature within the natural sphere and vice versa, we can always turn back to the natural attitude and there make use of all the insights we have won within the reduced sphere.

Let us take as an example Husserl's theory of noesis ("the experiencing") and noema ("the experienced") which leads us to the neighborhood of some tenets of James. As all cogitations are by their intentional character "consciousness of" something, a double manner of describing them will always exist: the first, the noematic, dealing with the "cogitatum," that is, with the intentional object of our specific thought as it appears in it, for instance as a certainty, possibly, or presumably existent object, or as a present, past, or future object; the second, the noetic, dealing with the acts of cogitation, with the experiencing itself (noesis) and with its modifications as: with the perceiving, retaining, recollecting, etc., and their peculiar differences of clarity and explicity.

Each specific noesis has its specific noematic correlate. There are modifications of thought which touch equally upon the whole noetico-noematic content as, e.g., the attentional modifications do; others which transform preponderantly either the noematic or the noetic side. But closer analysis (which can be performed only within the reduced sphere) shows that there is always a noematic nucleus or kernel in each intentional object which persists through all the modifications and which can be defined "as the meaning of the thought in the mode of its full realization."

Experience: Stream of Consciousness

Let us begin by considering Bergson's distinction between living within the stream of experience and living within the world of space and time. Bergson contrasts the inner stream of duration, the *durée*—a continuous coming-to-be and passing-away of heterogeneous qualities—with homogeneous time, which has been spatialized, quantified, and rendered discontinuous. In "pure duration" there is no "side-by-sideness," no mutual externality of parts, and no divisibility, but only a continuous flux, a stream of conscious states. However, the term "conscious states" is misleading, as it reminds one of the phenomena of the spatial world with its fixed entities, such as images, percepts, and physical objects. What we, in fact, experience in duration is not a being that is discrete and well-defined but a constant transition from a now-thus to a new now-thus. The stream of consciousness by its very nature has not yet been caught up in the net of reflection. Reflection, being a function of the intellect, belongs essentially in the spatiotemporal world of everyday life. The structure of our experience will vary according to whether we surrender ourselves to the flow of duration or stop to reflect upon it, trying to classify it into spatiotemporal concepts. We can, for example, experience motion as a continuously changing manifold—in other words, as a phenomenon of our inner life; we can, on the other hand, conceive this same motion as a divisible event in homogeneous space. In the latter case, however, we have not really grasped the essence of that motion which is ever coming to be and passing away. Rather, we have grasped motion that is no longer motion, motion that has run its course, in short, not the motion itself, but merely the space traversed. Now, we can look at human acts under the same double aspect. We can look at them as enduring conscious processes or as frozen, spatialized, already completed acts. This double aspect appears not merely in transcendent "temporal Objects," but throughout experience in general. . . .

Now how are the individual experiences within the stream of consciousness constituted into intentional unities? If we take as our starting point Bergson's concept of the *duree*, then it becomes clear that the difference between the flowing experiences in pure duration and the discrete discontinuous images in the space-time world is a difference between two levels of consciousness. In everyday life the Ego, as it acts and thinks, lives on the level of consciousness of the space-time world. Its "attention to life" (*attention à la vie*) prevents it from becoming submerged in the intuition of pure duration. However, if the "psychic tension" for any reason relaxes, the Ego will discover that what formerly seemed to be separate and sharply defined items are now dissolved into continuous transitions, that fixed images have become supplanted by a coming-to-be and passing-away that has no contours, no boundaries, and no differentiations. And so Bergson concludes that all distinctions, all attempts to "separate out" individual experiences from the one unity of duration, are artificial, i.e., alien to the pure *durée*, and all attempts to analyze process are merely cases of carrying over spatiotemporal modes of representation to the radically different *durée*.

Indeed, when I immerse myself in my stream of consciousness, in my duration, I do not find any clearly differentiated experiences at all. At one moment an experience waxes, then it wanes. Meanwhile something new grows out of what was something old and then gives place to something still newer. I cannot distinguish between the Now and the Earlier, between the later Now and the Now that has just been, except that I know that what has just been is different from what now is. For I experience my duration as a unidirectional, irreversible stream and find that between a moment ago and just now *I have grown older*. But I cannot become aware of this while still immersed in the stream. As long as my whole consciousness remains temporally uni-directional and irreversible, I am unaware either of my own growing older or of any difference between present and past. The very awareness of the stream of duration presupposes a turning-back against the stream, a special kind of attitude toward that stream, a "reflection," as we will call it. For only the fact that an earlier phase preceded this Now and Thus makes the Now to be Thus, and that earlier phase which constitutes the Now is given to me in this Now in the mode of remembrance (*Erinnerung*). The awareness of the experience in the pure stream of duration is changed at every moment into *remembered* having-just-been-thus; it is the remembering which lifts the experience out of the irreversible stream of duration and thus modifies the awareness, making it a remembrance.

Meaningful Experience

If we simply live immersed in the flow of duration, we encounter only undifferentiated experiences that melt into one another in a flowing continuum. Each Now differs essentially from its predecessor in that within the Now the predecessor is contained in retentional modification. However, I know nothing of this while I am simply living in the flow of duration, because it is only by an Act of reflective attention that I catch sight of the retentional modification and therewith of the earlier phase. Within the flow of duration there is only a living from moment to moment, which sometimes also contains in itself the retentional modifications of the previous phase. Then, as Husserl says, I live *in* my Acts, whose living intentionality carries me over from one Now to the next. But this Now should be construed as a punctiform instant, as a break in the stream of duration, as a cutting-in-two of the latter. For in order to effect such an artificial division within duration, I should have to get outside the flow itself. From the point of view of a being immersed in duration, the "Now" is a phase rather than a point, and therefore the different phases melt into one another along a continuum. The simple experience of living in the flow of duration goes forward in a uni-directional, irreversible movement, proceeding from manifold to manifold in a constant running-off process. Each phase of experience melts into the next without any sharp boundaries as it is being lived through; but each phase is distinct in its thusness, or quality, from the next insofar as it is held in the gaze of attention.

However, when, by my act of reflection, I turn my attention to my living experience, I am no longer taking up my position within the stream of pure duration, I am no longer simply living within that flow. The experiences are apprehended, distinguished, brought into relief, marked out from one another; the experiences which were constituted as phases within the flow of duration now become objects of attention as constituted experiences. What had first been constituted as a phase now stands out as a full-blown experience, no matter whether the Act of attention is one of reflection or of reproduction (in simple apprehension). *For the Act of attention*—and this is of major importance for the study of meaning—presupposes an elapsed, passed-away experience—in short, one that is already in the past, regardless of whether the attention in question is reflective or reproductive.

Therefore we must contrast those experiences which in their running-off are undifferentiated and shade into one another, on the one hand, with those that are discrete, already past, and elapsed, on the other. The latter we apprehend not by living through them but by an act of attention. This is crucial for the topic we are pursuing: Because the concept of meaningful experience always presupposes that the experience of which meaning is predicated is a discrete one, it now becomes quite clear that only a past experience can be called meaningful, that is, one that is present to the retrospective glance as already finished and done with.

Only from the point of view of the retrospective glance do there exist discrete experiences. Only the already experienced is meaningful, not that which is being experienced. For meaning is merely an operation of intentionality, which, however, only becomes visible to the reflective glance. From the point of view of passing experience, the predication of meaning is necessarily trivial, since meaning here can only be understood as the attentive gaze directed not at passing, but at already passed experience.

Is, however, the distinction just made between discrete and nondiscrete experience really justified? Is it not at least possible that the attentive glance can light upon each item of experience which has passed by, can "throw it into relief" and "distinguish" it from other items? We believe that the answer must be in the negative. There are, as a matter of fact, experiences which are experiences when they are present but which either cannot be reflected upon at all or can be reflected upon only through an extremely vague apprehension and whose reproduction, apart from the purely empty notion of "having experienced something"—in other words, in a clear way—is quite impossible. We will call this group "essentially actual" experiences because they are by their very nature limited to a definite temporal position within the inner stream of consciousness. They are known by their attachment or closeness to that innermost core of the Ego which Scheler in a happy turn of phrase called the "absolute personal privacy" (*absolut intime Person*) of an individual. About the absolute personal privacy of a person we know both that it must necessarily *be there* and that it remains *absolutely* closed to any sharing of its experience with others. But also in self-knowledge there is a sphere of absolute intimacy whose "being there" (*Dasein*) is just as indubitable as it is closed to our inspection. The experiences peculiar to this sphere are simply inaccessible to memory, and this fact pertains to their mode of being: memory catches only the "that" of these experiences. For the confirmation of this thesis (which can only be stated here and not fully proved), an observation which can be performed immediately furnishes support, namely, that the reproduction becomes all the less adequate to the experience the nearer it comes to the intimate core of the person. This diminishing adequacy has in consequence an ever greater vagueness of reproduced content. Concomitantly, the capacity for recapitulative reproduction diminishes, that is, the capacity for the complete reconstruction of the course of the experience. As far as reproduction is possible at all, it can only be accomplished by a simple act of apprehension. The "How" of the experience can, however, be reproduced only in recapitulative reconstruction. The recollection of an experience of the external world is relatively clear; an external course of events, a movement perhaps, can be recollected in free reproduction, that is, at arbitrary points of the duration. Incomparably more difficult is the reproduction of experiences of internal perception; those internal perceptions that lie close to the absolute private core of the person are irrecoverable as far as their How is concerned, and their That can be laid hold of only in a simple act of apprehension. Here belong, first of all, not only all experiences of the corporeality of the Ego, in other words, of the Vital Ego (muscular tensings and relaxings as correlates of the movements of the body, "physical" pain, sexual sensations, and so on), but also those psychic phenomena classified together under the vague heading of "moods," as well as "feelings" and "affects" (joy, sorrow, disgust, etc.). The limits of recall coincide exactly with the limits of "rationalizability," provided that one uses this equivocal word—as Max Weber does at times—in the broadest sense, that is, in the sense of "capable of giving a meaning." Recoverability to memory is, in fact, the first prerequisite of all rational construction. That which is irrecoverable—and this is in principle always something ineffable—can only be lived but never "thought": it is in principle incapable of being verbalized.

*Meaning-Endowed Conduct**

We must now answer the question, "How am I to distinguish my behavior from the rest of my experiences?" The answer is supplied by ordinary usage. A pain, for instance, is not generally called behavior. Nor would I be said to be behaving if someone else

---

* EDITOR'S NOTE: In this selection, the translators rendered the German term *Verhalten* by its literal English equivalent, "behavior." In his American period, Schutz became more and more aware of the unwarranted connotations that are attached to the term *behavior* due to the prevalence of psychological behaviorism. In order to circumvent the biomechanistic implications of a stimulus-response theory, he came to prefer the term *conduct*.

lifted my arm and then let it drop. But the *attitudes* I assume in either of these cases *are* called behavior. I may fight the pain, suppress it, or abandon myself to it. I may submit or resist when someone manipulates my arm. So what we have here are two different types of lived experiences that are fundamentally related. Experiences of the first type are merely "undergone" or "suffered." They are characterized by a basic passivity. Experiences of the second type consist of the attitudes taken toward experiences of the first type. To put it in Husserl's words, behavior is a "meaning-endowing experience of consciousness." When he studied the "important and difficult problem of the defining characteristics of thought," Husserl showed that not all experiences are meaning-endowing by nature. "Experiences of primordial passivity, associations, those experiences in which the original time-consciousness, the constitution of immanent temporality takes place, and other experiences of this kind, are all incapable of it" (that is, of conferring meaning). A meaning-endowing experience must rather be an "Ego-Act (attitudinal Act) or some modification of such an Act (secondary passivity, or perhaps a passively emerging judgment that suddenly 'occurs to me')."[5]

One can, if one wishes, define attitude-taking Acts as Acts of primary engendering activity, provided that, with Husserl, one includes here feelings and the constitution of values by feelings, whether these values be regarded as ends or means. Husserl uses the term "meaning-endowing conscious experiences" (*sinngebende Bewusstseinserlebnisse*) to cover all experiences given in intentionality in the form of spontaneous activity or in one of the secondary modifications thereof. Now, what are these modifications? The two principal ones are retention and reproduction. . . .

We define "behavior" as an experience of consciousness that bestows meaning through spontaneous Activity. Action and behavior [*in the narrower sense of conduct*—Trans.] form a subclass within behavior so conceived; we shall discuss them at length later. What distinguishes the objectivity of consciousness, which is constituted in original Activity and is therefore a case of behavior,

<hr />

5   Husserl, *Formale und transzendentale Logik*, p. 22.

from all other experiences of consciousness, and makes it "mean-ing-endowing" in Husserl's sense, becomes intelligible only under one condition, namely, that one apply the distinctions explained above between the constituting Act and the constituted objectivity also to the sphere of spontaneous Activity. If one does so, one will distinguish between the spontaneous Act itself and the object con-stituted within it. In the direction of the occurrence or running-off of the behavior, the spontaneous Act is nothing more than the mode of intentionality in which the constituting objectivity is given. In other words, behavior as it occurs is "perceived" in a unique way as primordial activity.

This perception functions as a primal impression, which of course undergoes the usual "shading" in the retentional process, just as all other impressions do. Activity is an experience which is constituted in phases in the transition from one Now to the next. The beam of reflection can only be directed at it from a later vantage point. This necessarily involves either retention or recol-lection. The latter may consist in a simple Act of apprehension or may involve reconstruction in phases. In any case the original in-tentionality of spontaneous Activity is preserved in intentional modification.

Applied to the theory of behavior, this means that one's own behavior, while it is actually taking place, is a *prephenomenal* experience. Only when it has already taken place (or if it occurs in successive phases, only when the initial phases have taken place) does it stand out as a discrete item from the background of one's other experiences. Phenomenal experience is, therefore, never of oneself behaving, only of having behaved. Yet the original experi-ence in another sense remains the same in memory as it was when it occurred. My past behavior is, after all, *my* behavior; it consists of *my* Act wherein *I* take up some attitude or other, even if I see it only "in profile" as something past. And it is precisely this atti-tudinal character which distinguishes it from all the rest of my experience. My elapsed experience is still mine, since it is I who once lived through it; this is simply another way of asserting that duration's elapse or "running-off" is continuous, that there is a fundamental unity in the time-constituting stream of consciousness.

Even experiences of primordial passivity are grasped retrospectively as *my* experiences. My behavior is distinguished from these by the fact that it refers back to my primal impression of spontaneous Activity.

Behavior, then, consists of a series of experiences which are distinguished from all other experiences by a primordial intentionality of spontaneous Activity which remains the same in all intentional modifications. Now it becomes clear what we meant when we said that behavior is merely experiences looked at in a certain light, that is, referred back to the Activity which originally produced them. The "meaning" of experiences is nothing more, then, than that frame of interpretation which sees them as behavior. So in the case of behavior, also, it turns out that only what is already over and done with has meaning. The prephenomenal experience of activity is, therefore, not meaningful. Only that experience which is reflectively perceived in the form of spontaneous Activity has meaning.

Attention to Life: Wide-Awakeness

One of the central points of Bergson's philosophy is his theory that our conscious life shows an indefinite number of different planes, ranging from the plane of action on one extreme to the plane of dream at the other. Each of these planes is characterized by a specific tension of consciousness, the plane of action showing the highest, that of dream the lowest degree of tension. According to Bergson these different degrees of tension of our consciousness are functions of our varying interest in life, action representing our highest interest in meeting reality and its requirements, dream being complete lack of interest. *Attention à la vie*, attention to life, is, therefore, the basic regulative principle of our conscious life. It defines the realm of our world which is relevant to us; it articulates our continuously flowing stream of thought; it determines the span and function of our memory; it makes us —in our language—either live within our present experiences, directed toward their objects, or turn back in a reflective attitude to our past experiences and ask for their meaning.

By the term *"wide-awakeness"* we want to denote a plane of consciousness of highest tension originating in an attitude of full attention to life and its requirements. Only the performing and especially the working self is fully interested in life and, hence, wide-awake. It lives within its acts and its attention is exclusively directed to carrying its project into effect, to executing its plan. This attention is an active, not a passive one. Passive attention is the opposite to full awakeness. In passive attention I experience, for instance, the surf of indiscernible small perceptions which are, as stated before, essentially actual experiences and not meaningful manifestations of spontaneity. Meaningful spontaneity may be defined with Leibnitz as the effort to arrive at other and always other perceptions. In its lowest form it leads to the delimitation of certain perceptions transforming them into apperception; in its highest form it leads to the performance of working which gears into the outer world and modifies it.

The concept of wide-awakeness reveals the starting point for a legitimate pragmatic interpretation of our cognitive life. The state of full awakeness of the working self traces out that segment of the world which is pragmatically relevant and these relevances determine the form and content of our stream of thought: the form, because they regulate the tension of our memory and therewith the scope of our past experiences recollected and of our future experiences anticipated; the content, because all these experiences undergo specific attentional modifications by the preconceived project and its carrying into effect.

Acting in the Outer World

Bergson's and also Husserl's investigations have emphasized the importance of our bodily movements for the constitution of the outer world and its time perspective. We experience our bodily movements simultaneously on two different planes: Inasmuch as they are movements in the outer world we look at them as events happening in space and spatial time, measurable in terms of the path run through; inasmuch as they are experienced together from within as happening changes, as manifestations of our spontaneity pertaining to our stream of consciousness, they partake of our inner time or *durée*. What occurs in the outer world belongs to the same time dimension in which events in inanimate nature occur. It can be registered by appropriate devices and measured by our chronometers. It is the spatialized, homogeneous time which is the universal form of objective or cosmic time. On the other hand it is the inner time or *durée* within which our actual experiences are connected with the past by recollections and retentions and with the future by protentions and anticipations. In and by our bodily movements we perform the transition from our *durée* to the spatial or cosmic time and our working actions partake of both. In simultaneity we experience the working action as a series of events in outer and in inner time, unifying both dimensions into a single flux which shall be called the *vivid present*. The vivid present originates, therefore, in an intersection of *durée* and cosmic time.

Living in the vivid present in its ongoing working acts, directed toward the objects and objectives to be brought about, the working self experiences itself as the originator of the ongoing actions and, thus, as an undivided total self. In experiences its bodily movements from within; it lives in the correlated essentially actual experiences which are inaccessible to recollection and reflection; its world is a world of open anticipations. The working self, and only the working self, experiences all this *modo presenti* and, experiencing itself as the author of this ongoing working, it realizes itself as a unity.

But if the self in a reflective attitude turns back to the working acts performed and looks at them *modo praeterito* this unity goes to pieces. The self which performed the past acts is no longer the undivided total self, but rather a partial self, the performer of this particular act that refers to a system of correlated acts to which it belongs. This partial self is merely the taker of a rôle or—to use with all necessary reserve a rather equivocal term which W. James and G. H. Mead have introduced into the literature—a Me. . . .

For our purpose the mere consideration that the inner experiences of our bodily movements, the essentially actual experiences, and the open anticipations escape the grasping by the reflective attitude shows with sufficient clearness that the past self can never be more than a partial aspect of the total one which realizes itself in the experience of its ongoing working.

One point relating to the distinction between (overt) working and (covert) performing has to be added. In the case of a mere performance, such as the attempt to solve mentally a mathematical problem, I can, if my anticipations are not fulfilled by the outcome and I am dissatisfied with the result, cancel the whole process of mental operations and restart from the beginning. Nothing will have changed in the outer world, no vestige of the annulled process will remain. Mere mental actions are, in this sense, revocable. Working, however, is irrevocable. My work has changed the outer world. At best, I may restore the initial situation by countermoves but I cannot make undone what I have done. That is why—from the moral and legal point of view—I am responsible for my deeds but not for my thoughts. That is also why I have the freedom of choice between several possibilities merely with respect to the mentally projected work, before this work has been carried through in the outer world or, at least, while it is being carried through in vivid present, and, thus, still open to modifications. In terms of the past there is no possibility for choice. Having realized my work or at least portions of it, I chose once for all what has been done and have now to bear the consequences. I cannot choose what I want to have done.

2

THE LIFE-WORLD

The World of the Natural Attitude

WE BEGIN with an analysis of the world of daily life which the wide-awake, grown-up man who acts in it and upon it amidst his fellow-men experiences with the natural attitude as a reality.

"World of daily life" shall mean the intersubjective world which existed long before our birth, experienced and interpreted by others, our predecessors, as an organized world. Now it is given to our experience and interpretation. All interpretation of this world is based upon a stock of previous experiences of it, our own experiences and those handed down to us by our parents and teachers, which in the form of "knowledge at hand" function as a scheme of reference.

To this stock of experiences at hand belongs our knowledge that the world we live in is a world of well circumscribed objects with definite qualities, objects among which we move, which resist us and upon which we may act. To the natural attitude the world is not and never has been a mere aggregate of colored spots, incoherent noises, centers of warmth and cold. Philosophical or psychological analysis of the constitution of our experiences may afterwards, retrospectively, describe how elements of this world affect our senses, how we passively perceive them in an indistinct and confused way, how by active apperception our mind singles out certain features from the perceptional field, conceiving them as well delineated things which stand out over against a more or

Reprinted from the following items in the Bibliography: 1945c, 533–34; 1953c, 6; 1959a, 77–79; 1944, 500–501.

less inarticulated background or horizon. The natural attitude does not know these problems. To it the world is from the outset not the private world of the single individual, but an intersubjective world, common to all of us, in which we have not a theoretical but an eminently practical interest. The world of everyday life is the scene and also the object of our actions and interactions. We have to dominate it and we have to change it in order to realize the purposes which we pursue within it among our fellow-men. Thus, we work and operate not only within but upon the world. Our bodily movements—kinaesthetic, locomotive, operative—gear, so to speak, into the world, modifying or changing its objects and their mutual relationships. On the other hand, these objects offer resistance to our acts which we have either to overcome or to which we have to yield. In this sense it may be correctly said that a pragmatic motive governs our natural attitude toward the world of daily life. World, in this sense, is something that we have to modify by our actions or that modifies our actions.

Biographically Determined Situation

Man finds himself at any moment of his daily life in a biographically determined situation, that is, in a physical and sociocultural environment as defined by him, within which he has his position, not merely his position in terms of physical space and outer time or of his status and role within the social system but also his moral and ideological position. To say that this definition of the situation is biographically determined means to say that it has its history; it is the sedimentation of all of man's previous experiences, organized in the habitual possessions of his stock of knowledge, at hand, and as such his unique possession, given to him and to him alone. This biographically determined situation includes certain possibilities of future practical or theoretical activities which shall be briefly called the "purpose at hand." It is this purpose at hand which defines those elements among all the others contained in such a situation which are relevant for this purpose. This system of relevances in turn determines what elements have to be made a substratum of generalizing typification, what traits of these have to be selected as characteristically typical and what others as unique and individual. . . .

Stock of Knowledge

Man in daily life . . . finds at any given moment a stock of knowledge at hand that serves him as a scheme of interpretation of his past and present experiences, and also determines his anticipations of things to come. This stock of knowledge has its particular history. It has been constituted in and by previous experiencing activities of our consciousness, the outcome of which has now become our habitual possession. Husserl, in describing the constituting process that is here involved, speaks graphically of the "sedimentation" of meaning.

On the other hand, this stock of knowledge at hand is by no means homogeneous, but shows a particular structure. I have already alluded to William James' distinction between "knowledge about" and "knowledge of acquaintance." There is a relatively small kernel of knowledge that is clear, distinct, and consistent in itself. This kernel is surrounded by zones of various gradations of vagueness, obscurity, and ambiguity. These follow zones of things just taken for granted, blind beliefs, bare suppositions, mere guesswork, zones in which it will do merely to "put one's trust." And finally, there are regions of our complete ignorance. . . .

First, let us consider what determines the structurization of the stock of knowledge at a particular Now. A preliminary answer is that it is the system of our practical or theoretical interest at this specific moment which determines not only what is problematic and what can remain unquestioned but also what has to be known and with what degree of clarity and precision it has to be known in order to solve the emergent problem. In other words, it is the particular problem we are concerned with that subdivides our stock of knowledge at hand into layers of different relevance for its solution, and thus establishes the borderlines of the various zones of our knowledge just mentioned, zones of distinctness and vagueness, of clarity and obscurity, of precision and ambiguity. Here is the root of the pragmatistic interpretation of the nature of our knowledge, the relative validity of which has to be recognized even by those who reject the other tenets of pragmatism, especially its theory of truth. To be sure, even within the restricted limits of commonsense knowledge of everyday life, the reference to "interests," "problems," "relevances" is not a sufficient explanation. All these terms are merely headings of highly complicated subject matters for further research.

Secondly, it must be emphasized that the stock of knowledge is in a continual flux, and changes from any Now to the next one not only in its range but also in its structure. It is clear that any supervening experience enlarges and enriches it. By reference to the stock of knowledge at hand at that particular Now, the actually emerging experience is found to be a "familiar" one if it is related by a "synthesis of recognition" to a previous experience in the modes of "sameness," "likeness," "similarity," "analogy," and the like. The emerging experience may, for example, be conceived as a pre-experienced "same which recurs" or as a pre-experienced "same but modified" or as of a type similar to a pre-experienced one, and so on. Or the emergent experience is found to be "strange" if it cannot be referred, at least as to its type, to pre-experiences at hand. In both cases it is the stock of knowledge at hand that serves as the scheme of interpretation for the actually emergent experience. This reference to already experienced acts presupposes memory and all of its functions, such as retention, recollection, recognition.

The Character of Practical Knowledge

. . . the knowledge of the man who acts and thinks within the world of his daily life is not homogeneous; it is (1) incoherent, (2) only partially clear, and (3) not at all free from contradictions.

1. It is incoherent because the individual's interests which determine the relevance of the objects selected for further inquiry are themselves not integrated into a coherent system. They are only partially organized under plans of any kind, such as plans of life, plans of work and leisure, plans for every social role assumed. But the hierarchy of these plans changes with the situation and with

the growth of the personality; interests are shifted continually and entail an uninterrupted transformation of the shape and density of the relevance lines. Not only the selection of the objects of curiosity but also the degree of knowledge aimed at changes.

2. Man in his daily life is only partially—and we dare say exceptionally—interested in the clarity of his knowledge, i.e., in full insight into the relations between the elements of his world and the general principles ruling those relations. He is satisfied that a well-functioning telephone service is available to him and, normally, does not ask how the apparatus functions in detail and what laws of physics make this functioning possible. He buys merchandise in the store, not knowing how it is produced, and pays with money, although he has only a vague idea what money really is. He takes it for granted that his fellow-man will understand his thought if expressed in plain language and will answer accordingly, without wondering how this miraculous performance may be explained. Furthermore, he does not search for the truth and does not quest for certainty. All he wants is information on likelihood and insight into the chances or risks which the situation at hand entails for the outcome of his actions. That the subway will run tomorrow as usual is for him almost of the same order of likelihood as that the sun will rise. If by reason of special interest he needs more explicit knowledge on a topic, a benign modern civilization holds ready for him a chain of information desks and reference libraries.

3. His knowledge, finally, is not a consistent one. At the same time he may consider statements as equally valid which in fact are incompatible with one another. As a father, a citizen, an employee, and a member of his church he may have the most different and the least congruent opinions on moral, political, or economic matters. This inconsistency does not necessarily originate in a logical fallacy. Men's thought is just spread over subject matters located within different and differently relevant levels, and they are not aware of the modifications they would have to make in passing from one level to another.

II. The Cognitive Setting
of the Life-World

3

SOCIAL INTERPRETATION AND
INDIVIDUAL ORIENTATION

I. *The Social Conception of the Community and the Individual*

THE SOCIAL WORLD TAKEN FOR GRANTED   We start from an examination of the social world in its various articulations and forms of organization which constitutes the social reality for men living within it. Man is born into a world that existed before his birth; and this world is from the outset not merely a physical, but also a sociocultural one. The latter is a preconstituted and preorganized world whose particular structure is the result of an historical process and is therefore different for each culture and society.

Certain features, however, are common to all social worlds because they are rooted in the human condition. Everywhere we find sex groups and age groups, and some division of labor conditioned by them; and more or less rigid kinship organizations that arrange the social world into zones of varying social distance, from intimate familiarity to strangeness. Everywhere we also find hierarchies of superordination and subordination, of leader and follower, of those in command and those in submission. Everywhere, too, we find an accepted way of life, that is, how to come to terms with things and men, with nature and the supernatural. There are everywhere, moreover, cultural objects, such as tools needed for the domination of the outer world, playthings for children, articles for adornment, musical instruments of some kind, objects serving as symbols for worship. There are certain ceremonies marking the great events in the life cycle of the individual (birth, initiation,

Reprinted from the following items in the Bibliography: 1957*a*, 36–38; 1944, 501–2; 1957*a*, 57–60, 52–54; 1944, 502–4, 505–7; 1957*a*, 61.

marriage, death), or in the rhythm of nature (sowing and harvesting, solstices, etc.). . . .

Thus, the social world into which man is born and within which he has to find his bearings is experienced by him as a tight knit web of social relationships, of systems of signs and symbols with their particular meaning structure, of institutionalized forms of social organization, of systems of status and prestige, etc. The meaning of all these elements of the social world in all its diversity and stratification, as well as the pattern of its texture itself, is by those living within it just taken for granted. The sum-total of the relative natural aspect the social world has for those living within it constitutes, to use William Graham Sumner's term, the folkways of the in-group, which are socially accepted as the good ways and the right ways for coming to terms with things and fellow men. They are taken for granted because they have stood the test so far, and, being socially approved, are held as requiring neither an explanation nor a justification.

These folkways constitute the social heritage which is handed down to children born into and growing up within the group. . . .

This is so, because the system of folkways establishes the standard in terms of which the in-group "defines its situation." Even more: originating in previous situations defined by the group, the scheme of interpretation that has stood the test so far becomes an element of the actual situation. To take the world for granted beyond question implies the deeprooted assumption that until further notice the world will go on substantially in the same manner as it has so far; that what has proved to be valid up to now will continue to be so, and that anything we or others like us could successfully perform once can be done again in a like way and will bring about substantially like results.

SELF-INTERPRETATION OF THE CULTURAL COMMUNITY*

The system of knowledge thus acquired—incoherent, inconsistent,

---

* EDITOR'S NOTE: Having discussed the characteristics and limitations of man's practical knowledge of everyday-life affairs (see "The Character of Practical Knowledge" in chapter 2 above), Schutz turned to the social foundations of this individual knowledge, as found in the cognitive system of the "in-group," the cultural community.

and only partially clear, as it is—takes on for the members of the in-group the appearance of a sufficient coherence, clarity, and consistency to give anybody a reasonable chance of understanding and of being understood. Any member born or reared within the group accepts the ready-made standardized scheme of the cultural pattern handed down to him by ancestors, teachers, and authorities as an unquestioned and unquestionable guide in all the situations which normally occur within the social world. The knowledge correlated to the cultural pattern carries its evidence in itself—or, rather, it is taken for granted in the absence of evidence to the contrary. It is a knowledge of trustworthy recipes for interpreting the social world and for handling things and men in order to obtain the best results in every situation with a minimum of effort by avoiding undesirable consequences. The recipe works, on the one hand, as a precept for actions and thus serves as a scheme of expression: whoever wants to obtain a certain result has to proceed as indicated by the recipe provided for this purpose. On the other hand, the recipe serves as a scheme of interpretation: whoever proceeds as indicated by a specific recipe is supposed to intend the correlated result. Thus it is the function of the cultural pattern to eliminate troublesome inquiries by offering ready-made directions for use, to replace truth hard to attain by comfortable truisms, and to substitute the self-explanatory for the questionable.

This "thinking as usual," as we may call it, corresponds to Max Scheler's idea of the "relatively natural conception of the world" (relativ natürliche Weltanschauung);[1] it includes the "of-course" assumptions relevant to a particular social group which Robert S. Lynd describes in such a masterly way—together with their inherent contradictions and ambivalence—as the "Middletown-spirit." Thinking as usual may be maintained as long as some basic assumptions hold true, namely: (1) that life and especially social life will continue to be the same as it has been so far, that is to say, that the same problems requiring the same solutions will recur

---

[1]   Max Scheler, "Probleme einer Soziologie des Wissens, *Die Wissensformen und die Gesellschaft* (Leipzig, 1926), pp. 58 ff; cf. Howard Becker and Hellmuth Otto Dahlke, "Max Scheler's Sociology of Knowledge," *Philosophy and Phenomenological Research* 2 (1942): 310–22, esp. p. 315.

and that, therefore, our former experiences will suffice for mastering future situations; (2) that we may relay on the knowledge handed down to us by parents, teachers, governments, traditions, habits, etc., even if we do not understand their origin and their real meaning; (3) that in the ordinary course of affairs it is sufficient to know something about the general type or style of events we may encounter in our life-world in order to manage or control them; and (4) that neither the systems of recipes as schemes of interpretation and expression nor the underlying basic assumptions just mentioned are our private affair, but that they are likewise accepted and applied by our fellow-men.

THE SUBJECTIVE MEANING OF GROUP MEMBERSHIP   The subjective meaning of the group, the meaning a group has for its members, has frequently been described in terms of a feeling among the members that they belong together, or that they share common interests. This is correct; but unfortunately, these concepts were only partially analyzed, namely, in terms of community and association (MacIver), *Gemeinschaft* and *Gesellschaft* (Toennies), primary and secondary groups (Cooley), and so on. . . .

. . . the subjective meaning the group has for its members consists in their knowledge of a common situation, and with it of a common system of typifications and relevances. This situation has its history in which the individual members' biographies participate; and the system of typification and relevances determining the situation forms a common relative natural conception of the world. Here the individual members are "at home," that is, they find their bearings without difficulty in the common surroundings, guided by a set of recipes of more or less institutionalized habits, mores, folkways, etc., that help them come to terms with beings and fellow men belonging to the same situation. The system of typifications and relevances shared with the other members of the group defines the social roles, positions, and statuses of each. This acceptance of a common system of relevances leads the members of the group to a homogeneous self-typification.

Our description holds good for both (a) existential groups with which I share a common social heritage, and (b) so-called voluntary groups joined or formed by me. The difference, however, is that in the first case the individual member finds himself within a preconstituted system of typifications, relevances, roles, positions, statuses not of his own making, but handed down to him as a social heritage. In the case of voluntary groups, however, this system is not experienced by the individual member as readymade; it has to be built up by the members and is therefore always involved in a process of dynamic evolution. Only some of the elements of the situation are common from the outset: the others have to be brought about by a common definition of the reciprocal situation.

Here a highly important problem is involved. How does the individual member of a group define his private situation within the framework of those common typifications and relevances in terms of which the group defines its situation? But before we proceed to an answer, a word of caution seems indicated.

Our description is a purely formal one and refers neither to the nature of the bond that holds the group together, nor to the extent, duration, or intimacy of the social contact. It is, therefore, equally applicable to a marriage or a business enterprise, to membership in a chess club or citizenship in a nation, to participation in a meeting or in Western culture. Each of these groups, however, refers to a larger one of which it is an element. A marriage or a business enterprise, of course, takes place within the general framework of the cultural setting of the larger group, and in accordance with the way of life (including its mores, morals, laws, and so forth) prevailing in this culture which is pregiven to the single actors as a scheme of orientation and interpretation of their actions. It is, however, up to the marriage or business partners to define, and continuously redefine, their individual (private) situation within this setting.

This is obviously the deeper reason why, to Max Weber, the existence of a marriage or a state means nothing but the mere chance (likelihood) that people act and will act in a specific way —or, in the terminology of this paper, in accordance with the general framework of typifications and relevances accepted beyond question by the particular sociocultural environment. Such a general framework is experienced by the individual members in terms of institutionalizations to be interiorized, and the individual has to define his personal unique situation by using the institutionalized pattern for the realization of his particular personal interests.

Here we have one aspect of the private definition of the individual's membership situation. A corollary to it is the particular attitude that the individual chooses to adopt toward the social role he has to fulfil within the group. One thing is the objective meaning of the social role and the role expectation as defined by the institutionalized pattern (say, the office of the Presidency of the United States); another thing is the particular subjective way in which the incumbent of this role defines his situation within it (Roosevelt's, Truman's, Eisenhower's interpretation of their mission).

The most important element in the definition of the private situation is, however, the fact that the individual finds himself always a member of numerous social groups. As Simmel has shown, each individual stands at the intersection of several social circles, and their number will be the greater the more differentiated the individual's personality. This is so because that which makes a personality unique is precisely that which cannot be shared with others.

According to Simmel, the group is formed by a process in which *many* individuals unite *parts* of their personalities—specific impulses, interests, forces—while what each personality really is, remains outside this common area. Groups are characteristically different according to the members' total personalities and those parts of their personalities with which they participate in the group. . . . In the individual's definition of his private situation the various social roles originating in his multiple membership in numerous groups are experienced as a set of self-typifications which in turn are arranged in a particular private order of domains of relevances that is, of course, continuously in flux. It is possible that exactly those features of the individual's personality which are to him of the highest order of relevance are irrelevant from the point of view of any system of relevances taken for granted by the group of which he is a member. This may lead to conflicts within the personality, mainly originating in the endeavor to live up to the various and frequently inconsistent role expectations inhering in the individual's membership in various social groups. As we have seen, it is only with respect to voluntary, and not to existential group membership that the individual is free to determine of which group he wants to be a member, and of which social role therein he wants to be the incumbent. It is, however, at least one aspect of freedom of the individual that he may choose for himself with which part of his personality he wants to participate in group memberships; that he may define his situation within the role of which he is the incumbent; and that he may establish his own private order of relevances in which each of his memberships in various groups has its rank.

II. *Outside and Inside Perspectives*

OUT-GROUP VIEW—IN-GROUP VIEW   The members of an out-group do not hold the ways of life of the in-group as self-evident truths. No article of faith and no historical tradition commits them to accept as the right and good ones the folkways of any group other than their own. Not only their central myth, but also the process of its rationalization and institutionalization are different. Other gods reveal other codes of the right and the good life, other things are sacred and taboo, other propositions of the Right of Nature are assumed.[2] The outsider measures the standards prevailing in the group under consideration in accordance with the system of relevances prevailing within the natural aspect the world has for his home-group. As long as a formula of transformation cannot be found which permits the translation of the system of relevances and typifications prevailing in the group under consideration into that of the home-group, the ways of the former remain un-understandable; but frequently they are considered to be of minor value and inferior.

This principle holds good, although in a slighter degree, even in the relationship between two groups that have many things in common, that is, where the two systems conform to a considerable extent. For example, Jewish immigrants from Iraq have consider-

---

[2]   T. V. Smith, in *The American Philosophy of Equality* (Chicago, 1927), p. 6, has pointed out that Locke used the State of Nature and Equality to overthrow tyrants, Hobbes to enthrone the "mortal God."

able difficulty in understanding that their practices of polygamy and child marriage are not permitted by the laws of Israel, the Jewish national home. Another example appears in the discussions in the French National Assembly of 1789, after Lafayette submitted his first draft of the Declaration of Human Rights modeled after the American pattern. Several speakers referred to the basic differences between American and French society: the situation of a new country, a colony having severed its relationship with its motherland, cannot be compared with that of a country which had enjoyed its own constitutional life for fourteen centuries. The principle of equality would have an entirely different function and meaning in the historical setting of both countries; the equal distribution of wealth and the equal way of life in America permit the application of equalitarian phraseology that would have the most disastrous consequences if applied to the highly differentiated French society.[3]

It is, however, important to understand that the self-interpretation by the in-group and the interpretation of the in-group's natural conception of the world by the out-groups are frequently interrelated, and this in a double respect:

a. On the one hand, the in-group feels itself frequently misunderstood by the out-group; such failure to understand its ways of life, so the in-group feels, must be rooted in hostile prejudices or in bad faith, since the truths held by the in-group are "matters of course," self-evident and, therefore, understandable by any human being. This feeling may lead to a partial shift of the system of relevances prevailing within the in-group, namely, by originating a solidarity of resistance against outside criticism. The out-group is then looked at with repugnance, disgust, aversion, antipathy, hatred, or fear.

b. On the other hand, a vicious circle[4] is thus set up because

[3]   Eric Voegelin, "Der Sinn der Erklärung der Menschen—und Bürgerrechte von 1789," *Zeitschrift für öffentliches Recht* 8 (1928) : 82–120.
[4]   On the problem of the vicious circle of prejudices, see R. M. MacIver, *The More Perfect Union* (New York, 1948), esp. pp. 68–81; also, United Nations, Memorandum of the Secretary-General, *The Main Types and Causes of Discrimination* Document E/Cn 4/Sub 2/40/Rev. of June 7, 1949, sections 56 ff.

the out-group, by the changed reaction of the in-group, is fortified in its interpretation of the traits of the in-group as highly detestable. In more general terms: to the natural aspect the world has for group A belongs not only a certain stereotyped idea of the natural aspect the world has for group B, but included in it also is a stereotype of the way in which group B supposedly looks at A. This is, on a major scale—i.e., in the relationship between groups—the same phenomenon which, in respect of relations between individuals, Cooley has called the "looking-glass effect."

Such a situation may lead to various attitudes of the in-group toward the out-group: the in-group may stick to its way of life and try to change the attitude of the out-group by an educational process of spreading information, or by persuasion, or by appropriate propaganda. Or the in-group may try to adjust its way of thinking to that of the out-group by accepting the latter's pattern of relevances at least partially. Or a policy of iron curtain or of appeasement might be established; and finally there will be no other way to disrupt the vicious circle but war at any temperature. A secondary consequence might be that those members of the in-group who plead for a policy of mutual understanding are designated by the spokesmen of radical ethnocentrism as disloyal or traitors, etc., a fact which again leads to a change in the self-interpretation of the social group.

STRANGER IN THE COMMUNITY The stranger . . . becomes essentially the man who has to place in question nearly everything that seems to be unquestionable to the members of the approached group.

To him the cultural pattern of the approached group does not have the authority of a tested system of recipes, and this, if for no other reason, because he does not partake in the vivid historical tradition by which it has been formed. To be sure, from the stranger's point of view, too, the culture of the approached group has its peculiar history, and this history is even accessible to him. But it has never become an integral part of his biography, as did the history of his home group. Only the ways in which his fathers and grandfathers lived become for everyone elements of his own way of life. Graves and reminiscences can neither be transferred nor conquered. The stranger, therefore, approaches the other group as a newcomer in the true meaning of the term. At best he may be willing and able to share the present and the future with the approached group in vivid and immediate experience; under all circumstances, however, he remains excluded from such experiences of its past. Seen from the point of view of the approached group, he is a man without a history.

To the stranger the cultural pattern of his home group continues to be the outcome of an unbroken historical development and an element of his personal biography which for this very reason has been and still is the unquestioned scheme of reference for his "relatively natural conception of the world." As a matter of course, therefore, the stranger starts to interpret his new social environment in terms of his thinking as usual. Within the scheme of reference brought from his home group, however, he finds a ready-made idea of the pattern supposedly valid within the approached group—an idea which necessarily will soon prove inadequate. . . .

First, the idea of the cultural pattern of the approached group which the stranger finds within the interpretive scheme of his home group has originated in the attitude of a disinterested observer. The approaching stranger, however, is about to transform himself from an unconcerned onlooker into a would-be member of the approached group. The cultural pattern of the approached group, then, is no longer a subject matter of his thought but a segment of the world which has to be dominated by actions. Consequently, its position within the stranger's system of relevance changes decisively, and this means, as we have seen, that another type of knowledge is required for its interpretation. Jumping from the stalls to the stage, so to speak, the former onlooker becomes a member of the cast, enters as a partner into social relations with his co-actors, and participates henceforth in the action in progress.

Second, the new cultural pattern acquires an environmental character. Its remoteness changes into proximity; its vacant frames become occupied by vivid experiences; its anonymous contents turn into definite social situations; its ready-made typologies disintegrate. In other words, the level or environmental experience of social objects is incongruous with the level of mere beliefs about unapproached objects; by passing from the latter to the former, any concept originating in the level of departure becomes necessarily inadequate if applied to the new level without having been restated in its terms.

Third, the ready-made picture of the foreign group subsisting within the stranger's home-group proves its inadequacy for the approaching stranger for the mere reason that it has not been formed with the aim of provoking a response from or a reaction of the members of the foreign group. The knowledge which it offers serves merely as a handy scheme for interpreting the foreign group and not as a guide for interaction between the two groups. Its validity is primarily based on the consensus of those members of the home group who do not intend to establish a direct social relationship with members of the foreign group. (Those who intend to do so are in a situation analogous to that of the approaching stranger.) Consequently, the scheme of interpretation refers to the members of the foreign group merely as objects of this interpretation, but not beyond it, as addressees of possible acts emanating from the outcome of the interpretive procedure and not as subjects of anticipated reactions toward those acts. Hence, this kind of knowledge is, so to speak, insulated; it can be neither verified nor falsified by responses of the members of the foreign group. The latter, therefore, consider this knowledge—by a kind of "looking-glass" effect[5]—as both irresponsive and irresponsible and complain of its prejudices, bias, and misunderstandings. The approaching stranger, however, becomes aware of the fact that an important element of his "thinking as usual," namely, his ideas of the foreign group, its cultural pattern, and its way of life, do not stand the test of vivid experience and social interaction.

The discovery that things in his new surroundings look quite different from what he expected them to be at home is frequently the first shock to the stranger's confidence in the validity of his habitual "thinking as usual." Not only the picture which the

[5]   In using this term, we allude to Cooley's well-known theory of the reflected or looking-glass self (Charles H. Cooley, *Human Nature and the Social Order*, rev. ed. [New York, 1922], p. 184).

stranger has brought along of the cultural pattern of the approached group but the whole hitherto unquestioned scheme of interpretation current within the home group becomes invalidated. It cannot be used as a scheme of orientation within the new social surroundings. For the members of the approached group their cultural pattern fulfils the functions of such a scheme. But the approaching stranger can neither use it simply as it is nor establish a general formula of transformation between both cultural patterns permitting him, so to speak, to convert all the co-ordinates within one scheme of orientation into those valid within the other—and this for the following reasons.

First, any scheme of orientation presupposes that everyone who uses it looks at the surrounding world as grouped around himself who stands at its center. He who wants to use a map successfully has first of all to know his standpoint in two respects: its location on the ground and its representation on the map. Applied to the social world this means that only members of the in-group, having a definite status in its hierarchy and also being aware of it, can use its cultural pattern as a natural and trustworthy scheme of orientation. The stranger, however, has to face the fact that he lacks any status as a member of the social group he is about to join and is therefore unable to get a starting point to take his bearings. He finds himself a border case outside the territory covered by the scheme of orientation current within the group. He is, therefore, no longer permitted to consider himself as the center of his social environment, and this fact causes again a dislocation of his contour lines of relevance.

Second, the cultural pattern and its recipes represent only for the members of the in-group a unit of coinciding schemes of interpretation as well as of expression. For the outsider, however, this seeming unity falls to pieces. The approaching stranger has to "translate" its terms into terms of the cultural pattern of his home group, provided that, within the latter, interpretive equivalents exist at all. If they exist, the translated terms may be understood and remembered; they can be recognized by recurrence; they are at hand but not in hand. Yet, even then, it is obvious that the stranger cannot assume that his interpretation of the new cultural pattern coincides with that current with the members of the in-group. On the contrary, he has to reckon with fundamental discrepancies in seeing things and handling situations.

Only after having thus collected a certain knowledge of the interpretive function of the new cultural pattern may the stranger start to adopt it as the scheme of his own expression. The difference between the two stages of knowledge is familiar to any student of foreign language and has received the full attention of psychologists dealing with the theory of learning. It is the difference between the passive understanding of a language and its active mastering as a means for realizing one's own acts and thoughts.

THE INSIDER'S VIEW AND THE STRANGER'S ORIENTATION
We may say that the member of the in-group looks in one single glance through the normal social situations occurring to him and that he catches immediately the ready-made recipe appropriate to its solution. In those situations his acting shows all the marks of habituality, automatism, and half-consciousness. This is possible because the cultural pattern provides by its recipes typical solutions for typical problems available for typical actors. In other words, the chance of obtaining the desired standardized result by applying a standardized recipe is an objective one; that is open to everyone who conducts himself like the anonymous type required by the recipe. Therefore, the actor who follows a recipe does not have to check whether this objective chance coincides with a subjective chance, that is, a chance open to him, the individual, by reason of his personal circumstances and faculties which subsists independently of the question whether other people in similar situations could or could not act in the same way with the same likelihood. Even more, it can be stated that the objective chances for the efficiency of a recipe are the greater, the fewer deviations from the anonymous typified behavior occur, and this holds especially for recipes designed for social interaction. This kind of recipe, if it is to work, presupposes that any partner expects the other to act or to react typically, provided that the actor himself acts typically. He who wants to travel by railroad has to behave in that typical way which the type "railroad agent" may reasonably expect as the

typical conduct of the type "passenger," and vice versa. Neither party examines the subjective chances involved. The scheme, being designed for everyone's use, need not be tested for its fitness for the peculiar individual who employs it.

For those who have grown up within the cultural pattern, not only the recipes and their efficiency chance but also the typical and anonymous attitudes required by them are an unquestioned "matter of course" which gives them both security and assurance. In other words, these attitudes by their very anonymity and typicality are placed not within the actor's stratum of relevance which requires explicit knowledge *of* but in the region of mere acquaintance in which it will do to put one's trust. This interrelation between objective chance, typicality, anonymity, and relevance seems to be rather important.

For the approaching stranger, however, the pattern of the approached group does not guarantee an objective chance for success but rather a pure subjective likelihood which has to be checked step by step, that is, he has to make sure that the solutions suggested by the new scheme will also produce the desired effect for him in his special position as outsider and newcomer who has not brought within his grasp the whole system of the cultural pattern but who is rather puzzled by its inconsistency, incoherence, and lack of clarity. He has, first of all, to use the term of W. I. Thomas, to *define* the situation. Therefore, he cannot stop at an approximate acquaintance with the new pattern, trusting in his vague knowledge *about* its general style and structure but needs an explicit knowledge *of* its elements, inquiring not only into their *that* but into their *why*. Consequently, the shape of his contour lines of relevance by necessity differs radically from those of a member of the in-group as to situations, recipes, means, ends, social partners, etc. Keeping in mind the above-mentioned interrelationship between relevance, on the one hand, and typicality and anonymity, on the other, it follows that he uses another yardstick for anonymity and typicality of social acts than the members of the in-group. For to the stranger the observed actors within the approached group are not—as for their co-actors—of a certain presupposed anonymity, namely, mere performers of typical functions, but individuals.

On the other hand, he is inclined to take mere individual traits as typical ones. Thus he constructs a social world of pseudo-anonymity, pseudo-intimacy, and pseudo-typicality. Therefore, he cannot integrate the personal types constructed by him into a coherent picture of the approached group and cannot rely on his expectation of their response. And even less can the stranger himself adopt those typical and anonymous attitudes which a member of the in-group is entitled to expect from a partner in a typical situation. Hence the stranger's lack of feeling for distance, his oscillating between remoteness and intimacy, his hesitation and uncertainty, and his distrust in every matter which seems to be so simple and uncomplicated to those who rely on the efficiency of unquestioned recipes which have just to be followed but not understood.

In other words, the cultural pattern of the approached group is to the stranger not a shelter but a field of adventure, not a matter of course but a questionable topic of investigation, not an instrument for disentangling problematic situations but a problematic situation itself and one hard to master.

These facts explain two basic traits of the stranger's attitude toward the group to which nearly all sociological writers dealing with this topic have rendered special attention, namely, (1) the stranger's objectivity and (2) his doubtful loyalty.

1. The stranger's objectivity cannot be sufficiently explained by his critical attitude. To be sure, he is not bound to worship the "idols of the tribe" and has a vivid feeling for the incoherence and inconsistency of the approached cultural pattern. But this attitude originates far less in his propensity to judge the newly approached group by the standards brought from home than in his need to acquire full knowledge *of* the elements of the approached cultural pattern and to examine for this purpose with care and precision what seems self-explanatory to the in-group. The deeper reason for his objectivity, however, lies in his own bitter experience of the limits of the "thinking as usual," which has taught him that a man may lose his status, his rules of guidance, and even his history and that the normal way of life is always far less guaranteed than it seems. Therefore, the stranger discerns, frequently with a grievous

clear-sightedness, the rising of a crisis which may menace the whole foundation of the "relatively natural conception of the "world," while all those symptoms pass unnoticed by the members of the in-group, who rely on the continuance of their customary way of life.

2. The doubtful loyalty of the stranger is unfortunately very frequently more than a prejudice on the part of the approached group. This is especially true in cases in which the stranger proves unwilling or unable to substitute the new cultural pattern entirely for that of the home group. Then the stranger remains what Park and Stonequist have aptly called a "marginal man," a cultural hybrid on the verge of two different patterns of group life, not knowing to which of them he belongs. But very frequently the reproach of doubtful loyalty originates in the astonishment of the members of the in-group that the stranger does not accept the total of its cultural pattern as the natural and appropriate way of life and as the best of all possible solutions of any problem. The stranger is called ungrateful, since he refuses to acknowledge that the cultural pattern offered to him grants him shelter and protection. But these people do not understand that the stranger in the state of transition does not consider this pattern as a protecting shelter at all, but as a labyrinth in which he has lost all sense of his bearings.

THE OBJECTIVE MEANING OF GROUP MEMBERSHIP   The objective meaning of group membership is that which the group has from the point of view of outsiders who speak of its members in terms of "They." In objective interpretation the notion of the group is a conceptual construct of the outsider. By the operation of *his* system of typifications and relevances he subsumes individuals showing certain particular characteristics and traits under a social category that is homogeneous merely from his, the outsider's, point of view.

It is of course possible that the social category constructed by the outsider corresponds to a social reality, namely, that the principles governing such typification are considered also by the individuals thus typified as elements of *their* situation as defined by *them* and as being relevant from *their* point of view. Even then, the interpretation of the group by the outsider will never fully coincide with the self-interpretation by the in-group. . . .

It is also possible, however, that people considering one another as heterogeneous may be placed by the outsider's typification under the same social category, which then is treated as if it were a homogeneous unit. The situation in which individuals are placed in this way by the outsider is of his, but not of their definition. For this reason the system of relevances leading to such typification is taken for granted merely by the outsider, but is not necessarily accepted by the individuals who may not be prepared to perform a corresponding self-typification.

4

SOCIAL MEANS OF ORIENTATION AND INTERPRETATION

Language and Social Knowledge

ONLY A VERY SMALL part of my knowledge of the world originates within my personal experience. The greater part is socially derived, handed down to me by my friends, my parents, my teachers and the teachers of my teachers. I am not only taught how to define the environment (that is, the typical features of the relative natural aspect of the world prevailing in the in-group as the unquestioned but always questionable sum total of things taken for granted until further notice), but also how typical constructs have to be formed in accordance with the system of relevances accepted from the anonymous unified point of view of the in-group. This includes ways of life, how to come to terms with the environment, efficient recipes for the use of typical means for bringing about typical ends in typical situations. The typifying medium *par excellence* by which socially derived knowledge is transmitted is the vocabulary and the syntax of everyday language. The vernacular of everyday life is primarily a language of named things and events, and any name includes a typification and generalization referring to the relevance system prevailing in the linguistic in-group which found the named thing significant enough to provide a separate term for it. The pre-scientific vernacular can be interpreted as a treasure house of ready-made pre-constituted types and characteristics, all socially derived and carrying along an open horizon of unexplored content.

Reprinted from the following items in the Bibliography: 1953c, 9–10; 1944, 504–5; 1955b, 156–57; 1955b, 157–59; 1967, 118–20, 120–23, 124–25.

Language in the Context of Culture

Language as a scheme of interpretation and expression does not merely consist of the linguistic symbols catalogued in the dictionary and of the syntactical rules enumerated in an ideal grammar. The former are translatable into other languages; the latter are understandable by referring them to corresponding or deviating rules of the unquestioned mother-tongue.[1] However, several other factors supervene.

1. Every word and every sentence is, to borrow . . . a term of William James, surrounded by "fringes" connecting them, on the one hand, with past and future elements of the universe of discourse to which they pertain, and surrounding them, on the other hand, with a halo of emotional values and irrational implications which themselves remain ineffable. The fringes are the stuff poetry is made of; they are capable of being set to music but they are not translatable.

2. There are in any language terms with several connotations. They, too, are noted in the dictionary. But, besides these standardized connotations, every element of the speech acquires its special secondary meaning derived from the context or the social environment within which it is used and, in addition, gets a special tinge from the actual occasion in which it is employed.

3. Idioms, technical terms, jargons, and dialects, whose use remains restricted to specific social groups, exist in every language, and their significance can be learned by an outsider too. But, in addition, every social group, be it ever so small (if not, every individual), has its own private code, understandable only by those who have participated in the common past experiences in which it took rise or in the tradition connected with them.

4. As Vossler has shown, the whole history of the linguistic group is mirrored in its way of saying things.[2] All the other ele-

[1] Therefore, the learning of a foreign language reveals to the student, frequently for the first time, the grammatical rules of his mother-tongue which he has followed so far as "the most natural thing in the world," namely, as recipes.

[2] Karl Vossler, *Geist und Kultur in der Sprache* (Heidelberg, 1925), pp. 117 ff.

ments of group life enter into it—above all, its literature. The erudite stranger, for example, approaching an English-speaking country is heavily handicapped if he has not read the Bible and Shakespeare in the English language, even if he grew up with translations of those books in his mother-tongue.

All the above-mentioned features are accessible only to the members of the in-group. They all pertain to the scheme of expression. They are not teachable and cannot be learned in the same way as, for example, the vocabulary. In order to command a language freely as a scheme of expression, one must have written love letters in it; one has to know how to pray and curse in it and how to say things with every shade appropriate to the addressee and to the situation. Only members of the in-group have the scheme of expression as a genuine one in hand and command it freely within their thinking as usual.

Marks

I experience the world within my actual reach as an element or phase of my unique biographical situation, and this involves a transcending of the Here and Now to which it belongs. To my unique biographical situation pertain, among many other things, my recollections of the world within my reach in the past but no longer within it since I moved from There to Here, and my anticipations of a world to come within my reach and which I must move from Here to another There in order to bring it into my reach. I know or assume that, disregarding technical obstacles and other limitations, such as the principal irretrievability of the past, I can bring my recollected world back into my actual reach if I return to whence I came (*world within restorable reach*); I expect also to find it substantially the same (although, perhaps, changed) as I had experienced it while it was within my actual reach; and I know or assume also that what is now within my actual reach will go out of my reach when I move away but will be, in principle, restorable if I later return.

The latter case is to me of an eminently practical interest. I expect that what is now within my actual reach will go out of my reach but will later on come into my actual reach again, and, especially, I anticipate that what is now in my manipulatory sphere will reenter it later and require my interference or will interfere with me. Therefore I have to be sure that I shall then find my bearings within it and come to terms with it as I can now while it is within my control. This presupposes that I shall be able to recognize those elements which I now find relevant in the world within my actual reach, especially within the manipulatory zone, and which (I assume by a general idealization, called the idealization of "I can do it again" by Husserl)[3] will prove relevant also when I return later on. I am, thus, *motivated* to single out and to *mark* certain objects. When I return I expect these marks to be useful as "subjective reminders" or "mnemonic devices" (Wild's terms).[4] It is immaterial whether such a mnemonic device consists of the breaking of the branch of a tree or the selecting of a particular landmark to mark the trail to the waterhole. A bookmark at the page where I stopped reading or underlining certain passages of this volume or pencil-strokes on the margin are also marks or subjective reminders. What counts is merely that all these marks, themselves objects of the outer world, will from now on be intuited not as mere "selves" in the pure apperceptual scheme. They entered for me, the interpreter, into an appresentational reference. The broken branch of the tree is more than just that. It became a mark for the location of the waterhole, or, if you prefer, a signal for me to turn left. In its appresentational function, which originates in the interpretational scheme bestowed upon it by me, the broken branch is now paired with its referential meaning: "Way to the waterhole."

This mark which functions as a subjective reminder is one of the simplest forms of the appresentational relationship; it is detached from any intersubjective context. The inherently arbitrary character of my selecting certain objects as "marks" should be emphasized. The mark has "nothing to do" with what it should remind me of, both are in an interpretational context merely because

---

3   Edmund Husserl, *Formale und transcendentale Logik* (Halle, 1929), sec. 74, p. 167.
4   John Wild, "Introduction to the Phenomenology of Signs," *Philosophy and Phenomenological Research* 8 (1947):224.

such a context was established by me. According to the principle of the relative irrelevance of the vehicle, I may replace the broken branch by a stonepile, according to the principle of figurative transference, I may dedicate this stonepile to a naiad, etc.

Indications

We mentioned before the stock of knowledge at hand as an element of my biographical situation. This stock of knowledge is by no means homogeneous. William James[5] has already distinguished between "knowledge about" and "knowledge of acquaintance." There are, moreover, zones of blind belief and ignorance. The structuration of my stock of knowledge at hand is determined by the fact that I am not *equally* interested in all the strata of the world within my reach. The selective function of interest organizes the world for me in strata of major and minor relevance. From the world within my actual or potential reach are selected as primarily important, those facts, objects, and events which actually are or will become possible ends or means, possible obstacles or conditions for the realization of my projects, or which are or will become dangerous or enjoyable or otherwise relevant to me.

Certain facts, objects, and events are known to me as being interrelated in a more or less typical way, but my knowledge of the particular kind of interrelatedness might be rather vague or even lack transparency. If I know that event B usually appears simultaneously or precedes or follows event A, then I take this as a manifestation of a typical and plausible relationship existing between A and B, although I know nothing of the nature of this relationship. Until further notice I simply expect or take it for granted that any future recurrence of an event of type A will be connected in typically the same way with a preceding, concomitant, or subsequent recurrence of an event of type B. I may then apprehend A not as an object, fact, or event standing for itself, but standing for something else, namely, referring to the past, present or future appearance of B. Here again we have a form of pairing by appre-

[5]   James, *Principles of Psychology* (New York, 1890), 1:221.

sentation which most authors subsume under the concept of sign. We prefer to reserve the term "sign" for other purposes and to call the appresentational relationship under scrutiny *indication*.

Husserl[6] has characterized this relationship of indication (*"Anzeichen"*) as follows: an object, fact, or event (*A*), actually perceptible to me, may be experienced as related to another past, present, or future fact or event (*B*), actually not perceptible to me, in such a way, that my conviction of the existence of the former (*A*) is experienced by me as an *opaque* motive for my conviction for, assumption of, or belief in the past, present, or future existence of the latter (*B*). This motivation constitutes for me a pairing between the indicating (*A*) and the indicated (*B*) elements. The indicating member of the pair is not only a "witness" for the indicated one, it does not only point to it, but it suggests the assumption that the other member exists, has existed, or will exist. Again the indicating member is not perceived as a "self," that is, merely in the apperceptual scheme, but as "wakening" or "calling forth" appresentationally the indicated one. It is, however, important that the particular nature of the motivational connection remain opaque. If there is clear and sufficient insight into the nature of the connection between the two elements, we have to deal not with the referential relation of indication but with the inferential one of *proof*. The qualification contained in the last statement eliminates, therefore, the possibility of calling the footprint of a tiger (recognized as such) an indication or "sign" of his presence in the locality. But the halo around the moon indicates coming rain, the smoke fire, a certain formation of the surface oil in the subsoil, a certain pigmentation of the face Addison's disease, the position of a needle on the dial of my car an empty gas tank, etc.

The relationship of indication as described covers most of the phenomena generally subsumed under the category of "natural signs." The knowledge of indications is of eminent importance from the practical point of view, because it helps the individual transcend the world within his actual reach by relating elements within it to elements outside it.

[6] Husserl, *Logische Untersuchungen I*, vol. 2/1, secs. 1–4, esp. p. 27.

Signs and Sign-Systems*

First of all, let us see how a sign gets constituted in the mind of the interpreter. We say that there exists between the sign and that which it signifies the relation of representation. When we look at a symbol, which is always in a broad sense an external object, we do not look upon it *as object* but *as representative* of something else. When we "understand" a sign, our attention is focused not on the sign itself but upon that for which it stands. Husserl repeatedly points out that it belongs to the essence of the signitive relation that "the sign and what it stands for have nothing to do with each other." The signitive relation is, therefore, obviously a particular relation between the interpretive schemes which are applied to those external objects here called "signs." When we understand a sign, we do not interpret the latter through the scheme adequate to it as an external object but through the schemes adequate to whatever it signifies. We are saying that an interpretive scheme is *adequate* to an experienced object if the scheme has been constituted out of polythetically lived-through experiences of this same object as a self-existent thing. For example, the following three black lines, *A*, can be interpreted (1) *adequately*, as the diagram of a certain black and white visual Gestalt, or (2) *nonadequately*, as a sign for the corresponding vocal sound. The adequate interpretive scheme for the vocal sound is, of course, constituted not out of visual but out of auditory experiences.

However, confusion is likely to arise out of the fact that the interpretation of signs in terms of what they signify is based on previous experience and is therefore itself the function of a scheme.

What we have said holds true of all interpretation of signs,

* EDITOR'S NOTE: In this selection, taken from his earliest publication, Schutz used the terms *signs* and *symbols* interchangeably. Thereby he was following a still widespread usage. In his later work, however, in part under the influence of ideas developed by William James, he made a sharp distinction between the two. The reader should keep in mind that wherever the term *symbol* occurs in this selection, it has the connotation of *sign*. For Schutz's later conception of *symbol*, see "Transcendences and Multiple Realities" in chapter 12 below.

whether the individual is interpreting his own signs or those of others. There is, however, an ambiguity in the common saying "a sign is always a sign for something." The sign is indeed the "sign for" what it means or signifies, the so-called "sign meaning" or "sign function." But the sign is also the "sign for" what it expresses, namely, the subjective experiences of the person using the sign. In the world of nature there are no signs (*Zeichen*) but only indications (*Anzeichen*). A sign is by its very nature something used by a person to express a subjective experience. Since, therefore, the sign always refers back to an act of choice on the part of a rational being—a choice of this particular sign—the sign is also an indication of an event in the mind of the sign-user. Let us call this the "expressive function" of the sign.

A sign is, therefore, always either an artifact or a constituted act-object.[7] The boundary between the two is absolutely fluid. Every act-object which functions as a sign-object (for instance, my finger pointing in a certain direction) is the end result of an action. But I might just as well have constructed a signpost, which would, of course, be classified as an artifact. In principle it makes no difference whether the action culminates in an act-object or in an artifact.

It should be noted that in interpreting a sign it is not necessary to refer to the fact that someone made the sign or that someone used it. The interpreter need only "know the meaning" of the sign. In other words, it is necessary only that a connection be established in his mind between the interpretive scheme proper to the object which is the sign and the interpretive scheme proper to the object which it signifies. Thus when he sees a road sign, he will say to himself, "Intersection to the left!" and not "Look at the wooden sign!" or "Who put that sign there?"

We can, therefore, define signs as follows: Signs are artifacts or act-objects which are interpreted not according to those inter-

---

7   [The words here translated "act-object" and "sign-object" are, respectively, *Handlungsgegenständlichkeit* and *Zeichengegenständlichkeit*. They refer to the act and sign considered as repeatable objects rather than as unique events.]

pretive schemes which are adequate to them as objects of the external world but according to schemes not adequate to them and belonging rather to other objects. Furthermore, it should be said that the connection between the sign and its corresponding non-adequate scheme depends on the past experience of the interpreter. As we have already said, the applicability of the scheme of that which is signified to the sign is itself an interpretive scheme based on experience. Let us call this last-named scheme the "sign system." A sign system is a meaning-context which is a configuration formed by interpretive schemes; the sign-user or the sign-interpreter places the sign within this context of meaning.

The Objective Meaning of Sign Systems

Now there is something ambiguous in this idea of a sign context. Surely no one will maintain that the connection in question exists independently of the actual establishment, use, or interpretation of the signs. For the connection is itself an example of meaning and therefore a matter of either prescription or interpretation. In a strict sense, therefore, meaning-connections hold, not between signs as such, but between their meanings, which is just another way of saying between the experiences of the knowing self establishing, using, or interpreting the signs. However, since these "meanings" are understood only in and through the signs, there holds between the latter the connection we call the "sign system."

The sign system is present to him who understands it as a meaning-context of a higher order between previously experienced signs. To him the German language is the meaning-context of each of its component words; the sign system of a map is the meaning-context of every symbol on that map; the system of musical-notation is the meaning-context of every written note; and so forth.

Knowing that a sign belongs to a certain sign system is not the same thing as knowing *what* that sign means and for what subjective experience of its user it is the expressive vehicle. Even though I do not know shorthand, still I know shorthand when I see it. Even though I may not know how to play a card game, still I can recognize the cards as *playing* cards, etc. The placing of a sign within its sign system is something I do by placing it within the total context of my experience. In doing this, all that is necessary is that I find within the store of my experience such a sign system together with the rules on the basis of which it is constituted. I do not have to understand the meaning of the individual signs or be fully conversant with the sign system. For instance, I can see that certain characters are Chinese without understanding their meaning.

As an *established* sign every sign is meaningful and therefore in principle intelligible. In general it is absurd to speak of a meaningless sign. A sign can properly be called meaningless only with respect to one or more established sign systems. However, to say that a sign is alien to one such system only means that it belongs to another. For instance, the meaninglessness per se of a definite auditory-visual symbol can never be determined but only its meaninglessness within a definite "language," in the broadest sense of that term. A letter combination which is quite unpronounceable can have a code meaning. It can be put together by one person according to the rules of the code and can then be interpreted by another person who knows those same rules. More than that, however, the audio-visual symbol "Bamalip" seems at first quite meaningless so far as the European languages are concerned. But the person who knows that "Bamalip" is the scholastic term for an entity of formal logic, namely, the first mood of the fourth figure of the syllogism, will be able to place it quite precisely within the structure of his own native language.

From this it follows that the sign meaning within a certain sign system must have been experienced previously. It is a question just what this phrase, "have been experienced," means. If we ask ourselves in what circumstances we have experienced the connection between the term "Bamalip" and the first mood of the fourth figure, we will find that we have learned it from a teacher or from a book. To have experienced the connection, however, means that we must on that occasion have established in our minds the term "Bamalip" as the sign of the first mood of the fourth figure. Therefore, the understanding of a sign (to be more precise, the possibility of its interpretation within a given system) points back to a previous decision on our part to accept and use this sign as an expression for a certain content of our consciousness.

Every sign system is therefore a scheme of our experience. This is true in two different senses. First, it is an *expressive scheme;* in other words, I have at least once used the sign for that which it designates, used it either in spontaneous activity or in imagination. Second, it is an *interpretive scheme;* in other words, I have already in the past interpreted the sign as the sign of that which it designates. This distinction is important, since, as already shown, I can recognize the sign system as an interpretive scheme, but only know that others do so. In the world of the solitary Ego the expressive scheme of a sign and its corresponding interpretive scheme necessarily coincide. If, for instance, I invent a private script, the characters of that code are established by me while I am inventing the script or using it to make notes. It is for me at such moments an expressive scheme. But the same scheme functions as an interpretive one for me when I later read what I have written or use it to make further notes.

To master fully a sign system such as a language, it is necessary to have a clear knowledge of the meaning of the individual signs within the system. This is possible only if the sign system and its component individual signs are known both as expressive schemes and as interpretive schemes for previous experiences of the knower. In both functions, as interpretive scheme and as expressive scheme, every sign points back to the experiences which preceded its constituting. As expressive scheme and as interpretive scheme a sign is only intelligible in terms of those lived experiences constituting it which it designates. Its meaning consists in its translatibility, that is, its ability to lead us back to somethng known in a different way. This may be either that scheme of experience in which the thing designated is understood, or another sign system. The philologist Meillet explains this point clearly as far as languages are concerned:

We cannot apprehend the sense of an unknown language intuitively. If we are to succeed in understanding the text of a language whose tradition has been lost, me must either have a faithful translation into a known language, that is, we must be closely related to one or more languages with which we are familiar. In other words, *we must already know it.*[8]

This property of "being already known" amounts to this: the meaning of the sign must be discoverable somewhere in the past experience of the person making use of the sign. To be fully conversant with a language, or in fact with any sign system, involves familiarity with given interpretive schemes on the basis of one's preceding experiences—even though this familiarity may be somewhat confused as to the implications of the schemes. It also involves the ability to transform these constituted objects into active experience of one's own, that is, in the ability to use expressively a sign system that one knows how to interpret.

We are now getting close to an answer to the question of what is meant by "connecting a meaning with a sign." . . . A meaning is connected with a sign, insofar as the latter's significance within a given sign system is understood both for the person using the sign and for the person interpreting it. Now we must be quite clear as to what we mean by speaking of the established membership of a sign in a given sign system. A sign has an "objective meaning" within its sign system when it can be intelligibly coordinated to what it designates within that system independently of whoever is using the sign or interpreting it. This is merely to say that he who "masters" the sign system will interpret the sign in its meaning-function to refer to that which it designates, regardless of who is using it or in what connection. The indispensable reference of the sign to previous experience makes it possible for the interpreter to repeat the syntheses that have constituted this interpretive or expressive scheme. Within the sign system, therefore, the sign has the ideality of the "I can do it again."

However, this is not to say that the signs within the previously known sign system cannot be understood without an Act of attention to those lived experiences out of which the knowledge of the sign was constituted. On the contrary: as a genuine interpretive

[8]   Quoted in Vossler, *Geist und Kultur in der Sprache*, p. 115. [Translated by Oscar Oeser as *The Spirit of Language in Civilization* (London, 1932), p. 104. The reference is to A. Meillet, *Aperçu d'une histoire de la langue grecque* (Paris, 1913), p. 48.]

scheme for previous lived experiences, it is invariant with respect to the lived experiences of the I in which it was constituted.

Expressive Function of Signs

What we have been considering is the objective meaning of the sign. The objective meaning is grasped by the sign-interpreter as a part of his interpretation of his own experience to himself. With this objective meaning of the sign we must contrast the sign's expressive function. The latter is its function as an indication of what actually went on in the mind of the communicator, the person who used the sign; in other words, of what was the communicator's own meaning-context.

If I want to understand the meaning of a word in a foreign language, I make use of a dictionary, which is simply an index in which I can see the signs arranged according to their objective meaning in two different sign systems or languages. However, the total of all the words in the dictionary is hardly the language. The dictionary is concerned only with the objective meanings of the words, that is, the meanings which do not depend on the users of the words or the circumstances in which they use them. In referring to subjective meanings, we do not here have in mind Husserl's "essentially subjective and occasional expressions." . . . Such essentially subjective expressions as "left," "right," "here," "there," "this," and "I" can, of course, be found in the dictionary and are in principle translatable; however, they also have an objective meaning insofar as they designate a certain relation to the person who uses them. Once I have spatially located this person, then I can say that these subjective occasional expressions have objective meaning. However, *all* expressions, whether essentially subjective in Husserl's sense or not, have for both user and interpreter, over and above their objective meaning, a meaning which is both subjective and occasional. Let us first consider the *subjective* component. Everyone using or interpreting a sign associates with the sign a certain meaning having its origin in the unique quality of the experiences in which he once learned to use the sign. This added meaning is a kind of aura surrounding the nucleus of the objective meaning.[9] Exactly what Goethe means by "demonic" can only be deduced from a study of his works as a whole. Only a careful study of the history of French culture aided by linguistic tools can permit us to understand the subjective meaning of the word "civilization" in the mouth of a Frenchman. Vossler applies this thesis to the whole history of language in the following way: "We study the development of a word; and we find that the mental life of all who have used it has been precipitated and crystallized in it."[10] However, in order to be able to "study" the word, we must be able to bring to bear from our previous experience a knowledge of the mental structure of all those who have used it. The particular quality of the experiences of the user of the sign at the time he connected the sign and the *signatum* is something which the interpreter must take into account, over and above the objective meaning, if he wishes to achieve true understanding.

We have said that the added meaning is not only subjective but *occasional*. In other words, the added meaning always has in it something of the context in which it is used. In understanding someone who is speaking, I interpret not only his individual words but his total articulated sequence of syntactically connected words —in short, "what he is saying." In this sequence every word retains its own individual meaning in the midst of the surrounding words and throughout the total context of what is being said. Still, I cannot really say that I understand the word until I have grasped the meaning of the whole statement. In short, what I need at the moment of interpretation is the total context of my experience. As the statement proceeds, a synthesis is built up step by step, from the point of view of which one can see the individual acts of meaning-interpretation and meaning-establishment. Discourse is, therefore, itself a kind of meaning-context. For both the speaker

[9]   In fact, we can even say that the understanding of the objective meaning is an unrealizable ideal, which means merely that the subjective and occasional component in the sign's meaning should be explained with the utmost clarity by means of rational concepts. That language is "precise" in which all occasional subjective meanings are adequately explained according to their circumstances.

[10]   Vossler, *Geist und Kultur in der Sprache*, p. 117 [Oeser trans., p. 106].

and the interpreter, the structure of the discourse emerges gradually. The German language expresses the point we are making precisely in its distinction between *Wörter* ("unconnected words") and *Worte* ("discourse"). We can, in fact, say that when unconnected words receive occasional meaning, they constitute a meaningful whole and become discourse.

5

SELECTIVE ATTENTION: RELEVANCES AND TYPIFICATION

Zones of Relevance

THE ZONE of things taken for granted may be defined as that sector of the world which, in connection with the theoretical or the practical problem we are concerned with at a given time, does not seem to need further inquiry, although we do not have clear and distinct insight into, and understanding of, its structure. What is taken for granted is, until invalidation, believed to be simply "given" and "given-as-it-appears-to-me"—that is, as I or others whom I trust have experienced and interpreted it. It is this zone of things taken for granted within which we have to find our bearings. All our possible questioning for the unknown arises only within such a world of supposedly preknown things, and presupposes its existence. Or, to use Dewey's terms, it is the indeterminate situation from which all possible inquiry starts with the goal of transforming it into a determinate one. Of course, what is taken for granted today may become questionable tomorrow, if we are induced by our own choice or otherwise to shift our interest and to make the accepted state of affairs a field of further inquiry.

In referring to a shift of our own interest we have touched upon the core of our problem. . . .

It is our interest at hand that motivates all our thinking, projecting, acting, and therewith establishes the problems to be solved by our thought and the goals to be attained by our actions. In other words, it is our interest that breaks assunder the unproblematic field of the preknown into various zones of various

Reprinted from the following items in the Bibliography: 1946, 467–70; 1957a, 48–50; 1950a, 388–89, 392–93; 1959a, 79–80; 1957a, 39–40, 43–45.

relevance with respect to such interest, each of them requiring a different degree of precision of knowledge.

For our purposes we may roughly distinguish four regions of decreasing relevance. First, there is that part of the world within our reach which can be immediately observed by us and also at least partially dominated by us—that is, changed and rearranged by our actions. It is that sector of the world within which our projects can be materialized and brought forth. This zone of primary relevance requires an optimum of clear and distinct understanding of its structure. In order to master a situation we have to possess the know-how—the technique and the skill—and also the precise understanding of why, when, and where to use them. Second, there are other fields not open to our domination but mediately connected with the zone of primary relevance because, for instance, they furnish ready-made tools to be used for attaining the projected goal or they establish the conditions upon which our planning itself or its execution depends. It is sufficient to be merely familiar with these zones of minor relevance, to be acquainted with the possibilities, the chances, and risks they may contain with reference to our chief interest. Third, there are other zones which, *for the time being,* have no such connection with the interests at hand. We shall call them relatively irrelevant, indicating thereby that we may continue to take them for granted as long as no changes occur within them which might influence the relevant sectors by novel and unexpected chances or risks. And, finally, there are the zones which we suggest calling absolutely irrelevant because no possible change occurring within them would—or so we believe—influence our objective in hand. For all practical purposes a mere blind belief in the That and the How of things within this zone of absolute irrelevancy is sufficient.

But this description is much too rough and requires several qualifications. First, we have spoken of an "interest at hand" which determines our system of relevances. There is, however, no such thing as an isolated interest at hand. The single interest at hand is just an element within a hierarchical system, or even a plurality of systems, of interests which in everyday life we call our plans—plans for work and thought, for the hour and for our life. To be sure, this system of interests is neither constant nor homogeneous. It is not constant because in changing from any Now to the succeeding Now the single interests obtain a different weight, a different predominance within the system. It is not homogeneous because even in the simultaneity of any Now we may have most disparate interests. The various social roles we assume simultaneously offer a good illustration. The interests I have in the same situation as a father, a citizen, a member of my church or of my profession, may not only be different but even incompatible with one another. I have, then, to decide which of these disparate interests I must choose in order to define the situation from which to start further inquiry. This choice will state the problem or set the goal in respect to which the world we are living in and our knowledge of it are distributed in zones of various relevance.

Second, the terms "zones" or "regions" of various relevance might suggest that there are closed realms of various relevance in our life-world and, correspondingly, of various provinces of our knowledge of it, each separated from the other by clean-cut border lines. The opposite is true. These various realms of relevances and precision are intermingled, showing the most manifold interpenetrations and enclaves, sending their fringes into neighbor provinces and thus creating twilight zones of sliding transitions. If we had to draw a map depicting such a distribution figuratively it would not resemble a political map showing the various countries with their well-established frontiers, but rather a topographical map representing the shape of a mountain range in the customary way by contour lines connecting points of equal altitude. Peaks and valleys, foothills and slopes, are spread over the map in infinitely diversified configurations. The system of relevances is much more similar to such a system of isohypses than to a system of coordinates originating in a center O and permitting measurement by an equidistant network.

Third, we have to define two types of systems of relevances which we propose to call the system of intrinsic, and the system of imposed, relevances. Again, these are merely constructive types which in daily life are nearly always intermingled with one another and are very rarely found in a pure state. Yet it is important to study them separately in their interaction. The intrinsic relevances are the outcome of our chosen interests, established by our spontaneous decision to solve a problem by our thinking, to attain a goal by our action, to bring forth a projected state of affairs. Surely we are free to choose what we are interested in, but this interest, once established, determines the system of relevances intrinsic to the chosen interest. We have to put up with the relevances thus set, to accept the situation determined by their internal structure, to comply with their requirements. And yet they remain, at least to a certain extent, within our control. Since the interest upon which the intrinsic relevances depend and in which they originate has been established by our spontaneous choice, we may at any time shift the focus of this interest and thereby modify the relevances intrinsic to it, obtaining thus an optimum of clarity by continued inquiry. This whole process will still show all the features of a spontaneous performance. The character of all these relevances as intrinsic relevances—that is, intrinsic to a chosen interest—will be preserved.

We are, however, not only centers of spontaneity, gearing into the world and creating changes within it, but also the mere passive recipients of events beyond our control which occur without our interference. Imposed upon us as relevant are situations and events which are not connected with interests chosen by us, which do not originate in acts of our discretion, and which we have to take just as they are, without any power to modify them by our spontaneous activities except by transforming the relevances thus imposed into intrinsic relevances. While that remains unachieved, we do not consider the imposed relevances as being connected with our spontaneously chosen goals. Because they are imposed upon us they remain unclarified and rather incomprehensible.

Social Domains of Relevance

The order of domains of relevances prevailing in a particular social group is itself an element of the relative natural conception of the world taken for granted by the in-group as an unquestioned way of life. In each group the order of these domains has its particular history. It is an element of socially approved and socially derived knowledge, and frequently is institutionalized. Manifold are the principles that are supposed to establish this order. In Plato's *Laws* (631C, 697B, 728E, 870), for example, all the details of the proposed legislation are derived from the order of goods: the divine ones (wisdom, temperance, courage, justice) and the human ones (health, beauty, strength, wealth); or the things in which every man has an interest have their specific rank: the interests about money have the lowest, next come the interests of the body, and of the highest rank are the interests of the soul (*Laws*, 743E). And Plato comes to the conclusion that a law must be wrong in which health has been preferred to temperance, or wealth to both.

But this is just one example of the many principles in accordance with which the domains of relevances can be ranked. Aristotle's statement that merit is differently estimated in different states, contains an important element of modern sociology of knowledge. We have to recall Max Scheler's findings that in any culture the highest rank is accorded to one of the three types of knowledge distinguished by him—knowledge for the sake of domination (*Beherrschungswissen*), knowledge for the sake of knowing (*Bildungswissen*)—knowledge for the sake of salvation (*Heilswissen*)—and therewith to one of the three types of men of knowledge: the scientist-technician, the sage, the saint. The social acceptance of this rank order determines the whole structure of the particular culture. Finally, Aristotle's statement recalls the concepts of modern anthropology (Linton) and sociology (Parsons-Shils) of ascription and achievement as basic determinants of status and role expectations within the social system.

Quite independently, however, of the particular principle according to which the order of the various domains of relevances has been established in a particular group, certain general statements as to their formal structure can be made:

1. The various domains of relevances are not commensurable

one with another; they are essentially heterogeneous. It is impossible to apply the criteria for excellence valid in one domain of relevances to another domain.

2. Both the relevance structure which constitutes the particular domains of relevances and the order of these domains itself are in continuous flux within each group. This is a main factor in the dynamics of the notions of equality and inequality accepted by a particular group. These concepts change, either (a) if for one reason or another the relevance structure which demarcates a *particular* domain of typification is no longer taken for granted beyond question but becomes questionable itself, a fact that might lead to a permeation of a particular domain of relevance by a heterogeneous one; or (b) if the *order* of the domains of relevances ceases to be socially approved and taken for granted.

3. Since, however, the domains of relevances and their order are themselves elements of the social situation, they might be defined in different ways in accordance with their subjective and objective meaning.

The Typification of Objects

The factual world of our experience . . . is experienced from the outset as a typical one. Objects are experienced as trees, animals, and the like, and more specifically as oaks, firs, maples, or rattlesnakes, sparrows, dogs. This table I am now perceiving is characterized as something recognized, as something foreknown and, nevertheless, novel. What is newly experienced is already known in the sense that it recalls similar or equal things formerly perceived. But what has been grasped once in its typicality carries with it a horizon of possible experience with corresponding references to familiarity, that is, a series of typical characteristics still not actually experienced but expected to be potentially experienced. If we see a dog, that is, if we recognize an object as being an animal and more precisely as a dog, we anticipate a certain behavior on the part of this dog, a typical (not individual) way of eating, of running, of playing, of jumping, and so on. Actually we do not see his teeth, but having experienced before what a dog's teeth typically look like, we may expect that the teeth of the dog before us will show the same typical features though with individual modifications. In other words, what has been experienced in the actual perception of one object is apperceptively transferred to any other similar object, perceived merely as to its type. Actual experience will or will not confirm our anticipation of the typical conformity of these other objects. If confirmed, the content of the anticipated type will be enlarged; at the same time, the type will be split up into subtypes. On the other hand, the concrete real object will prove to have its individual characteristics which, nevertheless, have a form of typicality. Now, and this seems to be of special importance, we *may* take the typically apperceived object as an example of a general type and allow ourselves to be led to the general concept of the type, but we do not *need* by any means to think of the concrete dog thematically as an exemplar of the general concept "dog." "In general," this dog here is a dog like any other dog and will show all the characteristics which the type "dog," according to our previous experience, implies; nevertheless, this known type carries along a horizon of still unknown typical characteristics pertaining not only to this or that individual dog but to dogs in general. Every empirical idea of the general has the character of an open concept to be rectified or corroborated by supervening experience.

Naming and Typifying

Language as used in daily life . . . is primarily a language of named things and events. Now any name includes a typification and is, in Husserl's sense, a nonessential empirical generalization. We may interpret the prescientific human language as a treasure house of preconstituted types and characteristics, each of them carrying along an open horizon of unexplored typical contents. By naming an experienced object, we are relating it by its typicality to pre-experienced things of similar typical structure, and we accept its open horizon referring to future experiences of the same type, which are therefore capable of being given the same name. To find a thing or event relevant enough to bestow a separate name upon it is again the outcome of the prevailing system of relevance. Here is an animal and this animal is a dog, but a dog of a particular kind which is unknown to me. I am, if sufficiently interested in this object, not satisfied with subsuming it under the name of "dog." The characteristics which it has in common with all other dogs are precisely those which are irrelevant to me; relevant, however, are those which lead to the building of a new subtype. I ask: What kind of dog is this? And my curiosity is satisfied if I learn that it is an Irish setter. At the same time, recognizing the animal as a dog, it is normally not relevant to me to continue the generalization: A dog is a mammal, an animal, a living thing, an object of the outer world, and so on. It is always the system of relevance that chooses from the vocabulary of my vernacular (and also from its syntactical structure) the relevant term, and that term is the typical pre-experienced generalization interesting me (or my interlocutor) in the present situation.

Experience and Typification

As Husserl . . . has convincingly shown, all forms of recognition and identification, even of real objects of the outer world, are based on a *generalized* knowledge of the *type* of these objects or of the *typical* style in which they manifest themselves. Strictly speaking, each experience is unique, and even the same experience that recurs is not the same, because it recurs. It is a recurrent sameness, and as such it is experienced in a different context and with different adumbrations. If I recognize this particular cherry tree in my garden as the same tree I saw yesterday, although in another light and with another shade of color, this is possible merely because I know the typical way in which this unique object appears in its surroundings. And the type "this particular cherry tree" refers to the pre-experienced types "cherry trees in general," "trees," "plants," "objects of the outer world." Each of these types has its typical style of being experienced, and the knowledge of this typical style is itself an element of our stock of knowledge at hand. The same holds good for the relations in which the objects stand to one another, for events and occurrences and their mutual relations, and so on.

Typification in Social Life

What the sociologist calls "system," "role," "status," "role expectation," "situation," and "institutionalization," is experienced by the individual actor on the social scene in entirely different terms. To him all the factors denoted by these concepts are elements of a network of typifications—typifications of human individuals, of their course-of-action patterns, of their motives and goals, or of the sociocultural products which originated in their actions. These types were formed in the main by others, his predecessors or contemporaries, as appropriate tools for coming to terms with things and men, accepted as such by the group into which he was born. But there are also self-typifications: man typifies to a certain extent his own situation within the social world and the various relations he has to his fellow men and cultural objects.

The knowledge of these typifications and of their appropriate use is an inseparable element of the sociocultural heritage handed down to the child born into the group by his parents and his teachers and the parents of his parents and the teachers of his teachers; it is, thus, socially derived. The sum-total of these various typifications constitutes a frame of reference in terms of which not only the sociocultural, but also the physical world has to be interpreted, a frame of reference that, in spite of its inconsistencies and its inherent opaqueness, is nonetheless sufficiently integrated and transparent to be used for solving most of the practical problems at hand.

It should be emphasized that the interpretation of the world in terms of types, as understood here, is not the outcome of a process of ratiocination, let alone of scientific conceptualization. The world, the physical as well as the sociocultural one, is experienced from the outset in terms of types: there are mountains, trees, birds, fishes, dogs, and among them Irish setters; there are cultural objects, such as houses, tables, chairs, books, tools, and among them hammers; and there are typical social roles and relationships, such as parents, siblings, kinsmen, strangers, soldiers, hunters, priests, etc. Thus, typifications on the commonsense level—in contradistinction to typifications made by the scientist, and especially the social scientist—emerge in the everyday experience of the world as taken for granted without any formulation of judgments or of neat propositions with logical subjects and predicates. They belong, to use a phenomenological term, to the prepredicative thinking. The vocabulary and the syntax of the vernacular of everyday language represent the epitome of the typifications socially approved by the linguistic group.

Systems of Relevance and Typification

A system of relevances and typifications as it exists at any historical moment, is itself a part of the social heritage and as such is handed down in the educational process to the members of the in-group. It has various important functions:

1. It determines which facts or events have to be treated as substantially—that is, typically—equal (homogeneous) for the purpose of solving in a typical manner typical problems that emerge or might emerge in situations typified as being equal (homogeneous).

2. It transforms unique individual actions of unique human beings into typical functions of typical social roles, originating in typical motives aimed at bringing about typical ends. The incumbent of such a social role is expected by the other members of the in-group to act in the typical way defined by this role. On the other hand, by living up to his role the incumbent typifies himself; that is, he resolves to act in the typical way defined by the social role he has assumed. He resolves to act in a way in which a businessman, soldier, judge, father, friend, gangleader, sportsman, buddy, regular fellow, good boy, American, taxpayer, etc., is supposed to act. Any role thus involves a self-typification on the part of the incumbent.

3. It functions as both a scheme of interpretation and as a

scheme of orientation for each member of the in-group and constitutes therewith a universe of discourse among them. Whoever (I
included) acts in the socially approved typical way is supposed
to be motivated by the pertinent typical motives and to aim at
bringing about the pertinent typical state of affairs. He has a reasonable chance, by such actions, of coming to terms with everyone
who accepts the same system of relevances and takes the typifications originating therein for granted. On the one hand, I have—in
order to understand another—to apply the system of typifications
accepted by the group to which both of us belong. For example, if
he uses the English language, I have to interpret his statements in
terms of the code of the English dictionary and the English grammar. On the other hand, in order to make myself understandable
to another, I have to avail myself of the same system of typifications as a scheme of orientation for my projected action. Of course,
there is a mere chance, namely, a mere likelihood, that the scheme
of typifications used by me as a scheme of orientation will coincide
with that used by my fellow man as a scheme of interpretation;
otherwise misunderstandings among people of goodwill would be
impossible. But at least as a first approximation we take it for
granted that we both mean what we say and say what we mean.

4. The chances of success of human interaction, that is, the
establishment of a congruency between the typified scheme used
by the actor as a scheme of orientation and by his fellow men as a
scheme of interpretation, is enhanced if the scheme of typification
is standardized, and the system of pertinent relevances institutionalized. The various means of social control (mores, morals,
laws, rules, rituals) serve this purpose.

5. The socially approved system of typifications and relevances is the common field within which the private typifications
and relevance structures of the individual members of the group
originate. This is so, because the private situation of the individual as defined by him is always a situation within the group, his
private interests are interests with reference to those of the group
(whether by way of particularization or antagonism), his private
problems are necessarily in a context with the group problems.
Again, this private system of domains of relevance might be in-

consistent in itself; it might also be incompatible with the socially approved one. For example, I may take entirely different attitudes toward the problems of rearmament of the United States in my social role as a father of a boy, as a taxpayer, as a member of my church, as a patriotic citizen, as a pacifist, and as a trained economist. Nevertheless, all these partially conflicting and intersecting systems of relevances, both those taken for granted by the group and my private ones, constitute particular domains of relevances; all objects, facts, and events are homogeneous in the sense that they are relevant to the same problem.

III. Acting in the Life-World

6

ACTING AND PLANNING

I. *Action, Motivation, Rationality*

CONDUCT, ACTION, WORKING Subjectively meaningful experiences emanating from our spontaneous life shall be called *conduct.* (We avoid the term "behavior" because it includes in present use also subjectively non-meaningful manifestations of spontaneity such as reflexes.) The term "conduct"—as used here —refers to all kinds of subjectively meaningful experiences of spontaneity, be they those of inner life or those gearing into the outer world. If it is permitted to use objective terms in a description of subjective experiences—and after the preceding clarification the danger of misunderstanding no longer exists—we may say that conduct can be an overt or a covert one. The former shall be called *mere doing,* the latter *mere thinking.* However the term "conduct" as used here does not imply any reference to intent. All kinds of so-called automatic activities of inner or outer life— habitual, traditional, affectual ones—fall under this class, called by Leibnitz the "class of empirical behavior."

Conduct which is devised in advance, that is, which is based upon a preconceived project, shall be called *action,* regardless of whether it is an overt or a covert one. As to the latter it has to be distinguished whether or not there supervenes on the project an intention to realize it—to carry it through, to bring about the projected state of affairs. Such an intention transforms the mere forethought into an aim and the project into a purpose. If an intention to reali-

Reprinted from the following items in the Bibliography: 1945*c*, 536–37; 1951*a*, 163–64; 1967, 63–65; 1943, 138–40, 140–43; 1959*a*, 80–82, 83–84, 84–85; 1951*a*, 165–66; 1959*a*, 86–87, 88.

zation is lacking, the projected covert action remains a phantasm, such as a day-dream; if it subsists, we may speak of a purposive action or a *performance*. An example of a covert action which is a performance is the process of projected thinking such as the attempt to solve a scientific problem mentally.

As to the so-called overt actions, that is, actions which gear into the outer world by bodily movements, the distinction between actions without and those with an intention to realization is not necessary. Any overt action is a performance within the meaning of our definition. In order to distinguish the (covert) performances of mere thinking from those (overt) requiring bodily movements we shall call the latter *working*.

Working, thus, is action in the outer world, based upon a project and characterized by the intention to bring about the projected state of affairs by bodily movements. Among all the described forms of spontaneity that of working is the most important one for the constitution of the reality of the world of daily life. . . . The wide-awake self integrates in its working and by its working its present, past, and future into a specific dimension of time; it realizes itself as a totality in its working acts; it communicates with others through working acts; it organizes the different spatial perspectives of the world of daily life through working acts.

MOTIVATION   It is frequently stated that actions within the meaning of our definition are motivated behavior. Yet the term "motive" is equivocal and covers two different sets of concepts which have to be distinguished. We may say that the motive of the murderer was to obtain the money of the victim. Here "motive" means the state of affairs, the end, which the action has been undertaken to bring about. We shall call this kind of motive the "in-order-to motive." From the point of view of the actor this class of motives refers to his future. In the terminology suggested, we may say that the projected act, that is the pre-phantasied state of affairs to be brought about by the future action constitutes the in-order-to motive of the latter. What is, however, motivated by such an in-order-to motive? It is obviously not the projecting itself. I may project in my phantasy to commit a murder without any supervening intention to carry out such a project. Motivated by the way of in-order-to, therefore, is the "voluntative fiat," the decision: "Let's go!" which transforms the inner fancying into a performance or an action gearing into the outer world.

Over against the class of in-order-to motives we have to distinguish another one which we suggest calling the "because" motive. The murderer has been motivated to commit his acts because he grew up in an environment of such and such a kind, because, as psycho-analysis shows, he had in his infancy such and such experiences, etc. Thus, from the point of view of the actor, the because-motive refers to his past experiences. These experiences have determined him to act as he did. What is motivated in an action in the way of "because" is the project of the action itself. In order to satisfy his needs for money, the actor had the possibility of providing it in several other ways than by killing a man, say by earning it in a remunerative occupation. His idea of attaining this goal by killing a man was determined ("caused") by his personal situation or more precisely, by his life history, as sedimented in his personal circumstances.

The distinction between in-order-to motives and because motives is frequently disregarded in ordinary language which permits the expression of most of the "in-order-to" motives by "because" sentences, although not the other way around. It is common usage to say that the murderer killed his victim *because* he wanted to obtain his money. Logical analysis has to penetrate the cloak of language and to investigate how this curious translation of "in-order-to" relations into "because" sentences becomes possible.

The answer seems to be a twofold one and opens still other aspects of the implications involved in the concept of motives. Motive may have a subjective and an objective meaning. Subjectively it refers to the experience of the actor who lives in his ongoing process of activity. To him, motive means what he has actually in view as bestowing meaning upon his ongoing action, and this is always the in-order-to motive, the intention to bring about a projected state of affairs, to attain a pre-conceived goal. As long as the actor lives in his ongoing action, he does not have in view its because motives. Only when the action has been accomplished, when in the suggested terminology it has become an act, he may turn back to his past action as an observer of himself and investigate by what circumstances he has been determined to do what he did. The same holds good if the actor grasps in retrospection the past initial phases of his still ongoing action. This retrospection may even be merely anticipated *modo futuri exacti*. Having, in my projecting phantasy, anticipated what I shall have done when carrying out my project, I may ask myself why I was determined to take this and no other decision. In all these cases the genuine because motive refers to past or future perfect experiences. It reveals itself by its very temporal structure only to the retrospective glance. This "mirror-effect" of temporal projection explains why, on the one hand, a linguistic "because form" may and is frequently used for expressing genuine "in-order-to relations" and why, on the other hand, it is impossible to express genuine because relations by an "in-order-to" sentence. In using the linguistic form "in-order-to," I am looking at the ongoing process of action which is still in the making and appears therefore in the time perspective of the future. In using the linguistic "because" form for expressing a genuine in-order-to relationship, I am looking at the preceding project and the therein *modo futuri exacti* anticipated act. The genuine because motive, however, involves, as we have seen, the time perspective of the past and refers to the genesis of the projecting itself.

So far we have analyzed the subjective aspect of the two categories of motives that is the aspect from the point of view of the actor. It has been shown that the in-order-to motive refers to the attitude of the actor living in the process of his ongoing action. It is, therefore, an essentially subjective category and is revealed to the observer only if he asks what meaning the actor bestows upon his action. The genuine because motive, however, as we have found, is an objective category, accessible to the observer who has to reconstruct from the accomplished act, namely from the state of affairs brought about in the outer world by the actor's action, the attitude of the actor to his action. Only insofar as the actor turns to his past and, thus, becomes an observer of his own acts, can he succeed in grasping the genuine because motives of his own acts.

CONSCIOUS ACTION   We must now ask what is meant by calling an action "conscious" in contrast to "unconscious" behavior. Our thesis is this: An action is conscious in the sense that, before we carry it out, we have a picture in our mind of what we are going to do. This is the "projected act." Then, as we do proceed to action, we are either continuously holding the picture before our inner eye (retention), or we are from time to time recalling it to mind (reproduction). The total experience of action is a very complex one, consisting of experiences of the activity as it occurs, various kinds of attention to that activity, retention of the projected act, reproduction of the projected act, and so on. This "map-consulting" is what we are referring to when we call the action conscious. Behavior without the map or picture is unconscious. To forestall confusion, let us mention that there are several other senses in which human experiences are distinguished as "conscious" versus "unconscious." Some are legitimate and others are not. For instance, there is the theory which alleges the existence of experiences totally alien to, and having no effect on, consciousness. We ourselves reject this concept as self-contradictory, since in our view experience implies consciousness. Then, of course, there is the very different sense in which one might call those experiences "unconscious" which have not yet been reflected upon. Regardless of the problems involved in such a usage, the dichotomy we are drawing is a quite different one. Our actions are conscious if we have previously mapped them out "in the future perfect tense."

Our next question concerns the mode of our knowledge of conscious action. What is the "evidence"[1] with which it presents itself, that is, how do we "encounter" the action in our experience? The answer is that the evidence or mode of presentation differs according to whether (1) the act is still in the "pure project" stage, (2)

1   "Evidence" (*Evidenz*) is used here in Husserl's sense as the specific experience of this "being conscious of." Cf. *Formale und transzendentale Logik*, pp. 437 ff., esp. p. 144.

the action as such has begun and the act is on its way to fulfillment, or (3) the act has been executed and is being looked back on as a *fait accompli*.

Let us look at the first situation. What kind of knowledge can we have of our project? As a matter of fact, it can be of any degree of clarity, from one of total vagueness to one of maximum detail. However, it must be remembered that our knowledge here is of the *project of the act*, not of the *act itself*. Naturally, the first is what its name implies, a mere sketch with many empty places and variables in it. These empty places are filled in, and the variables are given values as the action progresses step by step. At any moment we can compare our blueprint with what we are actually doing. Now we know each of these two items differently. We remember our blueprint or project, whereas we directly experience what we are doing. Naturally, memory-evidence is weaker and has less claim on us than direct, present experience. And the closer it is to the latter, the stronger it is. The various degrees of evidence in which experiences are presented to us in relation to their temporal positions have been developed at length by Husserl. We need concern ourselves with this diversity here only to the extent of noting that it exists and that it is very complex. To cite a frequent example: we may start out with a clear plan of action, then get rather confused while we are executing it, and in the end not be able to explain what we have done.

The number of possible variations is unlimited. However, we are *conscious* of an action only if we contemplate it as already over and done with, in short, as an *act*. This is true even of projects, for we project the intended action as an act in the future perfect tense.

When we were previously considering the thesis that conscious behavior is behavior with meaning attached to it, we said that "the meaning 'attached' to the behavior would consist precisely in the consciousness of the behavior." We now see in how many different ways this can be interpreted. But our main point remains unaffected: that the meaning of an action is the corresponding act. This follows strictly from our definition of action as behavior oriented to a previously made plan or project.

Beyond this, our analysis in terms of time has illuminated the radical difference between action before its execution, on the one hand, and the completed act, on the other. From this it follows that the question of what is the intended meaning of an act already performed requires one answer, whereas the question of the meaning of the concrete action first intended requires another.

What is this important difference? It is that while the action has yet to take place it is phantasied as that which will have taken place, that is, in the future perfect tense as something already performed. Thus what occurs is a reflective Act of attention to an action phantasied as over and done with. This Act of attention, of course, temporally precedes the action itself. Then as the action takes place and proceeds to its termination, the actor's experience is enlarged—he "grows older." What was inside the illuminated circle of consciousness during the moment of projection now falls back into the darkness and is replaced by later lived experiences which had been merely expected or protended. Let us imagine a person who projects a rational action that had been planned a long time before and whose goals, both final and intermediate, had, therefore, been clearly anticipated. It cannot be doubted that this person's attitude toward his plan will necessarily differ from his attitude toward the finished deed. This will be true even if the action proceeded according to plan. "Things look different the morning after."

WHAT IS "RATIONAL" CONDUCT?   1. "Rational" is frequently used as synonymous with "reasonable." Now we certainly act in our daily life in a reasonable way if we use the recipes we find in the store of our experience as already tested in an analogous situation. But acting rationally often means avoiding mechanical applications of precedents, dropping the use of analogies, and searching for a new way to master the situation.

2. Sometimes rational action is put on a par with acting deliberately, but the term "deliberately" itself implies many equivocal elements.

(a) Routine action of daily life is deliberated in so far as it always relates back to the original act of deliberation which once preceded the building up of the formula now taken by the actor as a standard for his actual behavior.

(*b*) Conveniently defined, the term "deliberation" may cover the insight into the applicability to a present situation of a recipe which has proved successful in the past.

(*c*) We can give the term "deliberation" a meaning covering the pure anticipation of the end—and this anticipation is always the motive for the actor to set the action going.

(*d*) On the other hand, the term "deliberation" as used, for instance, by Professor Dewey in his *Human Nature and Conduct,* means "a dramatic rehearsal in imagination of various competing possible lines of action." In this sense, which is of the greatest importance for the theory of rationality, we cannot classify as rational the type of every-day actions which we have examined up to now as deliberated actions. On the contrary, it is characteristic of these routine actions that the problem of choice between different possibilities does not enter into the consciousness of the actor. . . .

(3) Rational action is frequently defined as "planned" or "projected" action without a precise indication of the meaning of the terms "planned" or "projected." We cannot simply say that the non-rational routine acts of daily life are not consciously planned. On the contrary, they rest within the framework of our plans and projects. They are even instruments for realising them. All planning presupposes an end to be realised by stages, and each of these stages may be called, from one point of view or another, either means or intermediate ends. Now the function of all routine work is a standardisation and mechanisation of the means-end relations as such by referring standardised means to standardised classes of ends. The effect of this standardisation is that the intermediate ends disappear from the consciously envisaged chain of means which have to be brought about for performing the planned end. But here arises the problem of subjective meaning. . . . We cannot speak of the unit-act as if this unit were constituted or demarcated by the observer. We must seriously ask: when does one act start and when is it accomplished? We shall see that only the actor is in a position to answer this question.

Let us take the following example: Assume the professional life of a business man to be organised and planned to the extent that he intends to continue with his business for the next ten years, after which he hopes to retire. To continue his work involves going to his office every morning. For this purpose he has to leave his home at a certain hour, buy a ticket, take the train, etc. He did so yesterday and he will do so to-morrow if nothing extraordinary intervenes. Let us assume that one day he is late and that he thinks: "I shall miss my train—I shall be late at my office. Mr. 'X' will be there already, waiting for me. He will be in a bad humor, and perhaps he will not sign the contract on which so much of my future depends." Let us further assume that an observer watches this man rushing for the train "as usual" (as he thinks). Is his behavior planned, and if so, what is the plan? Only the actor can give the answer because he alone knows the span of his plans and projects. Probably all routine work is a tool for bringing about ends which are beyond routine work and which determine it.

4. "Rational" is frequently identified with "predictable." . . . We have . . . analysed the specific form of prediction in every-day knowledge as simply an estimate of likelihood.

5. According to the interpretation of some authors, "rational" refers to "logical." Professor Parsons' definition is one example and Pareto's theory of non-logical action to which he refers is another. In so far as the scientific concept of the rational act is in question, the system of logic may be fully applied. On the other hand, on the level of every-day experience, logic in its traditional form cannot render the services we need and expect. Traditional logic is a logic of concepts based on certain idealisations. In enforcing the postulate of clearness and distinctness of the concepts, for instance, traditional logic disregards all the fringes surrounding the nucleus within the stream of thought. On the other hand, thought in daily life has its chief interest precisely in the relation of the fringes which attach the nucleus to the actual situation of the thinker. This is clearly a very important point. It explains why Husserl classifies the greater part of our propositions in daily thought as "occasional propositions," that means, as valid and understandable only relative to the speaker's situation and to their

place in his stream of thought. It explains, too, why our every-day thoughts are less interested in the antithesis "true-false" than in the sliding transition "likely-unlikely." We do not make every-day propositions with the purpose of achieving a formal validity within a certain realm which could be recognised by someone else, as the logician does, but in order to gain knowledge valid only for our-selves and to further our practical aims. To this extent, but only to this extent, the principle of pragmatism is incontestably well founded. It is a description of the style of every-day thought, but not a theory of cognition.

6. A rational act presupposes, according to the interpretation of other authors, a choice between two or more means toward the same end, or even between two different ends, and a selection of the most appropriate. This interpretation will be analysed in the following section.

PLANNING AND "RATIONAL" CHOICE   As Professor John Dewey has pointed out, in our daily life we are largely preoccupied with the next step. Men stop and think only when the sequence of doing is interrupted, and the disjunction in the form of a problem forces them to stop and rehearse alternative ways—over, around or through—which their past experience in collision with this problem suggest. The image of a dramatic rehearsal of future ac-tion used by Professor Dewey is a very fortunate one. Indeed, we cannot find out which of the alternatives will lead to the desired end without imagining this act as already accomplished. So we have to place ourselves mentally in a future state of affairs which we consider as already realised, though to realise it would be the end of our contemplated action. Only by considering the act as accomplished can we judge whether the contemplated means of bringing it about are appropriate or not, or whether the end to be realised accommodates itself to the general plan of our life. I like to call this technique of deliberation "thinking in the future per-fect tense." But there is a great difference between action actually performed and action only imagined as performed. The really ac-complished act is irrevocable and the consequences must be borne whether it has been successful or not. Imagination is always revocable and can be revised again and again. Therefore, in simply rehearsing several projects, I can ascribe to each a different probability of success, but I can never be disappointed by its failure. Like all other anticipations, the rehearsed future action also has gaps which only the performance of the act will fill in. Therefore the actor will only retrospectively see whether his project has stood the test or proved a failure. . . .

Undoubtedly there are situations in which each of us sits down and thinks over his problems. In general he will do so at critical points in his life when his chief interest is to master a situation. But even then he will accept his emotions as guides in finding the most suitable solution as well as rational deliberation, and he is right in doing so, because these emotions also have their roots in his practical interest.

He will also appeal to his stock of recipes, to the rules and skill arising out of his vocational life or his practical experiences. He will certainly find many systematised solutions in his standardised knowledge. He may perhaps consult an expert, but again he will get nothing else than recipes and systematised solutions. His choice will be a deliberated one, and having rehearsed all the possibilities of action open to him in the future perfect tense, he will put in action that solution which seems to have the greatest chance of success.

But what are the conditions under which we may classify a deliberated act of choice as a rational one? It seems that we have to distinguish between the rationality of knowledge which is a prerequisite of the rational choice and the rationality of the choice itself. Rationality of knowledge is given only if all the elements from which the actor has to choose are clearly and distinctly conceived by him. The choice itself is rational if the actor selects from among all means within his reach the one most appropriate for realising the intended end.

We have seen that clearness and distinctness in the strict meaning of formal logic do not belong to the typical style of every-day thought. But it would be erroneous to conclude that, therefore, rational choice does not exist within the sphere of every-day life. Indeed, it would be sufficient to interpret the terms clearness and distinctness in a modified and restricted meaning, namely, as clearness and distinctness adequate to the requirements of the actor's practical interest. It is not our task to examine whether rational acts corresponding with the above-mentioned characteristics do or do not occur frequently in daily life. There is no doubt that "rational acts" together with their antithesis, defined by Max Weber as "traditional" or "habitual" acts, represent rather ideal types which will be found very seldom in their pure form in every-day action. What I wish to emphasise is only that the ideal of rationality is not and cannot be a peculiar feature of every-day thought, nor can it, therefore, be a methodological principle of the interpretation of human acts in daily life. This will become clearer if we discuss the concealed implications of the statement—or better, postulate—that rational choice would be present only if the actor had sufficient knowledge of the end to be realised as well as of the different means apt to succeed. This postulate implies:

(*a*) Knowledge of the place of the end to be realised within the framework of the plans of the actor (which must be known by him, too).

(*b*) Knowledge of its interrelations with other ends and its compatibility or incompatibility with them.

(*c*) Knowledge of the desirable and undesirable consequences which may arise as by-products of the realisation of the main end.

(*d*) Knowledge of the different chains of means which technically or even ontologically are suitable for the accomplishment of this end, regardless of whether the actor has control of all or several of their elements.

(*e*) Knowledge of the interference of such means with other ends or other chains of means including all their secondary effects and incidental consequences.

(*f*) Knowledge of the accessibility of those means for the actor, picking out the means which are within his reach and which he can and may set going.

The aforementioned points do not by any means exhaust the complicated analysis which would be necessary in order to break down the concept of rational choice in action. The complications increase greatly when the action in question is a social one, that is, when it is directed towards other people. In this case, the following elements become additional determinants for the deliberation of the actor:

First: The interpretation or misinterpretation of his own act by his fellow man.

Second: The reaction by the other people and its motivation.

Third: All the outlined elements of knowledge (*a* to *f*) which the actor, rightly or wrongly, attributes to his partners.

Fourth: All the categories of familiarity and strangeness, of intimacy and anonymity, of personality and type, which we have discovered in the course of our inventory of the organisation of the social world.

This short analysis shows that we cannot speak of an *isolated* rational act, if we mean by this an act resulting from deliberated choice, but only of a *system* of rational acts.[2]

II. *Anticipating and Projecting*

ANTICIPATION AND TYPIFICATION   It is . . . important . . . to realize that our actual experiences are not merely by retentions and recollections referred to our past experiences. Any experience refers likewise to the future. It carries along protentions of occurrences expected to follow immediately—they are so called by Husserl as a counterpart to retentions—and anticipations of temporally more distant events with which the present experience is expected to be related. In commonsense thinking these anticipations and expectations follow basically the typical structures that have held good so far for our past experiences and are incorporated in our stock of knowledge at hand.

Husserl handled this problem in investigating the underlying idealizations and formalizations that make anticipations in daily life possible at all. He has convincingly proved that idealizations and formalizations are by no means restricted to the realm of scientific thinking, but pervade also our commonsense experiences

2   See the excellent study which Professor Parsons has devoted to this problem under the heading "Systems of Action and Unit," at the end of his *Structure of Social Action*.

of the *Lebenswelt*. He calls them the idealization of "and so forth and so on" (*und so weiter*) and—its subjective correlate—the idealization of "I can do it again" (*ich kann immer weider*). The former idealization implies the assumption, *valid until counter-evidence appears*, that what has been proved to be adequate knowledge so far will also in the future stand the test. The latter idealization implies the assumption, *valid until counter-evidence appears*, that, in similar circumstances, I may bring about by my action a state of affairs similar to that I succeeded in producing by a previous similar action. In other words, these idealizations imply the assumption that the basic structure of the world as I know it, and therewith the type and style of my experiencing it and of my acting within it, will remain unchanged—unchanged, that is, until further notice.

Nevertheless—and again Husserl has pointed this out with utmost clarity—our protentions and anticipations of things to come are essentially empty references to the open horizons, and may be fulfilled by the future occurrences, or may, as he graphically calls it, "explode." In other words, any experience carries its own horizon of indeterminacy (perhaps an indeterminacy that is to a certain extent determinable), which refers to future experiences. How is this insight compatible with the basic idealization of "and so forth" and "I can do it again"?

I venture to propose two answers, for neither of which Husserl is responsible. First, our anticipations and expectations refer not to the future occurrences in their uniqueness and their unique setting within a unique context, but to occurrences of such and such a type typically placed in a typical constellation. The structurization of our stock of knowledge at hand in terms of types is at the foundation of the aforementioned idealizations. Yet because of their very typicality our anticipations are necessarily more or less empty, and this emptiness will be filled in by exactly those features of the event, once it is actualized, that make it a unique individual occurrence.

Secondly, we have to consider that . . . not only the range but also the structurization of our stock of knowledge at hand changes continually. The emergence of a supervening experience results by necessity in a change, be it ever so small, of our prevailing interests and therewith of our system of relevances. It is this system of relevances, however, that determines the structurization of the stock of knowledge at hand, and divides it into zones of various degrees of clarity and distinctness. Any shift in the system of relevances dislocates these layers and redistributes our knowledge. Some elements that belonged previously to the marginal zones enter the central domain of optimal clarity and distinctness; others are removed therefrom to the zones of increasing vagueness. Moreover, it is the system of relevances that determines the system of types under which our stock of knowledge at hand is organized. With the shift of my prevailing interests, therefore, also the types valid at the moment of anticipating will have changed when the anticipated event occurs and becomes an actual element of my vivid present.

Using the terms *in their strictest meaning* we may therefore say paradoxically that in the commonsense thinking of everyday life whatever occurs could not have been expected precisely as it occurs, and that whatever has been expected to occur will never occur as it has been expected. This is not in contradiction of the fact that for many useful purposes we may and we do in everyday life correctly anticipate things to come. Closer analysis shows that in such cases we are interested merely in the typicality of the future events. It may be said that an occurring event was expected if what really happens corresponds in its typicality with the typicalities at hand in our stock of knowledge at the time of our anticipating its occurrence. The important point to be emphasized, however, is the fact that merely in hindsight—*eventu*—does an occurrence turn out to have been expected or unexpected. Used in the present tense the statement "I expect" has an entirely different meaning. All anticipations in the commonsense thinking of daily life are made *modo potentiali,* in terms of chance. It is likely, presumable, conceivable, imaginable that "something of this or that type" will occur. Thus all anticipations refer in the mode of chance to the typicality of future events, and carry with them open horizons that may or may not be fulfilled when the anticipated event occurs in its uniqueness—provided it occurs at all—and becomes itself an element of our stock of knowledge then at hand. And again, this discrepancy between our expectations and their fulfillment or non-fulfillment by the anticipated facts is itself an element of our stock of knowledge at hand and has itself a particular cognitive style.

ANTICIPATION OF THINGS TO COME   The foregoing analysis of the dependency of our commonsense anticipations upon the stock of knowledge at hand has already referred to the prevailing interest that determines the structurization of our knowledge. I find myself at any moment of my existence within the *Lebenswelt* in a biographically determined situation. To this situation belong not only my position in space, time, and society, but also my experience that some of the elements of my *Lebenswelt* are imposed upon me, while others are either within my control or capable of being brought within my control and therefore modifiable. Thus the ontological structure of the universe is imposed upon me and constitutes the frame of all my possible spontaneous activities. Within this framework I have to find my bearings and I have to come to terms with its elements. For instance, the causal relations of the objective world are subjectively experienced as possible means for possible ends, as obstacles or supports for the spontaneous activities of my thinking and doing. They are experienced as contexts of interests, as a hierarchy of problems to be solved, as systems of projects and their inherent performabilities.

This is the reason why I am vitally interested in anticipating the things to come in the sector of the world that is imposed upon me and escapes my control. I am a mere onlooker of the ongoing happenings herein, but my very existence depends on these happenings. Hence my anticipations concerning events in the world beyond my control are codetermined by my hopes and fears. They are framed, in commonsense thinking, not only in the potential but also in the optative mode.

PROJECTING*   A special problem as to the anticipations of future events originates, however, in the sphere of human action.

---

*   EDITOR'S NOTE: Some of the aspects of projecting have been treated from a different angle in a previous selection. See the section "Conscious Action" in the earlier part of this chapter.

For the purpose of this paper the term "action" shall designate human conduct as an ongoing process that is devised by the actor in advance, that is, based on a preconceived project. The term "act" shall designate the outcome of this ongoing process, that is, the accomplished action or the state of affairs brought about by it. All projecting consists in an anticipation of future conduct by way of phantasying. . . . Yet projecting is more than mere phantasying. Projecting is motivated phantasying, motivated by the anticipated supervening intention of carrying out the project. The practicability of carrying out the projected action within the imposed frame of reality of the *Lebenswelt* is an essential characteristic of the project. This refers, however, to our stock of knowledge at hand at the time of projecting. Performability of the projected action means that according to my present knowledge at hand the projected action, at least as to its type, would have been feasible if the action had occurred in the past.

The project is in still another respect related to the stock of knowledge at hand. This becomes clear when we examine whether it is the future ongoing process of action, as it will roll on phase by phase, or the outcome of this future action, the act as having been accomplished, which is anticipated in phantasying or projecting. It can easily be seen that the latter, the act that will have been accomplished, is the starting point of all of our projecting. I have to visualize the state of affairs to be brought about by my future action before I can draft the single steps of my future acting from which that state of affairs will result. Metaphorically speaking, I have to have some idea of the structure to be erected before I can draft the blueprints. Thus in order to project my future action as it will roll on I have to place myself in my phantasy at a future time when this action will already have been accomplished, when the resulting act will already have been materialized. Only then may I reconstruct the single steps that *will have* brought forth this future act. What is thus anticipated in the project is, in the terminology proposed, not the future action, but the future act, and it is anticipated in the future perfect tense, *modo futuri exacti*.

Now as pointed out before, I base my projecting of the forthcoming act in the future perfect tense on my experiences of previously performed acts typically similar to the projected one. These pre-experiences are elements of my stock of knowledge at hand at the time of projecting. But that knowledge must needs be different from the stock of knowledge I shall have at hand when the now merely projected act will have been materialized. By then I shall have grown older and, if nothing else has changed, at least the experiences I shall have had while carrying out the project will have enlarged and restructurized my stock of knowledge. In other words, projecting, like any other anticipation of future events, carries along empty horizons that will be filled in merely by the materialization of the anticipated event; hence for the actor the meaning of the projected act must necessarily differ from the meaning of the accomplished one. Projecting (and still more, carrying out the project) is thus founded on the stock of knowledge at hand, with its particular structurization, at the time of projecting.

FANCYING AND PROJECTING   It is . . . the reference of projecting to a stock of knowledge at hand which distinguishes projecting from mere fancying. If I fancy to be superman or to be endowed with magic powers and dream what I will then perform, this is not projecting. In pure phantasy I am not hampered by any limits imposed by reality. It is in my discretion to ascertain what is within my reach, and to determine what is within my power. At my good pleasure I may fancy that all or some or none of the conditions upon which the attaining of my fancied goal by fancied means in a fancied situation depends, will have been fulfilled. In such a pure phantasying my mere wish defines my possible chances. It is a thinking in the optative mode.

Projecting of performances or overt actions, however, is a motivated phantasying, motivated namely by the anticipated supervening intention to carry out the project. The practicability of the project is a condition of all projecting which could be translated into a purpose. Projecting of this kind is, thus, phantasying within a given or better within an imposed frame, imposed namely by the reality within which the projected action will have to be carried out. It is not, as mere phantasying is, a thinking in the optative mode but a thinking in the potential one. This potentiality, this possibility of executing the project requires, for instance, that only ends and means believed by me to be within my actual or potential reach may be taken into account by my projecting in fancy; that I am not allowed to vary fictitiously in my phantasying those elements of the situation which are beyond my control; that all chances and risks have to be weighed in accordance with my present knowledge of possible occurrences of this kind in the real world; briefly that according to my present knowledge the projected action, *at least as to its type*, would have been feasible, its means and ends, *at least as to their types*, would have been available if the action had occurred in the past. The italicized restriction is important. It is not necessary that the "same" projected action in its individual uniqueness, with its unique ends and unique means has to be pre-experienced and, therefore, known. If this were the case nothing novel could ever be projected. But it is implied in the notion of such a project that the projected action, its end and its means remain compatible and consistent with these typical elements of the situation which according to our experience at hand at the time of projecting have warranted so far, the practicability, if not the success, of *typically* similar actions in the past.

PROJECTION AND INTEREST   The project once constituted modifies this structure decisively: the goal to be attained, the act to be accomplished, the problem to be solved becomes the dominating interest and selects what is and what is not relevant at this particular moment. It has to be added that neither this dominating interest nor the projecting in which it originates is isolated. Both are elements of *systems* of projects, interests, goals to be attained, problems to be solved, arranged in a hierarchy of preferences and interdependent in many respects. In ordinary language I call these systems my plans, plans for the hour or for the day, for work or for leisure, for life. These plans, themselves in continuous flux, determine the interests presently in focus and hence the structurization of the stock of knowledge at hand.

This double relationship between the project and the stock of knowledge—on the one hand the reference to my experiences of previously performed acts that I can perform again, on the other hand the reference of the project to my systems of hierarchically organized interest—has a highly important additional function. I have spoken, very loosely, of the particular moment of time, the Now, at which the stock of knowledge is at hand. But in truth this Now is not an instant. It is what William James and George H. Mead have called a specious present, containing elements of the past and the future. Projecting unifies this specious present and delimits its borderline. As far as the past is concerned, the limits of the specious present are determined by the remotest past experience, sedimented and preserved in that section of knowledge at hand that is still relevant to the present projecting. As far as the future is concerned, the limits of the specious present are determined by the span of the projects presently conceived, that is, by the temporally remotest acts still anticipated *modo futuri exacti*.

As long as we succeed, within this unified and delimited realm of the specious present, in keeping our projects consistent and compatible both with one another and with the stock of knowledge at hand, there exists a reasonable chance that our future action will conform, at least in type, to our project as anticipated *modo futuri exacti*. Such a chance will, however, be a subjective one; that is, it will exist merely for me, the actor, in the form of reasonable likelihood, and there is no warranty whatever that this subjective chance—chance for me—will coincide with objective probability, calculable in mathematical terms.

FORESIGHT AND HINDSIGHT   In the realm of future events that we assume can be influenced by our actions, we consider ourselves the makers of these events. Actually, what we preconceive in the projection of our action is an anticipated state of affairs that we imagine as having been materialized in the past. Nevertheless, in projecting our actions into the future, we are not merely retroverted historians. We are historians if we look from any Now back to our past experiences, and interpret them according to our stock of knowledge now at hand. But there is nothing open and empty in our past experiences. What was therein formerly anticipated has or has not been fulfilled. In projecting, on the other hand, we know that what we anticipate carries along open horizons. Once materialized, the state of affairs brought forth by our actions will necessarily have quite other aspects than those projected. In this case foresight is not distinguished from hindsight by the dimension of time in which we place the event. In both eventualities we look at the event as having occurred: in hindsight as having really occurred in the past; in foresight as having become quasi-existent in an anticipated past. What constitutes the decisive difference is the bare fact that genuine hindsight does not leave anything open and undetermined. The past is irrevocable and irretrievable. Foresight, an anticipated hindsight, depends on the stock of our knowledge at hand before the event, and therefore leaves open what will be irrevocably fulfilled merely by the occurrence of the anticipated event itself.

7

FREEDOM, CHOICE, AND INTEREST

Man as Free Actor

HE WHO LIVES in the social world is a free being: his acts proceed from spontaneous activity. Once the action has transpired, once it is over and done with, it has become an act and is no longer free but closed and determinate in character. Nevertheless, it was free at that time the action took place; and if the question concerning the intended meaning refers, as it does in Max Weber's case, to the point in time before the completion of the act, the answer must be that the actor always acts freely. . . .

Choice and Action

Once we strip away from the concept of will the meta-physical speculations and antinomies which have historically surrounded it, we are left with the simple experience of spontaneous Activity based on a previously formulated project. This experience lends itself readily to sober description. . . . An analysis of the phenomenal experience of will, the peculiar "fiat," as James calls it, by which the project is carried over into action, is not essential for our purposes and will, therefore, be dispensed with. . . .

Let us turn, then, to the second class of topics included under the heading "voluntary action": the problems of choice, decision, and freedom. If it is maintained that voluntary action is the criterion of meaningful behavior, then the "meaning" of this behavior consists only in the choice—in the freedom to behave one way rather than another. This would mean not only that the action is

---

Reprinted from the following items in the Bibliography: 1967, 227, 66–68; 1951a, 181–82; 1967, 68–69; 1951a, 169–70, 170–73, 173–74, 174–75.

"free" but that the aims of the act are known at the moment of decision; in short, that a free choice exists between at least two goals. It is the indisputable merit of Bergson that in his *Time and Free Will*,[1] published as long ago as 1888, he succeeded in clearing up the basic problem of determinism. In what follows, we will briefly summarize his arguments.

What does a choice between two possible acts X and Y mean? Both the determinists and the indeterminists tend to conceive X and Y as points in space: the deciding Ego stands at the crossroads O and can decide freely whether to go to X or to Y. But this very way of thinking is fallacious. The problem should not be conceived in terms of spatial goals, of pregiven pathways, of the coexistence of acts X and Y before one of them is performed. These goals do not exist at all before the choice, nor do the paths to them exist until and unless they are traversed. However, if the act—let us say X—has been performed, then the claim that, back at point O, Y could equally well have been chosen is necessarily meaningless. Equally meaningless is the assertion that, since the determining cause of X was already in existence back at O, only X could have been chosen. Both determinism and indeterminism read back "the deed already done" (*l'action accomplie*) to point O, seeking to attribute all its characteristics to the deed in the doing (*l'action s'accomplissante*). Behind both of these doctrines lurks the fallacious assumption that spatial modes of thought can be applied to duration, that duration can be explained through space, and succession through simultaneity. But the real way in which choice occurs is the following: The Ego imaginatively runs through a series of psychic states in each of which it expands, grows richer, and changes (*grossit, s'enrichit et change*), until "the free act detaches itself from it like an overripe fruit." The two "possibilities," "directions," or "tendencies" which we read back into the successive conscious states do not really exist there at all before the act is performed; what does exist is only an Ego, which, together with its motives, comprises an unbroken becoming. Both determinism and indeterminism treat this oscillation as if it were a spatial seesawing. The arguments of

[1]   Cf. especially chapter 3, "The Organization of Conscious States; Free Will." [We are referring to the English translation by F. L. Pogson (New York, 1912).]

determinism are based one and all on the formula, "The deed once done is done" (*l'acte une fois accompli, est accompli*). The arguments of indeterminism, on the other hand, are based on the formula, "The deed was not done until it was done" (*l'acte avant d'être accompli, ne l'était pas encore*). So much for Bergson.

What do we conclude from all this as far as our own argument is concerned? Let us bring together Bergson's thesis and the points we have previously made. We have seen that the project anticipates not the action itself but the act, and this in the future perfect tense. We have studied further the peculiar structural linkage between the project, the ongoing action, and the act which is seen in reflection either to fulfill or fail to fulfill the project. The project itself is a phantasy; it is only the shadow of an action, an anticipative reproduction, or, in Husserl's terminology, a "neutralizing representation."

On the other hand, the phantasy is a real lived experience which in turn can be reflected upon in all its modifications. How, then, does the "choice" take place? Apparently in this way: First of all, an act X is projected in the future perfect tense. *Thereupon* the actor becomes self-consciously aware of his phantasying the intentional Act and of its content. *Next* the act Y is projected; *then* the process of its projection becomes an object of the actor's reflective attention. These are retained, reproduced, compared reflectively in innumerable further intentional Acts following and lying over one another in an enormously complicated network of relationships. So far they are all neutralizing, noncommittal, ineffectual shadow actions. But these are not merely the "psychical states" of Bergson, for the latter are immersed in duration and are not reflective in nature. Indeed, and this is the crux of Bergson's argument, if these psychic states of his were reflective in character, they would be concerned with the deed already done rather than with the deed in the doing.

Choice and Interest

We now have to examine the origin of the "weight" of possibilities and counterpossibilities, of Leibniz' "good" and "evil" as the inherent positive weight of *"volonté antécédente"* or negative of a *"volonté moyenne."* Let us keep to our example of choosing between two different projects. Can it be said that the "weight," the "good" or "evil," attributed to either of them is inherent to the specific project? It seems that such a statement is meaningless. The standards of weights, of good and evil, of positive and negative, briefly of evaluation, are not created by the projecting itself, but the project is evaluated according to a pre-existent frame of reference. Any student of ethics is familiar with the age-old controversy on values and valuation here involved. For our problem, however, we need not embark upon discussing it. It is sufficient for us to point out that the problem of positive and negative weights transcends the actual situation of a concrete choice and decision and to give an indication how this fact can be explained without having recourse to the metaphysical question of the existence and nature of absolute values.

. . . There is no such thing for the actor as an isolated interest. Interests have from the outset the character of being interrelated with other interests in a system. It is merely a corollary of this statement that also actions, motives, ends and means, and, therefore, projects and purposes are only elements among other elements forming a system. Any end is merely a means for another end; any project is projected within a system of higher order. For this very reason any choosing between projects refers to a previously chosen system of connected projects of a higher order. In our daily life our projected ends are means within a preconceived particular plan—for the hour or the year, for work or for leisure—and all these particular plans are subject to our plan for life as the most universal one which determines the subordinate ones even if the latter conflict with one another. Thus, any choice refers to pre-experienced decisions of a higher order, upon which the alternative at hand is founded—as any doubt refers to a pre-experienced empirical certainty which becomes questionable in the process of doubting. It is our pre-experience of this higher organization of projects which is at the foundation of the problematic possibilities standing to choice and which determines the weight of either possibility: Its positive or negative character is positive or negative merely with reference to this system of higher order. For the purpose of this purely formal description, no assumption whatsoever is needed either as to the specific content of the higher system involved or as to the existence of so-called "absolute values," nor is any assumption needed as to the structure of our pre-knowledge, that is, as to its degree of clarity, explicitness, vagueness, etc. On the contrary, on any level of vagueness the phenomenon of choice can be repeated. As seen from the point of view of the actor in daily life, full clarity of all the elements involved in the process of choosing, that is, a *"perfectly"* rational action, is impossible. This is so because first, the system of plans upon which the constitution of alternatives is founded belongs to the because motives of his action and is disclosed merely to the retrospective observation, but hidden to the actor who lives in his acts oriented merely to his in-order-to motives which he has in view; secondly, because his knowledge, if our analysis is correct, is founded upon his biographically determined situation which selects the elements relevant to his purpose at hand from the world simply taken for granted and this biographically determined situation as prevailing at the time of the projecting changes in the course of oscillating between the alternatives, if for no other reason than because of the experience of this oscillating itself.

Intentional Action

Our analysis, aided as it is by Husserl, goes a considerable distance beyond Bergson's thesis. In our view the process of choice between successively pictured projects, plus the action itself right up to its completion, comprises a synthetic intentional Act (*Akt*) of a higher order, an Act that is inwardly differentiated into other Acts. Such an Act Husserl calls a *polythetic Act*.

Husserl distinguishes between intentional Acts which are continuous syntheses and intentional Acts which are discontinuous syntheses. For instance, an Act of consciousness which constituted the "thinghood" of a thing in space is a continuous synthesis. Discontinuous syntheses, on the other hand, are *bindings-together* of other discrete Acts. The unity formed is an *articulated* unity and is a unity of a higher order. This higher Act (which he calls a *polythetic* Act) is both polythetic and synthetic. It is polythetic because within it several different "theses" are posited. It is synthetic because they are posited together. As every constituent Act within the total Act has its object, so the total Act has its total object. But something distinctive happens in the constitution of this total object. It might be explained like this: The object of each constituent Act has a single shaft of attention or ray (*Strahl*) of awareness directed toward it. The synthetic Act which ensues is necessarily *many-rayed*, since it is to start with a synthetic *collection*. But it is not satisfied in being a *plural consciousness*. It transforms itself into a *single consciousness*, its complex collection of objects becoming the object of one ray, a "one-rayed object."

Now let us apply this to the Act (*Akt*) of choice. Originally, alternatives X and Y were projected. Each of these projective Acts directed a single ray of attention upon its object (the alternative in question). However, once the wavering between alternatives is resolved, once the choice is made, this choice appears to the reflective glance as a unified Act of projection or phantasy. The individual phantasy Acts or projections meanwhile drop out of view. Nevertheless, the total object of the new synthetic Act still has a projected status, a mere quasi-being; it is, in Husserl's terminology, "neutral" rather than "positional"; it is concerned, not with what *is*, but with what the actor has decided *will be*. On the other hand, once the deed (*Handlung*) is completed, the whole thing can be looked upon "positionally" as something actually existent. In any case the deed is now grasped in a monothetic intentional Act and is referred backward to the moment of choice, when there were originally only polythetic Acts. This is an illusion, as Bergson pointed out, but it is indulged in equally by determinists and indeterminists. The error is to suppose that the conscious state (*état psychique*), which only exists after the deed is done, lies back at some "point of duration" before the actual choice.

But this transformation from multiplicity to unity is of great importance from our point of view. For it means that the action, once completed, is a unity from original project to execution, regardless of the multiplicity and complexity of its component phases. This is the way in which the action presents itself to the Ego as long as the latter remains in the natural or naïve attitude.

Doubting and Questioning

The subjectively determined selection of elements relevant to the purpose at hand out of the objectively given totality of the world taken for granted gives rise to a decisive new experience: the experience of doubt, of questioning, of choosing and deciding, in short, of deliberation. Doubt might come from various sources; only one case important for our problem at hand will be discussed here. We said that there is no such thing as an isolated interest, that interests are from the outset interrelated with one another into systems. Yet interrelation does not necessarily lead to complete integration. There is always the possibility of overlapping and even conflicting interests and consequently of doubt whether the elements selected from our surrounding world taken for granted beyond question are really relevant to our purpose at hand. Is it indeed the p-being of S which I have to take into consideration and not its being q? Both are open possibilities within the general frame of the world taken for granted without question until counterproof. But now my biographically determined situation compels me to select either the p-being or the q-being of S as relevant for my purpose at hand. What has been unquestioned so far has now to be put into question, a situation of doubt occurs, a true alternative has been created. This situation of doubt, created by the selection of the actor in his biographically determined situation from the world taken for granted is what alone makes deliberation and choice possible. The fact that all choosing between projects refers to the situation of doubt has been acknowledged explicitly or implicitly by the greater number of the philosophers dealing with this problem. We quote the following passage from Dewey who has formulated the question in his masterful plastic language as follows: In deliberation, Dewey says, "each conflicting habit and impulse takes its turn in projecting itself upon the screen of imagination. It unrolls a picture of its future history, of the career it would have if it were given head. Although overt exhibition is checked by the pressure of contrary propulsive tendencies, this very inhibition gives habit a chance at manifestation in thought. . . . "In thought as well as in overt action the objects experienced in following out a course of action attract, repel, satisfy, annoy, promote and retard. Thus deliberation proceeds. To say that at last it ceases is to say that choice, decision, takes place. What then is choice? Simply hitting in imagination upon an object which furnishes an adequate stimulus to the recovery of overt action. "Choice is not the emergence of preference out of indifference. It is the emergence of a unified preference out of competing preferences."[2]

This analysis is in substance entirely acceptable also to those who are unable to share Dewey's fundamental view of interpreting human conduct in terms of habit and stimulus. Yet behind the problem discussed by Dewey another one emerges. What makes (in his terminology) habits and impulses conflict? What causes the pressure of contrary propulsive tendencies inhibiting one another? Which among our many preferences are competing and capable of being unified by the decision? In other words: I can choose only between projects which stand to choice. I am in a dilemma before an alternative. But what is the origin of such an alternative? It seems to us that Husserl has, although on another level, made a significant contribution to answering these questions.

Problematic and Open Possibilities

We owe to Husserl's investigation on the origin of the so-called modalizations of predicative judgments (such as certainty, possibility, probability) in the pre-predicative sphere the important distinction between what he calls problematic and open possibilities. This distinction is vital for the understanding of the problem of choice.

According to Husserl, any object of our experiences is originarily pregiven to our passive reception; it affects us, imposing itself upon the ego. Thus, it stimulates the ego to turn to the object, to attend to it, and this turning to the object is the lowest form of

[2]   John Dewey, *Human Nature and Conduct* (New York: Random House, Modern Library ed.), pp. 190 f.

activity emanating from the ego. Philosophers have frequently described this phenomenon as the receptivity of the ego, and psychologists have analyzed it under the heading of attention. Attention is first of all the tending of the ego toward the intentional object, but this tending is merely the starting point of a series of active *cogitationes* in the broadest sense: the initial phase of the starting activity carries along an intentional horizon of later phases of activity which will fulfill or not fulfill what has been anticipated in an empty way in a continuous synthetic process until the activity reaches its end or is interrupted, eventually in the form: "and so on." Taking as an example our actual belief in the existence of an outer object perceived we find that the ego's interest in this object induces it to manifold other activities, for instance to compare the image it has of the appearance of the perceptional object with other images of the same object, or to make accessible its back side if it appears from the front side, and so on. Each single phase of all these tendencies and activities carries along its specific horizon of protentional expectations, of anticipations, that is, of what may occur in the later phases of the fulfilling activity. If these expectations are not fulfilled there are several alternatives: (1) It may happen that the process is hampered for one reason or another either because the object disappears from the perceptional field or is covered by another object or because the original interest is superseded by another, stronger one. In these cases the process stops with the constitution of one single image of the object; (2) It may also happen that our interest in the perceptual object continues but that our anticipations are not fulfilled but disappointed by the supervening phases of the process. Here again two cases have to be distinguished: (a) the disappointment of our expectations is a complete one, for instance, the back side of this object which we expected to be an evenly red-colored sphere turns out to be not red but green and not spherical but deformed. This "not . . . but otherwise," this superimposition of a new meaning of the object over the pre-constituted meaning of the same object, whereby the new meaning supersedes the old one, leads in our example to the complete annihilation of the anticipating intention. The first impression ("this is an evenly red-colored sphere") is "stricken out," negated. (b) Yet it is possible that the first impression, instead of being completely annihilated, becomes merely doubtful in the course of the ongoing process. Is this something in the store window, a human being, say an employee occupied with window dressing, or a clothed dummy? There is a conflict between belief and belief, and for a certain time both perceptual apperceptions may coexist. While we doubt, neither of these two beliefs is cancelled; either of them continues in its own right; either is motivated, nay, even postulated, by the perceptual situation; but postulate stands against postulate, one contests the other and is contested by the other. Only our resolution of this doubt will annihilate one or the other. In case of a doubtful situation both beliefs of the alternative have the character of being "questionable," and that which is questionable is always contested in its being, namely, contested by something else. The ego oscillates between two tendencies to believe. Both beliefs are merely suggested as possibilities. The ego is in conflict with itself: it is inclined to believe now this, now that. This inclination means not merely the affective tendency of suggested possibilities, but these possibilities, says Husserl, are suggested to *me* as being, *I* follow now this, now that possibility in the process of taking a decision, bestow now on the one, now on the other validity in an act of "taking sides" although always hampered in carrying it through. This following of the ego is motivated by the weight of the possibilities themselves. Following actively one of the possibilities over at least a certain period I make so to speak an instantaneous decision, deciding for this possibility. But, then, I cannot proceed further because of the exigency of the counterpossibility which, too, will obtain its fair trial and makes me inclined to believe it. The decision is reached in a process of clarification of the contesting tendencies by which either the weakness of the counterpossibilities becomes more and more visible or by which new motives arise which reinforce the prevailing weight of the first.

Possibilities and counterpossibilities, contesting with one another, and originating in the situation of doubt are called by Husserl *problematic or questionable possibilities,* questionable, because the intention to decide in favor of one of them is a questioning intention. Only in the case of possibilities of this kind, that is of possibilities "for which something speaks," can we speak of likelihood. It is more likely that this is a man means: more circumstances speak for the possibility that this is a man than for the possibility that this is a dummy. Likelihood is, thus, a weight which belongs to the suggested beliefs in the existence of the intentional objects. From this class of problematic possibilities, originating in doubt, has to be distinguished the class of *open possibilities* originating in the unhampered course of empty anticipations. If I anticipate the color of the unseen side of an object of which I know only the front side that shows some pattern or patches, any specific color I anticipate is merely contingent, but that the unseen side will show "a" color is not. All anticipation has the character of indeterminacy, and this general indeterminacy constitutes a frame of free variability; what falls within the frame is one element among other elements of possibly *nearer* determination, of which I merely know that they will fit in the frame but which are otherwise entirely undetermined. This exactly is the concept of open possibilities.

The difference between problematic and open possibilities is first one of their origin. The problematic possibilities presuppose tendencies of belief which are motivated by the situation and in contest with one another; for each of them speaks something, each has a certain weight. None of the open possibilities has any weight whatsoever, they are all equally possible. There is no alternative preconstituted, but within a frame of generality all possible specifications are equally open. Nothing speaks for one which would speak against the other. An undetermined general intention, which itself shows the modality of certainty—although of an empirical or presumptive certainty—"until further notice"—carries along an implicit modalization of the certainty peculiar to its implicit specifications. On the other hand the field of problematic possibilities is unified: In the unity of contest and of being apprehended by disjunctive oscillation A, B, and C become known as being in opposition and, therefore, united. To be sure, it is quite possible that only one of these contesting possibilities stands out consciously whereas the others remain unnoticed in the background as empty and thematically unperformed representations. But this fact does not invalidate the pregivenness of a true alternative.

So far Husserl. His theory of choosing between alternatives is the more important for our problem as we will remember that any project leads to a true problematic alternative. Each project to do something carries with it the problematic counterpossibility of not doing it. . . .

The world as taken for granted is the general frame of open possibilities, none of them having its specific weight, none of them as long as believed beyond question, contesting the others. All are believed to be of empirical or presumptive certainty until further notice, that is, until counterproof. It is the selection made from things taken for granted by the individual in his biographically determined situation that transforms a selected set of these open possibilities into problematic ones which stand from now on to choice: Each of them has its weight, requires its fair trial, shows the conflicting tendencies of which Dewey speaks. How can this procedure of choosing be more precisely described?

Choosing Among Objects

To simplify the problem let us first consider the case in which I do not have to choose between two or more future states of affairs to be brought forth by my own future actions but between two objects, A and B, both actually and equally within my reach. I oscillate between A and B as between two equally available possibilities. A as well as B has a certain appeal to me. I am now inclined to take A, which inclination is then overpowered by an inclination to take B, this is again replaced by the first one, which finally prevails: I decide to take A and to leave B.

In this case everything takes place as described so far. A true alternative, preconstituted by our previous experiences, stands to choice: The objects A and B are equally within our reach, that is obtainable with the same effort. My total biographical situation, that is, my previous experiences as integrated into my actually prevailing system of interests, creates the principally problematic possibilities of conflicting preferences, as Dewey expresses it. This is the situation which most of the modern social sciences assume to be the normal one underlying human action. It is assumed that man finds himself at any time placed among more or less well-defined problematic alternatives or that a set of preferences enables him to determine the course of his future conduct. Even more, it is a methodological postulate of modern social science that the conduct of man has to be explained *as if* occurring in the form of choosing among problematic possibilities. Without entering here into details we want to give two illustrations:

Man acting in the social world among and upon his fellow men finds that the pre-constituted social world imposes upon him at any moment several alternatives among which he has to choose. According to modern sociology the actor has "to define the situation." By doing so he transforms his social environment of "open possibilities" into a unified field of "problematic possibilities" within which choice and decision—especially so-called "rational" choice and decision—becomes possible. The sociologist's assumption that the actor in the social world starts with the definition of the situation is, therefore, equivalent to the methodological postulate, that the sociologist has to describe the observed social actions *as if* they occurred within a unified field of true alternatives that is of problematic and not of open possibilities. Likewise the so-called "marginal principle," so important for modern economics, can be interpreted as the scientific postulate to deal with the actions of the observed economic subjects *as if* they had to choose between pregiven problematic possibilities.

Choosing Among Projects

We have studied so far the process of choosing between two objects actually within my reach, both equally obtainable. At first glance it might appear that the choice between two projects, between two courses of future action occurs in exactly the same manner. As a matter of fact most of the students of the problem of choice have failed to make any distinction. Perhaps the old distinction between . . . the art of producing and the art of acquiring, taken over by Plato and Aristotle from the Sophists, refers to this problem. The chief differences between the two situations seem to be as follows: In the case of choosing between two or more objects, all of them actually within my reach and equally available, the problematic possibilities are, so to speak, ready made and well circumscribed. As such their constitution is beyond my control, I have to take one of them or to leave both of them as they are. Projecting, however, is of my own making and in this sense within my control. But before I have rehearsed in my imagination the future courses of my actions, the outcome of my projecting action has not been brought within my reach and, strictly speaking, there are at the time of my projecting no problematic alternatives between which to choose. Anything that will later on stand to choice in the way of a problematic alternative has to be produced by me and in the course of producing it, I may modify it at my will within the limits of practicability. Moreover—and this point seems to be decisive—in the first case the alternatives which stand to my choice coexist in simultaneity in outer time: here are the two objects A and B, I may turn away from one of them and return to it; here it is still and unchanged. In the second case the several projects of my own future actions do not coexist in the simultaneity of outer time: The mind by its phantasying acts creates in succession in inner time the various projects, dropping one in favor of the other and returning to, or more precisely, re-creating, the first. But by and in the transition from one to the succeeding states of consciousness I have grown older. I have enlarged my experience, I am, returning to the first, no longer the "same" as I was when originally drafting it and consequently the project to which I return is no longer the same at that which I dropped; or, perhaps more exactly; it is the same, but modified. In the first case what stands to choice are problematic possibilities coexistent in outer time; in the second case the possibilities to choose between are produced successively and exclusively in inner time, within the *durée*.

IV. The World of Social Relationships

8

INTERACTIONAL RELATIONSHIPS

I. *Intersubjectivity and Understanding*

INTERSUBJECTIVITY If we retain the natural attitude as men among other men, the existence of others is no more questionable to us than the existence of an outer world. We are simply born into a world of others, and as long as we stick to the natural attitude we have no doubt that intelligent fellow-men do exist. Only if radical solipsists or behaviorists demand proof of this fact does it turn out that the existence of intelligent fellow-men is a "soft datum" and incapable of verification (Russell). But in their natural attitude even those thinkers do not doubt this "soft datum." Otherwise they could not meet others in congresses where it is reciprocally proved that the intelligence of the other is a questionable fact. As long as human beings are not concocted like homunculi in retorts but are born and brought up by mothers, the sphere of the "We" will be naïvely presupposed.

FELLOW MEN TAKEN FOR GRANTED The world of my daily life is by no means my private world but is from the outset an intersubjective one, shared with my fellow men, experienced and interpreted by others; in brief, it is a world common to all of us. The unique biographical situation in which I find myself within the world at any moment of my existence is only to a very small extent of my own making. I find myself always within an historically given world which, as a world of nature as well as a sociocultural

Reprinted from the following items in the Bibliography: 1942, 337–38; 1955b, 160, 161; 1953a, 404–5; 1942, 342–44; 1967, 107–13, 113–16, 116–18; 1960, 213–16; 1953c, 8–9; 1967, 163–64, 164–65, 166–67, 167–71, 171–72, 172–74, 174–76; 1953c, 20.

world, had existed before my birth and which will continue to exist after my death. This means that this world is not only mine but also my fellow men's environment; moreover, these fellow men are elements of my own situation, as I am of theirs. Acting upon the others and acted upon by them, I know of this mutual relationship, and this knowledge also implies that they, the others, experience the common world in a way substantially similar to mine. They, too, find themselves in a unique biographical situation within a world which is, like mine, structured in terms of actual and potential reach, grouped around their actual Here and Now at the center in the same dimensions and directions of space and time, an historically given world of nature, society, and culture, etc. . . . Man takes for granted the bodily existence of fellow men, their conscious life, the possibility of intercommunication, and the historical giveness of social organization and culture, just as he takes for granted the world of nature into which he was born.

APPRESENTATION OF THE OTHER   Knowledge of another's mind is possible only through the intermediary of events occurring on or produced by another's body. This is, in Husserl's terminology, an outstanding case of appresentational reference. According to him, the other is from the outset given to me as both a material object with its position in space and a subject with its psychological life. His body, like all other material objects, is given to my original perception or, as Husserl says, in originary presence. His psychological life, however, is not given to me in originary presence but only in copresence; it is not presented, but appresented. By the mere continuous visual perception of the other's body and its movements, a system of appresentations, of well ordered indications of his psychological life and his experiences is constituted.

THE COMMUNICATIVE COMMON ENVIRONMENT   To be related to a common environment and to be united with the Other in a community of persons—these two propositions are inseparable. We could not be persons for others, even not for ourselves, if we could not find with the others a common environment as the counterpart of the intentional interconnectedness of our conscious lives. This common environment is established by comprehension, which in turn, is founded upon the fact that the subjects reciprocally motivate one another in their spiritual activities. Thus, relationships of mutual understanding (*Wechselverständnis*) and consent (*Einverständnis*) and, therewith, a *communicative common environment* originate. It is characterized by the fact that it is relative to the persons who find one another within this environment and the environment itself as their counterpart (*als ihr Gegenüber*). The persons participating in the communicative environment are given one to the other not as objects but as counter-subjects, as consociates in a societal community of persons. Sociality is constituted by communicative acts in which the I turns to the others, apprehending them as persons who turn to him, and both know of this fact. Nevertheless, the comprehension of the other person occurs merely by appresentation, everyone having merely his own experiences given in originary presence. This leads to the fact that within the common environment any subject has his particular subjective environment, his private world, originarily given to him and to him alone. He perceives the same object as his partner but with adumbrations dependent upon his particular Here and his phenomenal Now. Any subject participates in several time dimensions: There is first his particular inner time, the flux of immanent time, in which the constituting experiences have their place; secondly the time dimension of the constituted experiences, the (still subjective) space-time. By reason of the relationships of simultaneity, of "before" and "after," prevailing between both dimensions the primarily constituted unity of the appearing thing is, as to its duration, simultaneous with the continuity of perception and its noetical duration. There is, thirdly, the objective intersubjective time which forms *a priori* a single order of time with all the subjective times: The objective time and the objective space "appear" as "valid" phenomena in the subjective orders of space-time. This is the true reason of the exchangeability of places mentioned herein before. The communicative common environment presupposes that the same thing given to me *now* (namely in an intersubjective Now) in a particular adumbration can be given to the other in the same modus *thereafter* in the flux of intersubjective time and vice versa.

GENERAL THESIS OF THE ALTER EGO   Now let us go back again to the naïve attitude of daily life in which we live in our acts directed toward their objects. Among those objects which we experience in the vivid present are other people's behavior and thoughts. In listening to a lecturer, for instance, we seem to participate immediately in the development of his stream of thought. But —and this point is obviously a decisive one—our attitude in doing so is quite different from that we adopt in turning to our own stream of thought by reflection. We catch the other's thought in its vivid presence and not *modo preterito;* that is, we catch it as a "Now" and not as a "Just now." The other's speech and our listening are experienced as a vivid simultaneity. Now he starts a new sentence, he attaches word to word; we do not know how the sentence will end, and before its end we are uncertain what it means. The next sentence joins the first, paragraph follows paragraph; now he has expressed a thought and passes to another, and the whole is a lecture among other lectures and so on. It depends on circumstances how far we want to follow the development of his thought. But as long as we do so we participate in the immediate present of the other's thought.

The fact that I can grasp the other's stream of thought, and this means the subjectivity of the alter ego in its vivid present,[1] whereas I cannot grasp my own self but by way of reflection in its past, leads us to a definition of the alter ego: the alter ego is that subjective stream of thought which can be experienced in its vivid present. In order to bring it into view we do not have to stop fictitiously the other's stream of thought nor need we transform its "Nows" into "Just Nows." It is simultaneous with our own stream of consciousness, we share together the same vivid present—in one word: we grow old together. The alter ego therefore is that stream of con-

[1]   It is not necessary to refer to an example of social interrelationship bound to the medium of speech. Whoever has played a game of tennis, performed chamber music, or made love has caught the other in his immediate vivid present.

sciousness whose activities I can seize in their present by my own simultaneous activities.

This experience of the other's stream of consciousness in vivid simultaneity I propose to call the *general thesis of the alter ego's existence*. It implies that this stream of thought which is not mine shows the same fundamental structure as my own consciousness. This means that the other is like me, capable of acting and thinking; that his stream of thoughts show the same through and through connectedness as mine; that analogous to my own life of consciousness his shows the same time-structure, together with the specific experiences of retentions, reflections, protentions, anticipations, connected therewith and its phenomena of memory and attention, of kernel and horizon of the thought, and all the modifications thereof. It means, furthermore, that the other can live, as I do, either in his acts and thoughts, directed toward their objects or turn to his own acting and thinking; that he can experience his own Self only *modo praeterito*, but that he may look at my stream of consciousness in a vivid present; that, consequently, he has the genuine experience of growing old with me as I know that I do with him.

As a potentiality each of us may go back into his past conscious life as far as recollection goes, whereas our knowledge of the other remains limited to that span of his life and its manifestations observed by us. In this sense each of us knows more of himself than of the other. But in a specific sense the contrary is true. In so far as each of us can experience the other's thoughts and acts in the vivid present whereas either can grasp his own only as a past by way of reflection, I know more of the other and he knows more of me than either of us knows of his own stream of consciousness. This present, common to both of us, is the pure sphere of the "We." . . . We participate . . . without an act of reflection in the vivid simultaneity of the "We," whereas the I appears only after the reflective turning. . . . We cannot grasp our own acting in its actual present; we can seize only those past of our acts which have already gone by; but we experience the other's acts in their vivid performance.

All that we have described as the "general thesis of the alter ego" is a description of our experiences in the mundane sphere. It is a piece of "phenomenological psychology," as Husserl calls it in antithesis to "transcendental phenomenology." But the results of an analysis of the mundane sphere, if true, cannot be impugned by any basic assumption (metaphysical or ontological) which migh be made in order to explain our belief in the existence of others. Whether or not the origin of the "We" refers to the transcendental sphere at all, our immediate and genuine experience of the alter ego within the mundane sphere cannot be gainsaid. In any event, however, the general thesis of the alter ego, as outlined above, is a sufficient frame of reference for the foundation of empirical psychology and social sciences. For all our knowledge of the social world, even of its most anonymous and remotest phenomena and of the most diverse types of social communities is based upon the possibility to experience an alter ego in vivid presence.

UNDERSTANDING ANOTHER PERSON   There are ambiguities in the ordinary notion of understanding another person. Sometimes what is meant is intentional Acts directed toward the other self; in other words, my lived experiences of you. At other times what is in question is *your* subjective experiences. Then, the arrangements of all such experiences into meaning-contexts (Weber's comprehension of intended meaning) is sometimes called "understanding of the other self," as is the classification of others' behavior into motivation contexts. The number of ambiguities associated with the notion of "understanding another person" becomes even greater when we bring in the question of understanding the signs he is using. On the one hand, what is understood is the sign itself, then again *what* the other person means by using this sign, and finally the significance of the fact *that* he is using the sign, here, now, and in this particular context.

In order to sort out these different levels in the meaning of the term, let us first give it a generic definition. Let us say that understanding (*Verstehen*) as such is correlative to meaning, for all understanding is directed toward that which has meaning (*auf ein Sinnhaftes*) and only something understood is meaningful (*sinnvoll*). . . . all intentional Acts which are interpretations of one's own subjective experiences would be called Acts of understanding (*verstehende Akte*). We should also designate as "understanding" all the lower strata of meaning-comprehension on which such self-explanation is based.

The man in the natural attitude, then, understands the world by interpreting his own lived experiences of it, whether these experiences be of inanimate things, of animals, or of his fellow human beings. And so our initial concept of the understanding of the other self is simply the concept "our explication of our lived experiences of our fellow human beings as such." The fact that the Thou who confronts me is a fellow man and not a shadow on a movie screen— in other words, that he has duration and consciousness—is something I discover by explicating my own lived experiences of him.

Furthermore, the man in the natural attitude perceives changes in that external object which is known to him as the other's body. He interprets these changes just as he interprets changes in inanimate objects, namely, by interpretation of his own lived experiences of the events and processes in question. Even this second phase does not go beyond the bestowing of meaning within the sphere of the solitary consciousness.

The transcending of this sphere becomes possible only when the perceived processes come to be regarded as lived experiences belonging to another consciousness, which, in accordance with the general thesis of the other self, exhibits the same structure as my own. The perceived bodily movements of the other will then be grasped not merely as *my* lived experience of these movements within *my* stream of consciousness. Rather it will be understood that, simultaneous with *my* lived experience of you, there is *your* lived experience which belongs to you and is part of your stream of consciousness. Meanwhile, the specific nature of your experience is quite unknown to me, that is, I do not know the meaning-contexts you are using to classify those lived experiences of yours, provided, indeed, you are even aware of the movements of your body.

However, I can know the meaning-context into which I classify my own lived experiences of you. . . . This is not your intended meaning in the true sense of the term. What can be comprehended is always only an "approximate value" of the limiting concept of "the other's intended meaning."

However, talk about the meaning-context into which the Thou orders its lived experience is again very vague. The very question of whether a bodily movement is purposive or merely reactive is a question which can only be answered in terms of the other person's own context of meaning. And then if one considers the further questions that can be asked about the other person's schemes of experience, for instance about his motivational contexts, one can get a good idea of how complex is the theory of understanding the other self. It is of great importance to penetrate into the structure of this understanding far enough to show that we can only interpret lived experiences belonging to other people in terms of our own lived experiences of them.

In the above discussion we have limited our analysis exclusively to cases where other people are present bodily to us in the domain of directly experienced social reality. In so doing, we have proceeded as if the understanding of the other self were based on the interpretation of the movements of his body. A little reflection shows, however, that this kind of interpretation is good for only one of the many regions of the social world; for even in the natural standpoint, a man experiences his neighbors even when the latter are not at all present in the bodily sense. He has knowledge not only of his directly experienced consociates[2] but also about his more distant contemporaries. He has, in addition, empirical information about his historical predecessors. He finds himself surrounded by objects which tell him plainly that they were produced by other people; these are not only material objects but all kinds of linguistic and other sign systems, in short, artifacts in the broadest sense. He interprets these first of all by arranging them within his own contexts of experience. However, he can at any time ask further questions about the lived experiences and meaning-contexts of their creators, that is, about why they were made.

We must now carefully analyze all these complex processes. We shall do so, however, only to the extent required by our theme, namely, "the understanding of the other person within the social

---

[2]   [Schutz used the English term "consociates" (among others) to mean those whom we directly experience. We shall be using it in this technical sense to translate references to people in our *Umwelt* (domain of directly experienced social reality).]

world." For this purpose we must begin with the lowest level and clarify those Acts of self-explication which are present and available for use in interpreting the behavior of other people. For the sake of simplicity, let us assume that the other person is present bodily. We shall select our examples from various regions of human behavior by analyzing first an action without any communicative intent and then one whose meaning is declared through signs.

As an example of the "understanding of a human act" without any communicative intent, let us look at the activity of a woodcutter.

Understanding that wood is being cut can mean:

1. That we are noticing only the "external event," the ax slicing the tree and the wood splitting into bits, which ensues. If this is all we see, we are hardly dealing with what is going on in another person's mind. Indeed, we need hardly bring in the other person at all, for woodcutting is woodcutting, whether done by man, by machine, or even by some natural force. Of course, meaning *is* bestowed on the observed event by the observer, in the sense that he understands it as "woodcutting." In other words, he inserts it into his own context of experience. However, this "understanding" is merely the explication of his own lived experiences. . . . The observer perceives the event and orders his perceptions into polythetic syntheses, upon which he then looks back with a monothetic glance, and arranges these syntheses into the total context of his experience, giving them at the same time a name. However, the observer in our case does not as yet perceive the *woodcutter* but only *that the wood is being cut,* and he "understands" the perceived sequence of events as "woodcutting." It is essential to note that even this interpretation of the event is determined by the total context of knowledge available to the observer at the moment of observation. Whoever does not know how paper is manufactured will not be in a position to classify the component processes because he lacks the requisite interpretive scheme. Nor will he be in a position to formulate the judgment "This is a place where paper is manufactured." And this holds true, as we have established, for all arrangements of lived experiences into the context of knowledge.

But understanding that wood is being cut can also mean:

2. That changes in another person's body are perceived, which

changes are interpreted as indications that he is alive and conscious. Meanwhile, no further assumption is made that an action is involved. But this, too, is merely an explication of the observer's own perceptual experiences. All he is doing is identifying the body as that of a living human being and then noting the fact and manner of its changes.

Understanding that someone is cutting wood can, however, mean:

3. That the center of attention is the woodcutter's own lived experiences as actor. The question is not one about external events but one about lived experiences: "Is this man acting spontaneously according to a project he had previously formulated? If so, what is this project? What is his in-order-to motive? In what meaning-context does this action stand for *him*?" And so forth. These questions are concerned with neither the facticity of the situation as such nor the bodily movements as such. Rather, the outward facts and bodily movements are understood as indications (*Anzeichen*) of the lived experiences of the person being observed. The attention of the observer is focused not on the indications but on what lies behind them. This is *genuine understanding of the other person.*

Now, let us turn our attention to a case where signs are being used and select as our example the case of a person talking German. The observer can direct his attention:

1. Upon the bodily movements of the speaker. In this case he interprets his own lived experience on the basis of the context of experience of the present moment. First the observer makes sure he is seeing a real person and not an image, as in a motion-picture film. He then determines whether the person's movements are actions. All this is, of course, self-interpretation.

2. Upon the perception of the sound alone. The observer may go on to discover whether he is hearing a real person or a tape recorder. This, too, is only an interpretation of his own experiences.

3. Upon the specific pattern of the sounds being produced. That is, he identifies the sounds first as words, not shrieks, and then as German words. They are thus ordered within a certain scheme, in which they are signs with definite meanings. This ordering within the scheme of a particular language can even take place without

knowledge of the meanings of the words, provided the listener has some definite criterion in mind. If I am traveling in a foreign country, I know when two people are talking to each other, and I also know that they are talking the language of the country in question without having the slightest idea as to the subject of their conversation.

In making any of these inferences, I am merely interpreting my own experiences, and nothing is implied as to a single lived experience of any of the people being observed.

The observer "understands," in addition:

4. The word as the sign of its own word meaning. Even then he merely interprets his own experiences by coordinating the sign to a previously experienced sign system or interpretive scheme, say the German language. As the result of his knowledge of the German language, the observer connects with the word *Tisch* the idea of a definite piece of furniture, which he can picture with approximate accuracy. It matters not at all whether the word has been uttered by another person, a phonograph, or even a parrot. Nor does it matter whether the word is spoken or written, or, if the latter, whether it is traced out in letters of wood or iron. It does not matter when or where it is uttered or in what context. As long, therefore, as the observer leaves out of account all questions as to why and how the word is being used on the occasion of observation, his interpretation remains self-interpretation. He is concerned with the *meaning of the word*, not the *meaning of the user of the word*. When we identify these interpretations as self-interpretations, we should not overlook the fact that all previous knowledge of the other person belongs to the interpreter's total configuration of experience, which is the context from whose point of view the interpretation is being made.

The observer can, however, proceed to the genuine understanding of the other person if he:

5. Regards the meaning of the word as an indication (*Anzeichen*) of the speaker's subjective experiences—regards the meaning, in short, as *what the speaker meant*. For instance, he can try to discover what the speaker intended to say and what he meant by saying it on this occasion. These questions are obviously

aimed at conscious experiences. The first question tries to establish the context of meaning within which the speaker understands the words he is uttering, while the second seeks to establish the motive for the utterance. It is obvious that the genuine understanding of the other person involved in answering such questions can only be attained if the objective meaning of the words is first established by the observer's explication of his own experiences. . . .

Let us now state in summary which of our interpretive acts referring to another self are interpretations of our own experience. There is first the interpretation that the observed person is really a human being and not an image of some kind. The observer establishes this solely by interpretation of his own perceptions of the other's body. Second, there is the interpretation of all the external phases of action, that is, of all bodily movements and their effects. Here, as well, the observer is engaging in interpretation of his own perceptions, just as when he is watching the flight of a bird or the stirring of a branch in the wind. In order to understand what is occurring, he is appealing solely to his own past experience, not to what is going on in the mind of the observed person.[3] Finally, the same thing may be said of the perception of all the other person's expressive movements and all the signs which he uses, provided that one is here referring to the general and objective meaning of such manifestations and not their occasional and subjective meaning.

But, of course, by "understanding the other person" much more is meant, as a rule. This additional something, which is really the only strict meaning of the term, involves grasping what is really going on in the other person's mind, grasping those things of which the external manifestations are mere indications. To be sure, interpretation of such external indications and signs in terms of interpretation of one's own experiences must come first. But the interpreter will not be satisfied with this. He knows perfectly well from the total context of his own experience that, corresponding to the outer objective and public meaning which he has just deciphered, there is this other, inner, subjective meaning. He asks, then, "What is that

---

[3]   Of course, all such interpretations presume acceptance of the General Thesis of the Alter Ego, according to which the external object is understood to be animated, that is, to be the body of another self.

woodcutter really thinking about? What is he up to? What does all this chopping mean to him?" Or, in another case, "What does this person mean by speaking to me in this manner, at this particular moment? For the sake of what does he do this (what is his in-order-to motive)? What circumstance does he give as the reason for it (that is, what is his genuine because-motive)? What does the choice of these words indicate?" Questions like these point to the other person's *own* meaning-contexts, to the complex ways in which his own lived experiences have been constituted polythetically and also to the monothetic glance with which he attends to them.

GENUINE SUBJECTIVE UNDERSTANDING   Having established that all genuine understanding of the other person must start out from Acts of explication performed by the observer on his own lived experience, we must now proceed to a precise analysis of this genuine understanding itself. From the examples we have already given, it is clear that our inquiry must take two different directions. First we must study the genuine understanding of actions which are performed *without any communicative intent*. The action of the woodcutter would be a good example. Second we would examine cases where such communicative intent was present. The latter type of action involves a whole new dimension, the using[4] and interpreting of signs.

Let us first take actions performed without any communicative intent. We are watching a man in the act of cutting wood and wondering what is going on in his mind. Questioning him is ruled out, because that would require entering into a social relationship with him, which in turn would involve the use of signs.

Let us further suppose that we know nothing about our woodcutter except what we see before our eyes. By subjecting our own perceptions to interpretation, we know that we are in the presence of a fellow human being and that his bodily movements indicate he is engaged in an action which we recognize as that of cutting wood.

Now how do we know what is going on in the woodcutter's mind? Taking this interpretation of our own perceptual data as a

---

[4]   [*Setzung*; literally "positing" or "establishing."]

starting point, we can plot out in our mind's eye exactly how *we* would carry out the action in question. Then we can actually imagine ourselves doing so. In cases like this, then, we project the other person's goal as if it were our own and fancy ourselves carrying it out. Observe also that we here project the action in the future perfect tense as completed and that our imagined execution of the action is accompanied by the usual retentions and reproductions of the project, although, of course, only in fancy. Further, let us note that the imagined execution may fulfill or fail to fulfill the imagined project.

Or, instead of imagining for ourselves an action wherein we carry out the other person's goal, we may recall in concrete detail how we once carried out a similar action ourselves. Such a procedure would be merely a variation on the same principle.

In both these cases, we put ourselves in the place of the actor and identify our lived experiences with his. It might seem that we are here repeating the error of the well-known "projective" theory of empathy. For here we are reading our own lived experiences into the other person's mind and are therefore only discovering our own experiences. But, if we look more closely, we will see that our theory has nothing in common with the empathy theory except for one point. This is the general thesis of the Thou as the "other I," the one whose experiences are constituted in the same fashion as mine. But even this similarity is only apparent, for we start out from the general thesis of the other person's flow of duration, while the projective theory of empathy jumps from the mere fact of empathy to the belief in other minds by an act of blind faith. Our theory only brings out the implications of what is already present in the self-explicative judgment "I am experiencing a fellow human being." We know with certainty that the other person's subjective experience of his own action is in principle different from our own imagined picture of what we would do in the same situation. The reason, as we have already pointed out, is that the intended meaning of an action is always in principle subjective and accessible only to the actor. The error in the empathy theory is twofold. First, it naïvely tries to trace back the constitution of the other self within the ego's consciousness to empathy, so that the latter becomes the direct source of knowledge of the other. Actually, such a task of discovering the constitution of the other self can only be carried out in a transcendentally phenomenonological manner. Second, it pretends to a knowledge of the other person's mind that goes far beyond the establishment of a structural parallelism between that mind and my own. In fact, however, when we are dealing with actions having no communicative intent, all that we can assert about their meaning is already contained in the general thesis of the alter ego.

It is clear, then, that we imaginatively project the in-order-to motive of the other person as if it were our own and then use the fancied carrying-out of such an action as a scheme in which to interpret his lived experiences. However, to prevent misunderstanding, it should be added that what is involved here is only a reflective analysis of another person's completed act. It is an interpretation carried out after the fact. When an observer is directly watching someone else to whom he is attuned in simultaneity, the situation is different. Then the observer's living intentionality carries him along without having to make constant playbacks of his own past or imaginary experiences. The other person's action unfolds step by step before his eyes. In such a situation, the identification of the observer with the observed person is not carried out by starting with the goal of the act as already given and then proceeding to reconstruct the lived experiences which must have accompanied it. Instead, the observer keeps pace, as it were, with each step of the observed person's action, identifying himself with the latter's experiences within a common "we-relationship." . . .

So far we have assumed the other person's bodily movement as the only datum given to the observer. It must be emphasized that, if the bodily movement is taken by itself in this way, it is necessarily isolated from its place within the stream of the observed person's living experience. And this context is important not only to the observed person but to the observer as well. He can, of course, if he lacks other data, take a mental snapshot of the observed bodily movement and then try to fit it into a phantasied filmstrip in accordance with the way he thinks he would act and feel in a similar situation. However, the observer can draw much more reliable conclusions about his subject if he knows something about his past and something about the over-all plan into which this action fits. To come back to Max Weber's example, it would be important for the observer to know whether the woodcutter was at his regular job or just chopping wood for physical exercise. An adequate model of the observed person's subjective experiences calls for just this wider context. We have already seen, indeed, that the unity of the action is a function of the project's span. From the observed bodily movement, all the observer can infer is the single course of action which has directly led to it. If, however, I as the observer wish to avoid an inadequate interpretation of what I see another person doing, I must "make my own" all those meaning-contexts which make sense of this action on the basis of my past knowledge of this particular person.

EXPRESSIVE ACTION   So far we have studied only cases where the actor seeks merely to bring about changes in the external world. He does not seek to "express" his subjective experiencs. By an "expressive" action we mean one in which the actor seeks to project outward (*nach aussen zu projizieren*) the contents of his consciousness, whether to retain the latter for his own use later on (as in the case of an entry in a diary) or to communicate them to others. In each of these two examples we have a genuinely planned or projected action (*Handeln nach Entwurf*) whose in-order-to motive is that someone take cognizance of something. In the first case this someone is the other person in the social world. In the second it is oneself in the world of the solitary Ego. Both of these are expressive acts. We must clearly distinguish the "expressive act" (*Ausdruckshandlung*) from what psychologists call the "expressive movement" (*Ausdrucksbewegung*). The latter does not aim at any communication or at the expression of any thoughts for one's own use or that of others. Here there is no genuine action in our sense, but only behavior: there is neither project nor in-order-to motive. Examples of such expressive movements are the gestures and facial expressions which, without any explicit intention, enter into every conversation.

From my point of view as observer, your body is presented to me as a field of expression on which I can "watch" the flow of your lived experiences. I do this "watching" simply by treating *both* your expressive movements and your expressive acts as indications of your lived experiences. But we must look at this point in greater detail.

If I understand, as Weber says, certain facial expressions, verbal interjections, and irrational movements as an outbreak of anger, this understanding itself can be interpreted in several different ways. It can mean, for instance, nothing more than self-elucidation, namely my arrangement and classification of my own experiences of your body. It is only when I perform a further Act of attention involving myself intimately with *you*, regarding *your* subjective experiences as flowing simultaneously with *my* subjective experiences *of* you, that I really grasp or "get with" *your* anger. This turning to the genuine understanding of the other person is possible for me only because I have previously had experiences similar to yours even if only in phantasy, or if I have encountered it before in external manifestations. The expressive movement does, then, enter into a meaning-context, but only for the *observer*, for whom it is an indication of the lived experiences of the person he is observing. The latter is barred from giving meaning to his own expressive movements as they occur by the mere fact that he has not yet noticed them; they are, in our terminology, prephenomenal.

Expressive movements, then, have meaning only for the observer, not for the person observed. It is precisely this that distinguishes them from expressive acts. The latter always have meaning for the actor. Expressive acts are always genuine communicative acts (*Kundgabehandlungen*) which have as a goal their own interpretation.

The mere occurrence of a piece of external behavior, therefore, gives the interpreter no basis for knowing whether he is dealing with an expressive movement or an expressive act. He will be able to determine this only by appealing to a different context of experience. For instance, the play of a man's features and gestures in everyday life may be no different from those of an actor on the stage. Now we look upon the facial expressions and gestures of the latter as set signs that the stage actor is utilizing to express certain subjective experiences. In everyday life, on the other hand, we never quite know whether another person is "acting" in this sense or not unless we pay attention to factors other than his immediate movements. For instance, he may be imitating someone else for our benefit, or he may be playing a joke on us, or he may be hypocritically feigning certain feelings in order to take advantage of us.

It is quite immaterial to the understanding of expressive acts whether they consist of gestures, words, or artifacts. Every such act involves the use of signs.

MOTIVATIONAL UNDERSTANDING   I cannot understand other people's acts without knowing the in-order-to or the because motives of such acts. To be sure, there are manifold degrees of understanding. I must not (even more, I cannot) grasp the full ramifications of other people's motives, with their horizons of individual life plans, their background of individual experiences, their references to the unique situation by which they are determined. As we said before, such an ideal understanding would presuppose the full identity of my stream of thought with that of the alter ego, and that would mean an identity of both our selves. It suffices, therefore, that I can reduce the other's act to its typical motives, including their reference to typical situations, typical ends, typical means, etc.

On the other hand, there are also different degrees of my knowledge of the actor himself, degrees of intimacy and anonymity. I may reduce the product of human activity to the agency of an alter ego with whom I share present time and present space, and then it may occur that this other individual is an intimate friend of mine or a passenger I meet for the first time and will never meet again. It is not necessary even that I know the actor personally in order to have an approach to his motives. I can for instance understand the acts of a foreign statesman and discuss his motives without having ever met him or even without having seen a picture of him. The same is true for individuals who have lived long before my own time; I can understand the acts and motives of Caesar as well as of the cave-man who left no other testimony of his existence than the firestone hatchet exhibited in the showcase of the museum. But it is not even necessary to reduce human acts to a more or less well known individual actor. To understand them it is sufficient to find typical motives of typical actors which explain the act as a typical one arising out of a typical situation. There is a certain conformity in the acts and motives of priests, soldiers, servants, farmers everywhere and at every time. Moreover, there are acts of such a general type that it is sufficient to reduce them to "somebody's" typical motives for making them understandable.

. . . Social things are only understandable if they can be reduced to human activities; and human activities are only made understandable by showing their in-order-to or because motives. The deeper reason for this fact is that as I naively live within the social world I am able to understand other people's acts only if I can imagine that I myself would perform analogous acts if I were in the same situation, directed by the same because motives, or oriented by the same in-order-to motives all these terms understood in the restricted sense of the "typical" analogy, the "typical" sameness, as explained before.

That this assertion is true can be demonstrated by an analysis of the social action in the more precise sense of this term, namely of an action which involves the attitudes and actions of others and is oriented to them in its course.[5] As yet we have dealt in this study only with action as such without entering into the analysis of the modification which the general scheme undergoes with the introduction of social elements proper: mutual correlation and intersubjective adjustment. We have, therefore, observed the attitude of an isolated actor without making any distinction as to whether

[5]   Max Weber, *Wirtschaft und Gesellschaft* (Tübingen, 1922; new ed., 1956). Parts of this important work are available in English translation in H. H. Gerth and C. Wright Mills, eds., *From Max Weber: Essays in Sociology* (New York, 1946) ; other parts in the English translation by Talcott Parsons, under the title *The Theory of Social and Economic Organization* (New York, 1947).

this actor is occupied with the handling of a tool or acting with others and for others, motivated by others and motivating them.

This topic is very complicated to analyze and we have to restrict ourselves to sketching its outlines. It can be proved that all social relations as they are understood by me, a human being living naively in the social world which is centered around myself, have their prototype in the social relation connecting myself with an individual alter ego with whom I am sharing space and time. My social act, then, is oriented not only to the physical existence of this alter ego but to the other's act which I expect to provoke by my own action. I can, therefore, say that the other's reaction is the in-order-to motive of my own act. The prototype of all social relationship is an intersubjective connection of motives. If I imagine, projecting my act, that you will understand my act and that this understanding will induce you to react, on your part, in a certain way, I anticipate that the in-order-to motives of my own acting will become because motives of your reaction, and vice-versa.

Let us take a very simple example. I ask you a question. The in-order-to motive of my act is not only the expectation that you will understand my question, but also to get your answer; or more precisely, I reckon *that* you will answer, leaving undecided what the content of your answer may be. *Modo futuri exacti* I anticipate in projecting my own act that you will have answered my question in some way or other, and this means I think there is a fair chance that the understanding of my question will become a because motive for your answer, which I expect. The question, so we can say, is the because motive of the answer, as the answer is the in-order-to motive of the question. This interrelationship between my own and your motives is a well tested experience of mine, though, perhaps, I have never had explicit knowledge of the complicated interior mechanism of it. But I myself had felt on innumerable occasions induced to react to another's act, which I had interpreted as a question addressed to me, with a kind of behavior of which the in-order-to motive was my expectation that the other, the questioner, might interpret my behavior as an answer. Over against this experience I know that I have succeeded frequently in provoking another person's answer by my own act called questioning and so on. Therefore I feel I have a fair chance of getting your answer when I shall have once realized my action of questioning.

RECIPROCITY OF PERSPECTIVES   In the natural attitude of common-sense thinking of daily life I take it for granted that intelligent fellow men exist. This implies that the objects of the world are, as a matter of principle, accessible to their knowledge, namely, either known to them or knowable by them. This I know and take for granted beyond question. But I know also and take for granted that, strictly speaking, the "same" object must mean something different to me and to any of my fellow men. This is so because

(i) I, being "here," am at another distance from and experience other aspects as being typical of the objects than he, who is "there." For the same reason, certain objects are out of my reach (of my seeing, hearing, my manipulatory sphere, etc.) but within his and vice versa.

(ii) My and my fellow man's biographically determined situations, and therewith my and his purpose at hand and my and his system of relevances originating in such purposes, must needs differ, at least to a certain extent.

Common sense thinking overcomes the differences in individual perspectives resulting from these factors by two basic idealizations:

(i) The idealization of the interchangeability of the standpoints: I take it for granted—and assume my fellow man does the same—that if I change places with him so that his "here" becomes mine, I would be at the same distance from things and see them in the same typicality as he actually does; moreover, the same things would be in my reach which are actually in his. (All this vice versa.)

(ii) The idealization of the congruency of the system of relevances: Until counter-evidence I take it for granted—and assume my fellowman does the same—that the differences in perspectives originating in my and his unique biographical situations are irrelevant for the purpose at hand of either of us and that he and I, that "We" assume that both of us have selected and interpreted the actually or potentially common objects and their features in an identical manner or at least an "empirically identical" manner, namely, sufficient for all practical purposes.

It is obvious that both idealizations, that of the interchangeability of the standpoints and that of the congruency of relevances —both together constituting the *general thesis of reciprocal perspectives*—are typifying constructs of objects of thought which supersede the thought objects of my and my fellow man's private experience. By the operation of these constructs of common-sense thinking it is assumed that the sector of the world taken for granted by me is also taken for granted by you, my individual fellow man, even more, that it is taken for granted by "Us," but this "We" does not merely include you and me but "everyone who belongs to us," namely everyone whose system of relevances is substantially (sufficiently) in conformity with yours and mine. Thus, the general thesis of reciprocal perspectives leads to the apprehension of objects and their aspects actually known by me and potentially known by you as everyone's knowledge. Such knowledge is conceived to be objective and anonymous, namely detached from and independent of my fellow man's definition of the situation, my and his unique biographical circumstances and the actual and potential purposes at hand therein involved.

The terms "objects" and "aspect of objects" have to be interpreted in the broadest possible sense as objects of knowledge taken for granted.

II. *We-Relationship*

FACE-TO-FACE SITUATION: THOU-ORIENTATION   I speak of another person as within reach of my direct experience when he shares with me a community of space and a community of time. He shares a community of space with me when he is present in person and I am aware of him as such, and, moreover, when I am aware of him as this person *himself*, this *particular* individual, and of his body as the field upon which play the symptoms of his inner consciousness. He shares a community of time with me when his experience is flowing side by side with mine, when I can at any moment look over and grasp his thoughts as they come into being, in other words, when we are growing older together. Persons thus in reach of each other's direct experience I speak of as being in the "face-to-face" situation. The face-to-face situation presupposes, then, an actual simultaneity with each other of two separate streams of consciousness. We have already made this point clear . . . when we were dealing with the general thesis of the alter ego. We are now adding to it the corollary of the spatial immediacy of the Other, in virtue of which his body is present to me as a field of expression for his subjective experiences.

This spatial and temporal immediacy is essential to the face-to-face situation. All acts of Other-orientation and of affecting-the-other, and therefore all orientations and relationships within the face-to-face situation, derive their own specific flavor and style from this immediacy.

Let us first look at the way in which the face-to-face situation is constituted from the point of view of a participant in that situation. In order to become aware of such a situation, the participant must become intentionally conscious of the person confronting him. He must assume a face-to-face Other-orientation toward the partner. We shall term this attitude "Thou-orientation," and shall now proceed to describe its main features.

First of all, the Thou-orientation is the pure mode in which I am aware of another human being as a person. I am already Thou-oriented from the moment that I recognize an entity which I directly experience as a fellow man (as a Thou), attributing life and consciousness to him. However, we must be quite clear that we are *not* here dealing with a conscious *judgment*. This is a prepredicative experience in which I become aware of a fellow human being *as a person*. The Thou-orientation can thus be defined as the intentionality of those Acts whereby the Ego grasps the existence of the other person in the mode of the original self. Every such external experience in the mode of the original self presupposes the actual presence of the other person and my perception of him as there.

Now, we wish to emphasize that it is precisely the being there (*Dasein*) of the Other toward which the Thou-orientation is directed, not necessarily the Other's specific characteristics. The concept of the Thou-orientation does not imply awareness of what is

going on in the Other's mind. In its "pure" form the Thou-orientation consists merely of being intentionally directed toward the
pure being-there of another alive and conscious human being. To
be sure, the "pure" Thou-orientation is a formal concept, an intellectual construct, or, in Husserl's terminology, an "ideal limit."
In real life we never experience the "pure existence" of others; instead we meet real people with their own personal characteristics
and traits. The Thou-orientation as it occurs in everyday life is
therefore not the "pure" Thou-orientation but the latter *actualized*
and *rendered determinate* to some degree or other.

WE-RELATIONSHIP   Now the fact that I look upon you as a
fellow man does not mean that I am also a fellow man for you, unless you are aware of me. And, of course, it is quite possible that
you may not be paying any attention to me at all. The Thou-
orientation can, therefore, be either one-sided or reciprocal. It is
one-sided if only one of us notices the presence of the other. It is
reciprocal if we are mutually aware of each other, that is, if each
of us is Thou-oriented toward the other. In this way there is constituted out of the Thou-orientation the face-to-face relationship (or
directly experienced social relationship). . . . The face-to-face relationship in which the partners are aware of each other and sym-
pathetically participate in each other's lives for however short a
time we shall call the "pure We-relationship." But the "pure We-
relationship" is likewise only a limiting concept. The directly experienced social relationship of real life is the pure We-relationship
concretized and actualized to a greater or lesser degree and filled
with content.

Let us illustrate this with an example. Suppose that you and I
are watching a bird in flight. The thought "bird-in-flight" is in
each of our minds and is the means by which each of us interprets
his own observations. Neither of us, however, could say whether
our lived experiences on that occasion were identical. In fact,
neither of us would even try to answer that question, since one's
own subjective meaning can never be laid side by side with another's and compared.

Nevertheless, during the flight of the bird you and I have

"grown older together"; our experiences have been simultaneous. Perhaps while I was following the bird's flight I noticed out of the corner of my eye that your head was moving in the same direction as mine. I could then say that the two of us, that *we*, had watched the bird's flight. What I have done in this case is to coordinate temporally a series of my own experiences with a series of yours. But in so doing I do not go beyond the assertion of a mere *general* correspondence between my perceived "bird in flight" and your experiences. I make no pretense to any knowledge of the content of your subjective experiences or of the particular way in which they were structured. It is enough for me to know that you are a fellow human being who was watching the same thing that I was. And if you have in a similar way coordinated my experiences with yours, then we can both say that *we* have seen a bird in flight.

The basic We-relationship is already given to me by the mere fact that I am born into the world of directly experienced social reality. From this basic relationship is derived the original validity of all my direct experiences of particular fellow men and also my knowledge that there is a larger world of my contemporaries whom I am not now experiencing directly.

CONVERSATION IN WE-RELATIONSHIP   To explain how our experiences of the Thou are rooted in the We-relationship, let us take conversation as an example. Suppose you are speaking to me and I am understanding what you are saying. As we have already seen, there are two senses of this understanding. First of all I grasp the "objective meaning" of your words, the meaning which they would have had, had they been spoken by you or anyone else. But second, of course, there is the subjective meaning, namely, what is going on in your mind as you speak. In order to get to your subjective meaning, I must picture to myself your stream of consciousness as flowing side by side with my own. Within this picture I must interpret and construct your intentional Acts as you choose your words. To the extent that you and I can mutually experience this simultaneity, growing older together for a time, to the extent that we can live in it together, to *that* extent we can live in each other's subjective contexts of meaning. However, our ability to apprehend each other's subjective contexts of meaning should not be confused with the We-relationship itself. For I get to your subjective meaning in the first place only by starting out with your spoken words as given and then by asking how you came to use those words. But this question of mine would make no sense if I did not already assume an actual or at least potential We-relationship between us. For it is only within the We-relationship that I can concretely experience you at a particular moment of your life. To put the point in terms of a formula: I can live in your subjective meaning-contexts only to the extent that I directly experience you within an actualized content-filled We-relationship.

This is true for all stages of understanding another person in which attention to his subjective meaning is involved. For all my lived experiences of the other person (above all the directly apprehended other person), whether they manifest agreement or discrepancy, have their origin in the sphere of the We-relationship. Attention to the We-relationship in turn broadens the objective knowledge of other people which I have gained from the interpretation of my own experiences of them. It likewise broadens my objective knowledge of the particular person involved with me in this particular We-relationship. Thus the contents of the one undivided stream of the We are always enlarging and contracting. In this sense the We resembles my stream of consciousness in the flow of its duration. But this similarity is balanced by a difference. The We-relationship is spatial as well as temporal. It embraces the body of the other person as well as his consciousness. And because I grasp what is going on in his mind only through the medium of his perceived bodily movements, this Act of grasping is for me a lived experience that transcends my own stream of consciousness. Nevertheless, it should be emphasized that, among all self-transcending experiences, the We-experience remains closest to the stream of consciousness itself.

Moreover, while I am living in the We-relationship, I am really living in *our* common stream of consciousness. And just as I must, in a sense, step outside my own stream of consciousness and "freeze" my subjective experiences if I am going to reflect on them, the same requirement holds for the We-relationship. When you and I are immediately involved with each other, every experience is colored by that involvement. To the extent that we are going to think about the experiences we have together, we must to that degree withdraw from each other. If we are to bring the We-relationship into the focus of our attention, we must stop focusing on each other. But that means stepping out of the face-to-face relationship, because only in the latter do we live *in* the We. And here we can apply at a higher level everything that we said about phenomenal time in our analysis of the solitary Ego. Attention to the lived experiences of the We-relationship likewise presupposes that these experiences are full blown and have already elapsed. And our retrospective grasp of the We-experiences can fall anywhere in the continuum from maximum clarity to complete confusion. And it can be characterized by all degrees of consciousness, just as self-awareness can. In particular, the greater my awareness of the We-relationship, the less is my involvement in it, and the less am I genuinely related to my partner. The more I reflect, the more my partner becomes transformed into a mere object of thought.

FACE-TO-FACE RELATIONSHIPS   If the *pure* We-relationship were merely a modification of social relationship in general, it could be identified equally with direct social orientation and with social interaction. But, strictly speaking, the pure We-relationship is given *prior* to either of these. The pure We-relationship is merely the reciprocal form of the pure Thou-orientation, that is, the pure awareness of the *presence* of another person. His presence, it should be emphasized, not his specific traits. The pure We-relationship involves our awareness of each other's presence and also the knowledge of each that the other is aware of him. But, if we are to have a social relationship, we must go beyond this. What is required is that the Other-orientation of each partner become colored by a specific knowledge of the specific manner in which he is being regarded by the other partner. This in turn is possible only within directly experienced social reality. Only here do our glances actually meet; only here can one actually note how the other is looking at him.

But one cannot become aware of this basic connection between the pure We-relationship and the face-to-face relationship while still a participant in the We-relationship. *One must step out of it and examine it.* The person who is still a participant in the We-relationship does not experience it in its pure form, namely, as an awareness *that* the other person is there. Instead, he simply lives within the We-relationship in the fullness of its concrete content. In other words, the pure We-relationship is a mere limiting concept which one uses in the attempt to get a theoretical grasp of the face-to-face situation. But there are no specific concrete experiences which correspond to it. For the concrete experiences which do occur within the We-relationship in real life grasp their object—the We—as something unique and unrepeatable. And they do this in *one* undivided intentional Act.

Concrete We-relationships exhibit many differences among themselves. The partner, for instance, may be experienced with different degrees of immediacy, different degrees of intensity, or different degrees of intimacy. Or he may be experienced from different points of view. He may appear within the center of attention or at its periphery.

These distinctions apply equally to orientation relationships and to social interactions, determining in each of them the directness with which the partners "know" each other. Compare, for instance, the knowledge two people have of each other in conversation with the knowledge they have of each other in sexual intercourse. What different degrees of intimacy occur here, what different levels of consciousness are involved! Not only do the partners experience the We more deeply in the one case than in the other, but each experiences himself more deeply and his partner more deeply. It is not only the *object,* therefore, that is experienced with greater or lesser directness; it is the *relationship* itself, the being turned toward the object, the relatedness.

These are only two *types* of relationship. But now consider the different ways in which they can actually take place! The conversation, for instance, can be animated or offhand, eager or casual, serious or light, superficial or quite personal.

The fact that we may experience others with such different degrees of directness is very important. It is, as a matter of fact, the key to understanding the transition from the direct experience of others to the indirect which is characteristic of the world of mere contemporaries. . . .

First of all, let us remember that in the face-to-face situation I literally see my partner in front of me. As I watch his face and his gestures and listen to the tone of his voice, I become aware of much more than what he is deliberately trying to communicate to me. My observations keep pace with each moment of his stream of consciousness as it transpires. The result is that I am incomparably better attuned to him than I am to myself. I may indeed be more aware of my own past (to the extent that the latter can be captured in retrospect) than I am of my partner's. Yet I have never been face to face with myself as I am with him now; hence I have never caught myself in the act of actually living through an experience.

To this encounter with the other person I bring a whole stock of previously constituted knowledge. This includes both general knowledge of what another person is as such and any specific knowledge I may have of the person in question. It includes knowledge of other people's interpretive schemes, their habits, and their language. It includes knowledge of the taken-for-granted in-order-to and because-motives of others as such and of this person in particular. And when I am face to face with someone, my knowledge of him is increasing from moment to moment. My ideas of him undergo continuous revision as the concrete experience unfolds. For no direct social relationship is one isolated intentional Act. Rather it consists of a continuous series of such Acts. The orientation relationship, for instance, consists of a continuous series of intentional Acts of Other-orientation, while social interaction consists in a continuous series of Acts of meaning-establishment and meaning-interpretation. All these different encounters with my fellow man will be ordered in multiple meaning-contexts: they are encounters with a human being as such, with this particular human being, and with this particular human being at this particular moment of time. And these meaning-contexts of mine will be "subjective" to the extent that I am attending to your actual conscious experiences themselves and not merely to my own lived experiences of you. Furthermore, as I watch you, I shall see that you are oriented to me, that you are seeking the subjective meaning of my words, my actions, and what I have in mind insofar as you are concerned. And I will in turn take account of the fact that you are thus oriented to me, and this will influence both my intentions with respect to you and how I act toward you. This again you will see, I will see that you have seen it, and so on. This interlocking of glances, this thousand-faceted mirroring of each other, is one of the unique features of the face-to-face situation. We may say that it is a constitutive characteristic of this particular social relationship. However, we must remember that the pure We-relationship, which is the very form of every encounter with another person, is not itself grasped *reflectively* within the face-to-face situation. Instead of being observed, it is lived through. The many different mirror images of Self within Self are not therefore caught sight of one by one but are experienced as a continuum within a single experience. Within the unity of this experience I can be aware simultaneously of what is going on in my mind and in yours, *living through* the two series of experiences as one series—what we are experiencing together.

This fact is of special significance for the face-to-face situation. Within the face-to-face situation I can be a witness of your projects and also of their fulfillment or frustration as you proceed to action. Of course, once I know what you are planning to do, I may momentarily *suspend* the We-relationship in order to estimate *objectively* your chances of success. But it is only within the intimacy of the We-relationship itself that one can actually *live through* a course of action from its birth as a project to its ultimate outcome.

It is further essential to the face-to-face situation that you and I have the same environment.[6] First of all I ascribe to you an environment corresponding to my own. Here, in the face-to-face situation, but only here, does this presupposition prove correct, to the extent that I can assume with more or less certainty within the directly experienced social realm that the table I see is identical (and identical in all its perspective variations) with the table you see, to the extent that I can assume this even if you are only my contemporary or my predecessor. Therefore, when I am in a face-

6   By "environment" I mean that part of the external world which I can directly apprehend. This would include not only the physical but also the social environment with all of its cultural artifacts, languages, etc.

to-face situation with you, I can point to something in our common environment, uttering the words "this table here" and, by means of the identification of lived experiences in the environmental object, I can assure the adequacy of my interpretive scheme to your expressive scheme. For practical social life it is of the greatest significance that I consider myself justified in equating my own interpretation of my lived experiences with your interpretation of yours on those occasions when we are experiencing one and the same object.

We have, then, the same undivided and common environment, which we may call "our environment." The world of the We is not private to either of us, but is our world, the one common intersubjective world which is right there in front of us. It is only from the face-to-face relationship, from the common lived experience of the world in the We, that the intersubjective world can be constituted. This alone is the point from which it can be deduced.

I can constantly check my interpretations of what is going on in other people's minds, due to the fact that, in the We-relationship, I share a common environment with them. In principle, it is only in the face-to-face situation that I can address a question to you. But I can ask you not only about the interpretive schemes which you are applying to our common environment. I can also ask you how you are interpreting your lived experiences, and, in the process, I can correct, expand, and enrich my own understanding of you. This becoming-aware of the correctness or incorrectness of my understanding of you is a higher level of the We-experience. On this level I enrich not only my experience of you but of other people generally.

RECIPROCAL WITNESSING   If I know that you and I are in a face-to-face relationship, I also know something about the manner in which each of us is attuned to his conscious experiences, in other words, the "attentional modifications" of each of us. This means that the way we attend to our conscious experiences is actually modified by our relationship to each other. This holds for both of us. For there is a true social relationship only if you reciprocate my awareness of you in some manner or other. As soon as this happens, as soon as we enter the face-to-face situation, each of us begins to attend to his own experiences in a new way. This particular attentional modification in which the two partners of a directly experienced social relationship are mutually aware of each other has special implications for the social interaction which occurs in that situation. *Whenever I am interacting with anyone, I take for granted as a constant in that person a set of genuine because- or in-order-to motives.* I do this on the ground of my own past experience of that particular person as well as of people generally. My own behavior toward that person is based in the first instance upon this taken-for-granted constellation of motives, regardless of whether they are his real motives or not. And here emerges the peculiarity of face-to-face interaction. It consists not in a specific structure of the reciprocal motivation context itself but in a specific *disclosure* of the motives of the other person. Even in face-to-face interactions I only project in phantasy the behavior of the other person as I plan my own action. This phantasy is, of course, merely the other's *expected* behavior, without the details as yet filled in and without, as yet, any confirmation. I have yet to see what my partner will actually do. But because he and I continually undergo modifications of attention with respect to each other in the We-relationship, I can actually live through and participate in the constitution of his motivational context. I interpret the present lived experiences which I impute to you as the in-order-to motives of the behavior I expect from you or as the consequences of your past experiences, which I then regard as their because-motives. I "orient" my action to these motivational contexts of yours, as you "orient" yours to mine. However, this "orienting oneself" takes place within the directly experienced social realm in the particular mode of "witnessing." When interacting with you within this realm, I *witness* how you react to my behavior, how you interpret my meaning, how my in-order-to motives trigger corresponding because-motives of your behavior. In between my expectation of your reaction and that reaction itself I have "grown older" and perhaps wiser, taking into account the realities of the situation, as well as my own hopes of what you would do. But in the face-to-face situation you and I grow older together, and I can add to my expectation of what you are going to do the actual sight of you making up your mind, and then of your action itself in all its constituent phases. During all this time we are aware of each other's stream of consciousness as contemporaneous with our own; we share a rich, concrete We-relationship without any need to reflect on it. In a flash I see your whole plan and its execution in action. This episode of my biography is full of continuous lived experiences of you grasped within the We-relationship; meanwhile, you are experiencing me in the same way, and I am aware of the fact.

III. *Social Observation*

DIRECT OBSERVATION   So far we have been studying the directly experienced social relationship in order to bring out the peculiar characteristics of the face-to-face situation in its purest form. Our analysis would, however, be incomplete unless we dealt with the case where I am aware of someone else while knowing that he is *unaware* of me. Especially important under this heading is the observation of another's behavior. The analysis of such observation is, as a matter of fact, the key to the understanding of the manner in which the data of the social sciences are established. . . .

. . . Our task will be to throw light upon the special kind of Thou-orientation which the observer takes up toward the person he is directly observing. We shall be paying special attention to the ways in which his interpretive schemes differ from those used in the face-to-face relationship.

In the face-to-face relationship the Thou-orientation is *reciprocal* between the two partners. In direct social observation, however, it is *one-sided*. Let us imagine that we have a case of the latter. Say that I am observing someone else's behavior and that he either does not know that he is being observed or is paying no attention to it. Now the problem is, How do I know what is going on in his mind? Well, even if I am merely observing him, his body is still a field of expression for his inner life. I may, as I watch him, take my own perceptions of his body as signs of his conscious experiences. In so doing, I will take his movements, words, and so forth, into account as evidence. I will direct my attention to the subjective rather than to the objective meaning-contexts of the indications I perceive. As a direct observer I can thus in one glance take in both the outward manifestations—or "products"—and the processes in which are constituted the conscious experiences lying behind them. This is possible because the lived experiences of the Other are occurring simultaneously with my own objective interpretations of his words and gestures.

The other person is quite as much present in a bodily sense to the observer as he is to someone who is participating in a social relationship with him. His words can be heard and his gestures seen: there is as great a wealth of indications of his inner life as in the case of a direct relationship. Every additional experience the observer has of the other person increases his knowledge of the latter. Their two environments are congruent, and therefore their conscious experiences probably correspond. But this probability cannot in principle be raised to certainty. Here the situation differs from what obtains in a face-to-face relationship. In the latter I can, at will, verify my assumption that my experiences correspond to those of the other person. I can do this by direct appeal to an object of the external world which is common to both of us. But in any direct social observation carried on outside a social relationship, my interpretation of another's behavior cannot be checked against his own self-interpretation, unless of course I exchange my role as an observer for that of a participant. *When I start asking questions of the person observed, I am no longer a mere observer.* Still the point must be stressed that direct social observation can be converted at will into a face-to-face relationship, thereby making such interrogation possible, whereas that cannot be said of observation of one's mere contemporaries or predecessors.

Since the observer's Thou-orientation to his subject is one-sided, the subjective meaning-context in which he interprets the lived experiences of the other person has no opposite number. Absent, therefore, is the many-faceted mutual mirroring characteristic of the face-to-face relationship, in which the conscious content of the two partners is mutually identified. The behavior of the observed person, instead of being oriented to the observer's behavior, is completely independent of the latter. The participant in the face-to-face relationship knows with probability or certainty that his partner's behavior is oriented to his own, and he is even aware of the modifications of attention underlying his partner's conscious experiences. He can compare these modifications of attention with his own toward the partner. The observer lacks this access to the other person's attentional modifications; he can at least acquire no information about these modifications from looking into his own consciousness. Nor is he in a position to influence the behavior of the observed nor to be influenced by him. He cannot project his own in-order-to motive in such a way as to have it become the because-motive of the observed. The observer cannot judge from the mere behavior of the Other whether the latter is succeeding in carrying out his plans or not. In extreme cases, as when seeing an expressive movement, he can even be in doubt whether he is observing an action at all. Perhaps it is pure purposeless behavior that he is watching.

OBSERVATION AND INTERPRETATION   The observer who seeks to interpret his subject's motives will have to be satisfied with three indirect approaches:

1. He can search his memory for similar actions of his own and, finding such, can draw from them a general principle concerning the relation of their in-order-to and because-motives. He can then assume that this principle holds true for the other person's actions as well as for his own and can proceed to interpret the other person's actions by "putting himself in his place." This reading of one's own hypothetical motives into another's behavior can take place either at once, on the spot, or through a later consideration of what could have made the person act as he did.

2. Lacking such a guideline, he can resort to his own knowledge of the customary behavior of the person observed and from this deduce the latter's in-order-to and because-motives. If a visitor from Mars were to enter a lecture hall, a courtroom, and a church, the three places would seem quite the same to him in outward appearance. From the internal arrangements of none of the three would he be able to comprehend what the presiding official was about. But let him be told that one is a professor, another a judge,

and the third a priest, and he would then be able to interpret their actions and assign motives to them.

3. But it may be that the observer lacks significant information about the person he is observing. His last resort will then be to try to infer the in-order-to motive from the act by asking whether such and such a motive would be furthered by the act in question. He must, while observing the ongoing action, interpret it in terms of the effect which it actually has and assume that the effect is what was intended.

It is obvious that these three types of motivational understanding are not equally reliable. The further away from the concrete We-relationship (and, therefore, the more abstract) the interpretation is, the less chance it has of hitting its mark. The second type of understanding would, for instance, come up against this kind of pitfall: the priest speaking from the pulpit might not be delivering a sermon at all. The third type must face the hazard of the leap from the completed act to its in-order-to motive, a hazard still greater, since the act may not have turned out as the actor intended.

In the case of trying to discover the genuine because-motives of another, the contrast between participation and mere observation is considerably lessened. Here the observer is not much worse off than the participant in the face-to-face relationship. Even the latter is forced to reconstruct the motives of his partner ex post facto. The only advantage the direct participant has is that the data with which he starts are more vivid.

The direct observation of social relationships is, to be sure, more complicated than the observation of individual behavior. However, it does not differ in principle. Here, too, the observer must fall back upon his experience of social relationships in general, of this particular social relationship, and of the particular partners now involved. The observer's interpretive schemes cannot be identical with those of either of the partners in the relationship for the simple reason that his modifications of attention differ from theirs in a fundamental way. Moreover, he is aware of both of them, whereas they are aware only of each other. It can even happen that he knows one of the two people better than the latter is known by his partner and, therefore, is better acquainted with his interpretive schemes. Thus the nonparticipating listener can realize that two partners to a discussion are merely talking past one another, whereas they themselves may be totally unaware of this. On the other hand, the observer is at a disadvantage as compared to the participants: since he is not always sure of the in-order-to motives of one participant, he can hardly identify them with the because-motives of the other.

THE OBSERVER   The observer does not participate in the complicated mirror-reflexes by which in the interaction pattern among contemporaries the actor's in-order-to motives become understandable to the partner as his own because motives and vice versa. Precisely this fact constitutes the so-called 'disinterestedness' or detachment of the observer. He is not involved in the actor's hopes and fears whether or not they will understand one another and achieve their end by the interlocking of motives. Thus his system of relevances differs from that of the interested parties and permits him to see at the same time more and less than what is seen by them. But under all circumstances, it is merely the manifested fragments of the actions of *both* partners that are accessible to his observation. In order to understand them the observer has to avail himself of his knowledge of typically similar patterns of interaction in typically similar situational settings and has to construct the motives of the actors from that sector of the course of action which is patent to his observation. The constructs of the observer are, therefore, different ones than those used by the participants in the interaction, if for no other reason than the fact that the purpose of the observer is different from that of the interactors and therewith the systems of relevances attached to such purposes are also different. There is a mere chance, although a chance sufficient for many practical purposes, that the observer in daily life can grasp the subjective meaning of the actor's acts. This chance increases with the degree of anonymity and standardization of the observed behavior.

9

INTERPERSONAL COMMUNICATION

Vehicles of Thought

It is true that, as Husserl stated, any comprehension of the other's thought—always disregarding telepathy—requires as vehicle, carrier, or medium the apprehension of an object, fact, or event in the outer world, which, however, is not apprehended as a self in the mere apperceptual scheme but appresentationally as expressing cogitations of a fellow man. The term "cogitation" is here used in the broadest Cartesian sense, denoting feelings, volitions, emotions, etc. We propose, for the purpose of this paper, to use the term *"sign"* for designating objects, facts, or events in the outer world, whose apprehension appresents to an interpreter cogitations of a fellow man.

Apprehension

The objects, facts, and events which are interpreted as signs must directly or indirectly refer to another's bodily existence. In the simplest case, that of a face-to-face relationship, another's body, events occurring on his body (blushing, smiling), including bodily movements (wincing, beckoning), activities performed by it (talking, walking, manipulating things) are capable of being apprehended by the interpreter as signs. If there is no face-to-face relationship, but distance in space or time, we have to keep in mind (i) that apprehension does not necessarily presuppose actual per-

Reprinted from the following items in the Bibliography: 1955*b*, 166, 166–67, 167, 167–68, 168–70, 170–71; 1945*c*, 542–43, 543–44; 1955*b*, 171–72; 1951*b*, 87–92, 93–94, 94–96, 96–97.

ception, but that the appresenting member of the appresentational pair may also be a recollection or even a phantasm; I remember (or: I can imagine) the facial expression of my friend when he learned (or will learn) some sad news. I can even phantasy a sad looking centaur; (ii) that the result or product of another's activity refers to the action from which it resulted and, thus, can function as a sign for his cogitations; (iii) that the principle of the relative irrelevance of the vehicle is applicable. (The printed lecture refers to the talk of the lecturer.)

Manifestation

That an object, fact, or event in the outer world is interpreted as a sign for a fellow man's cogitation does not necessarily presuppose (i) that the other meant to manifest his cogitation by this sign, even less that he did so with communicative intent. An involuntary facial expression, a furtive glance, blushing, trembling, the other's gait, in brief, any physiognomical event can be interpreted as a sign for a fellow man's cogitation. A certain hesitation in the other's voice can convince me that he lies although he tries to hide that he does. The letter writer wants to convey the content of a message, but the graphologist disregards the content and takes the handwriting as such, that is, the static result of the unintentional gestures performed by the writer, as signs. (ii) If the sign was meant to function in a communicative context, the interpreter was not necessarily intended to be the addressee. (iii) It is, moreover, not necessarily presupposed that the two partners of a communicative sign-relation are known to each other (example: whoever erected this signpost wanted to show any passerby the direction).

Three Types of Signs

In his excellent book, *Der Aufbau der Sprache*,[1] Bruno Snell developed a theory of three basic forms of bodily movement which, according to him, have corollaries in different kinds of

[1]   (Hamburg, 1952), chaps. 1 and 2.

sounds, words, morphological elements, the syntactical structure of Western languages, forms of literature, and even in types of philosophy. He distinguishes purposive, expressive, and mimetic movements (*Zweck-, Ausdrucks-, und Nachahmungsbewegungen*). The first category, the purposive movements, may consist in gestures, such as nodding, pointing, beckoning, but also talking; the second, the expressive movements, are exteriorizations of inner experiences, primarily without purposive intent; the spatial-temporal differentiation of movements, according to high and low, wide and narrow, fast and slow, gives certain gestures their expressive meaning; the third category, the mimetic gesture, imitates or represents another being with whom the actor identifies himself. The animal and fertility dances, well known to the anthropologist, are examples. Snell also points out that the pure purposive gesture reveals expressive characteristics, for example, in the pitch and speed of the voice in talking, and that all three types of gesture can be used for communicative purposes (for example, expressive ones by the actor on the stage, mimetic ones by the pantomimist). According to Snell, the purposive gesture indicates what the performer wants, the expressive gesture what he feels, and the mimetic gesture what he is or what he pretends to be.

The expressive and mimetic gestures (or, in our terminology, signs) are of particular importance as foundations of higher appresentational forms, namely, symbols. Communication as such is based foremost on purposive signs, as the communicator has at least the intention of making himself understandable to the addressee if not to induce him to react appropriately. But certain requirements have to be fulfilled to make communication possible.

Signs in Communication

(i) The sign used in communication is always a sign addressed to an individual or anonymous interpreter. It originates within the actual manipulatory sphere of the communicator, and the interpreter apprehends it as an object, fact, or event in the world within his reach. . . . It is not necessary that the interpreter's world within his reach overlap spatially the manipulatory sphere of the communicator (telephone, television), nor that the production of the sign occur simultaneously with its interpretation (Egyptian papyrus, monuments), nor that the *same* physical object or event used by the communicator as carrier of the communication be apprehended by the interpreter (principle of the relative irrelevance of the vehicle). In more complicated cases of communication, which cannot be studied here, any number of human beings or mechanical devices might be inserted into the communicatory process between the original communicator and the interpreter. The main point of importance for the following is the insight that communication requires under all circumstances both events in the outer world, produced by the communicator, and events in the outer world apprehensible by the interpreter. In other words, *communication can occur only within the reality of the outer world.* . . .

(ii) The sign used in communication is always preinterpreted by the communicator in terms of its expected interpretation by the addressee. To be understood the communicator has, before producing the sign, to anticipate the apperceptual, appresentational, and referential scheme under which the interpreter will subsume it. The communicator has, therefore, as it were, to perform a rehearsal of the expected interpretation and to establish such a context between his cogitations and the communicative sign that the interpreter, guided by the appresentational scheme he will apply to the latter, will find the former an element of the related referential scheme. This context . . . is, however, nothing else than the interpretational scheme itself. In other words, communication presupposes that the interpretational scheme which the communicator relates and that which the interpreter will relate to the communicative sign in question will *substantially* coincide.

(iii) The italicized qualification is important. Strictly speaking, a full identity of both interpretational schemes, that of the communicator and that of the interpreter, is, at least in the commonsense world of everyday life, impossible. The interpretational scheme is closely determined by the biographical situation and the system of relevances originating therein. If there were no other differences between the biographical situations of the communicator and that of the interpreter, then at least the "Here" of either one is a "There" to the other. This fact alone sets insurmountable limits for a fully successful communication in the ideal sense. But, of course, communication might be and indeed is highly successful for many good and useful purposes and may reach an optimum in highly formalized and standardized languages such as in technical terminology. These considerations, seemingly of a highly theoretical nature, have important practical consequences: successful communication is possible only between persons, social groups, nations, etc., who share a substantially similar system of relevances. The greater the differences between their system of relevances, the fewer the chances for the success of the communication. Complete disparity of the systems of relevances makes the establishment of a universe of discourse entirely impossible.

(iv) To be successful, any communicative process must, therefore, involve a set of common abstractions or standardizations. We mentioned . . . the idealization of the congruency of the system of relevances which leads to the superseding of the thought objects of private experience by typifying constructs of public objects of thought. Typification is indeed that form of abstraction which leads to the more or less standardized, yet more or less vague, conceptualization of commonsense thinking and to the necessary ambiguity of the terms of the ordinary vernacular. This is because our experience, even in what Husserl calls the prepredicative sphere, is organized from the outset under certain types. The small child who learns his mother tongue is at an early age capable of recognizing an animal as a dog or a bird or a fish, an element of his surroundings as a stone or a tree or a mountain, a piece of furniture as a table or a chair. But, as a glance in the dictionary shows, these are the terms most difficult to define in ordinary language. Most of the communicative signs are language signs, so the typification required for sufficient standardization is provided by the vocabulary and the syntactical structure of the ordinary vernacular of the mother tongue.

Linguistic Presentation

The structure of language as a set of signs combinable under syntactical rules, its function as a vehicle of discursive (propositional) thinking, its power not only to name things but also to express relations among them, not only to build propositions but also to formulate relations among propositions. . . . It is of the essence of language that normally any linguistic communication involves a time process; a speech is built up by sentences, a sentence by the step by step articulation of successive elements (polythetically, as Husserl calls it), whereas the meaning of the sentence or the speech can be projected by the speaker and grasped by the listener in one single ray (monothetically). The stream of articulating cogitations of the speaker is thus simultaneous with the outer event of producing the sounds of the speech and the perceiving of the latter simultaneously with the comprehending cogitations of the listener. Speech is, therefore, one of the intersubjective time-processes—others are making music together, dancing together, making love together—by which the two fluxes of inner time, that of the speaker and that of the listener, become synchronous one with the other and both with an event in outer time. The reading of a written communication establishes in the same sense a quasi-simultaneity between the events within the inner time of the writer and that of the reader.

Oral Communication

Social actions involve communication, and any communication is necessarily founded upon acts of working. In order to communicate with others I have to perform overt acts in the outer world which are supposed to be interpreted by the others as signs of what I mean to convey. Gestures, speech, writing, etc., are based upon bodily movements. So far, the behavioristic interpretation of communication is justified. It goes wrong by identifying the vehicle of communication, namely the working act, with the communicated meaning itself.

Let us examine the mechanism of communication from the point of view of the interpreter. I may find as given to my interpretation either the ready-made outcome of the other's communicating acts or I may attend in simultaneity the ongoing process of his communicating actions as they proceed. . . . The latter relation prevails, for instance, if I am listening to my partner's talk. . . . He builds up the thought he wants to convey to me step by step, adding word to word, sentence to sentence, paragraph to paragraph. While he does so, my interpreting actions follow his communicating ones in the same rhythm. We both, I and the other, experience the ongoing process of communication in a vivid present. Articulating his thought, while speaking, in phrases, the communicator does not merely experience what he actually utters; a complicated mechanism of retentions and anticipations connects within his stream of consciousness one element of his speech with what preceded and what will follow to the unity of the thought he wants to convey. All these experiences belong to his inner time. And there are, on the other hand, the occurrences of his speaking, brought about by him in the spatialized time of the outer world. Briefly, the communicator experiences the ongoing process of communicating as a working in his vivid present.

And I, the listener, experience for my part my interpreting actions also as happening in my vivid present, although this interpreting is not a working, but merely a performing within the meaning of our definitions. On the one hand, I experience the occurrences of the other's speaking in outer time; on the other hand, I experience my interpreting as a series of retentions and anticipations happening in my inner time interconnected by my aim to understand the other's thought as a unit.

Now let us consider that the occurrence in the outer world—the communicator's speech—is, while it goes on, an element common to his and my vivid present, both of which are, therefore, simultaneous. My participating in simultaneity in the ongoing process of the other's communicating establishes therefore a new dimension of time. He and I, *we* share, while the process lasts, a common vivid present, *our* vivid present, which enables him and me to say: "*We* experienced this occurrence together." By the We-relation, thus established, we both—he, addressing himself to me, and I, listening to him,—are living in our mutual vivid present, directed toward the thought to be realized in and by the communicating process. *We grow older together.*

Gestural Expression

So far our analysis of communication in the vivid present of the We-relation has been restricted to the time perspective involved. We have now to consider the specific functions of the other's bodily movements as an expressional field open to interpretation as signs of the other's thought. It is clear that the extension of this field, even if communication occurs in vivid present, may vary considerably. It will reach its maximum if there exists between the partners community not only of time but also of space, that is, in the case of what sociologists call a face-to-face relation.

To make this clearer let us keep to our example of the speaker and the listener and analyze the interpretable elements included in such a situation. There are first the words uttered in the meaning they have according to dictionary and grammar in the language used plus the additional fringes they receive from the context of the speech and the supervening connotations originating in the particular circumstances of the speaker. There is, furthermore, the inflection of the speaker's voice, his facial expression, the gestures which accompany his talking. Under normal circumstances merely the conveyance of the thought by appropriately selected words has been projected by the speaker and constitutes, therefore, "working" according to our definition. The other elements within the interpretable field are from the speaker's point of view not planned and, therefore, at best mere conduct (mere doing) or even mere reflexes and, then, essentially actual experiences without subjective meaning. Nevertheless, they, too, are integral elements of the listener's interpretation of the other's state of mind. The community of space permits the partner to apprehend the other's bodily expressions not merely as events in the outer world, but as factors of the communicating process itself, although they do not originate in working acts of the communicator.

Visual Presentation

Visual presentations, . . . as Mrs. Langer has correctly shown,[2] are structurally different by their nondiscursive character. They are not composed of elements having independent meanings, that is, they have no vocabulary. They cannot be defined in terms of other signs as can discursive signs. Their primary function is that of conceptualizing the flux of sensations. Mrs. Langer sees the appresentational relationship of a pictorial presentation founded in the fact that the proportion of parts, their position, and relative dimension correspond to our conception of the depicted object. That is the reason we recognize the same house in a photograph, a painting, a pencil sketch, an architect's elevation drawing, and a builder's diagram. To Husserl, the characteristic of the picture (in contradistinction to all other signs) consists in the fact that the picture is related to the depicted thing by similarity, whereas most of the other signs (disregarding, for example, onomatopoeia) have no content in common with that which is signified. (That is the reason many authors emphasize the "arbitrariness" of linguistic signs.) Nevertheless, the appresentational relationship prevails also in pictorial presentations, although sometimes in a rather complicated way of interconnected levels. Looking, for instance, at Dürer's print, "The Knight, Death, and The Devil," we distinguish first—as we would say, in the apperceptual scheme—the print as such, this thing in the portfolio; second, still in the apperceptual scheme, the black lines on paper as small colorless figures; third, these figures are *appresented* as "depicted realities" as they appear in the picture, "the knight of flesh and blood" of whom, as Husserl states, we are aware in his quasibeing, which is "neutrality modification" of being. Here Husserl stops, but we could and have to continue to follow the appresentational process further. These three figures, the knight, death, and the devil, as appresented in the neutrality modification of their quasibeing, appresent, in turn, in an appresentation of the second degree, so to speak, a meaningful context, and it is especially this meaning which Dürer wanted to convey to the beholder: the knight between death and the devil

[2]   Langer, *Philosophy in a New Key*, pp. 55 ff. and 77 ff.

teaches us something about the condition of man between two supernatural forces. This is the *symbolic* appresentation. . . .

Communication by expressive and mimetic gestures has so far not found the attention it deserves from students of semantics. Examples for the former are gestures of greeting, paying respect, applauding, showing disapproval, gestures of surrender, of paying honor, etc. The latter combine features of the pictorial presentation, namely, similarity with the depicted object, with the time-structure of speech. Even a kind of mimetic vocabulary can be developed, as, for instance, in the highly standardized use of the fan by the Japanese *Kabuki* dancer.

Musical Communication: Composer and Beholder

In the situation we have chosen to investigate—the actual performance of a piece of music—the genesis of the stock of knowledge at hand with all its hidden social references is, so to speak, prehistoric. The web of socially derived and socially approved knowledge constitutes merely the setting for the main social relationship into which our piano player (and also any listener or mere reader of music) will enter: that with the composer of the sonata before him. It is the grasping of the composer's musical thought and its interpretation by re-creation which stand in the center of the player's field of consciousness or, to use a phenomenological term, which become "thematic" for his ongoing activity. This thematic kernel stands out against the horizon of preacquired knowledge, which knowledge functions as a scheme of reference and interpretation for the grasping of the composer's thought. It is now necessary to describe the structure of this social relationship between composer and beholder,[3] but before entering into its analysis it might be well to forestall a possible misunderstanding. It is by no means our thesis that a work of music (or of art in general) cannot be understood except by reference to its individual author or to the circumstances—biographical or other—in which he created

[3]   The term "beholder" shall include the player, listener, and reader of music.

this particular work. It is certainly not a prerequisite for the understanding of the musical content of the so-called Moonlight Sonata to take cognizance of the silly anecdotes which popular belief attaches to the creation of this work; it is not even indispensable to know that the sonata was composed by a man called Beethoven who lived then and there and went through such and such personal experiences. Any work of art, once accomplished, exists as a meaningful entity independent of the personal life of its creator. The social relationship between composer and beholder as it is understood here is established exclusively by the fact that a beholder of a piece of music participates in and to a certain extent re-creates the experiences of the—let us suppose, anonymous—fellow man who created this work not only as an expression of his musical thoughts but with communicative intent.

For our purposes a piece of music may be defined—very roughly and tentatively, indeed—as a meaningful arrangement of tones in inner time. It is the occurrence in inner time, Bergson's *durée,* which is the very form of existence of music. The flux of tones unrolling in inner time is an arrangement meaningful to both the composer and the beholder, because and in so far as it evokes in the stream of consciousness participating in it an interplay of recollections, retentions, protentions, and anticipations which interrelate the successive elements. To be sure, the sequence of tones occurs in the irreversible direction of inner time, in the direction, as it were, from the first bar to the last. But this irreversible flux is not irretrievable. The composer, by the specific means of his art, has arranged it in such a way that the consciousness of the beholder is led to refer what he actually hears to what he anticipates will follow and also to what he has just been hearing and what he has heard ever since this piece of music began. The hearer, therefore, listens to the ongoing flux of music, so to speak, not only in the direction from the first to the last bar but simultaneously in a reverse direction back to the first one.

It is essential for our problem to gain a clearer understanding of the time dimension in which music occurs. It was stated above that the inner time, the *durée,* is the very form of existence of music.

Of course, playing an instrument, listening to a record, reading a page of music—all these are events occurring in outer time, the time that can be measured by metronomes and clocks, that is, the time that the musician "counts" in order to assure the correct "tempo." But to make clear why we consider inner time the very medium within which the musical flow occurs, let us imagine that the slow and the fast movement of a symphony each fill a twelve-inch record. Our watches show that the playing of either record takes about three and a half minutes. This is a fact which might possibly interest the program maker of a broadcasting station. To the beholder it means nothing. To him it is not true that the time he lived through while listening to the slow movement was of "equal length" with that which he dedicated to the fast one. While listening he lives in a dimension of time incomparable with that which can be subdivided into homogeneous parts. The outer time is measurable; there are pieces of equal length; there are minutes and hours and the length of the groove to be traversed by the needle of the record player. There is no such yardstick for the dimension of inner time the listener lives in; there is no equality between its pieces, if pieces there were at all. It may come as a complete surprise to him that the main theme of the second movement of Beethoven's Pianoforte Sonata in d-minor, Op. 31, No. 2, takes as much time in the mere clock sense—namely, one minute —as the last movement of the same sonata up to the end of the exposition.

The preceding remarks serve to clarify the particular social relationship between composer and beholder. Although separated by hundreds of years, the latter participates with quasi simultaneity in the former's stream of consciousness by performing with him step by step the ongoing articulation of his musical thought. The beholder, thus, is united with the composer by a time dimension common to both, which is nothing other than a derived form of the vivid present shared by the partners in a genuine face-to-face relation such as prevails between speaker and listener. . . .

The meaning of a musical work, however, is essentially of a polythetical structure. It cannot be grasped monothetically. It consists in the articulated step-by-step occurrence in inner time, in the very polythetic constitutional process itself. I may give a name to a specific piece of music, calling it "Moonlight Sonata" or "Ninth Symphony"; I may even say, "These were variations with a finale in the form of a passacaglia," or characterize, as certain program notes are prone to do, the particular mood or emotion this piece of music is supposed to have evoked in me. But the musical content itself, its very meaning, can be grasped merely by reimmersing oneself in the ongoing flux, by reproducing thus the articulated musical occurrence as it unfolds in polythetic steps in inner time, a process itself belonging to the dimension of inner time. And it will "take as much time" to reconstitute the work in recollection as to experience it for the first time. In both cases I have to re-establish the quasi simultaneity of my stream of consciousness with that of the composer described hereinbefore.

We have therefore the following situation: two series of events in inner time, one belonging to the stream of consciousness of the composer, the other to the stream of consciousness of the beholder, are lived through in simultaneity, which simultaneity is created by the ongoing flux of the musical process. It is the thesis of the present paper that this sharing of the other's flux of experiences in inner time, this living through a vivid present in common, constitutes . . . the mutual tuning-in relationship, the experience of the "We," which is at the foundation of all possible communication. The peculiarity of the musical process of communication consists in the essentially polythetic character of the communicated content, that is to say, in the fact that both the flux of the musical events and the activities by which they are communicated, belong to the dimension of inner time. This statement seems to hold good for any kind of music. There is, however, one kind of music—the polyphonic music of the western world—which has the magic power of realizing by its specific musical means the possibility of living simultaneously in two or more fluxes of events. In polyphonic writing each voice has its particular meaning; each represents a series of, so to speak, autarchic musical events; but this flux is designed to roll on in simultaneity with other series of musical events, not less autarchic in themselves, but coexisting with the former and combining with them by this very simultaneity into a new meaningful arrangement.

Musical Communication: Performer and Listener

It is the eminent social function of the performer—the singer or player of an instrument—to be the intermediary between composer and listener. By his re-creation of the musical process the performer partakes in the stream of consciousness of the composer as well as of the listener. He thereby enables the latter to become immersed in the particular articulation of the flux of inner time which is the specific meaning of the piece of music in question. It is of no great importance whether performer and listener share together a vivid present in face-to-face relation or whether through the interposition of mechanical devices, such as records, only a quasi simultaneity between the stream of consciousness of the mediator and the listener has been established. The latter case always refers to the former. The difference between the two shows merely that the relationship between performer and audience is subject to all variations of intensity, intimacy, and anonymity. This can be easily seen by imagining the audience as consisting of one single person, a small group of persons in a private room, a crowd filling a big concert hall, or the entirely unknown listeners of a radio performance or a commercially distributed record. In all these circumstances performer and listener are "tuned-in" to one another, are living together through the same flux, are growing older together while the musical process lasts. This statement applies not only to the fifteen or twenty minutes of measurable outer time required for the performance of this particular piece of music, but primarily to the coperformance in simultaneity of the polythetic steps by which the musical content articulates itself in inner time. Since, however, all performance as an act of communication is based upon a series of events in the outer world—in our case the flux of audible sounds—it can be said that the social relationship between performer and listener is founded upon the common experience of living simultaneously in several dimensions of time.

Musical Communication: Making Music Together

The same situation, the pluridimensionality of time simultaneously lived through by man and fellow man, occurs in the relationship between two or more individuals making music together, which we are now prepared to investigate. If we accept Max Weber's famous definition, according to which a social relationship is "the conduct of a plurality of persons which according to their subjective meaning are mutually concerned with each other and oriented by virtue of this fact," then both the relationship prevailing between intermediary and listener and that prevailing between coperformers fall under this definition. But there is an important difference between them. The listener's coperforming of the polythetic steps in which the musical content unfolds is merely an internal activity (although as an "action involving the action of others and being oriented by them in its course" undoubtedly a social action within Weber's definition). The coperformers (let us say a soloist accompanied by a keyboard instrument) have to execute activities gearing into the outer world and thus occurring in spatialized outer time. Consequently, each coperformer's action is oriented not only by the composer's thought and his relationship to the audience but also reciprocally by the experiences in inner and outer time of his fellow performer. Technically, each of them finds in the music sheet before him only that portion of the musical content which the composer has assigned to his instrument for translation into sound. Each of them has, therefore, to take into account what the other has to execute in simultaneity. He has not only to interpret his own part, which as such remains necessarily fragmentary, but he has also to anticipate the other player's interpretation of his—the other's—part and, even more, the other's anticipations of his own execution. Either's freedom of interpreting the composer's thought is restrained by the freedom granted to the other. Either has to foresee by listening to the other, by protentions and anticipations, any turn the other's interpretation may take and has to be prepared at any time to be leader or follower. Both share not only the inner *durée* in which the content of the music played actualizes itself; each, simultaneously, shares in vivid present the other's stream of consciousness in immediacy. This is possible because making music together occurs in a true face-to-face relationship—inasmuch as the participants are sharing not only a section of time but also a sector of space. The other's facial expressions, his gestures in handling his instrument, in short all the activities of performing, gear into the outer world and can be grasped by the partner in immediacy. Even if performed without communicative intent, these activities are interpreted by him as indications of what the other is going to do and therefore as suggestions or even commands for his own behavior. Any chamber musician knows how disturbing an arrangement can be that prevents the coperformers from seeing each other. Moreover, all the activities of performing occur in outer time, the time which can be measured by counting or the metronome or the beat of the conductor's baton. The coperformers may have recourse to these devices when for one reason or another the flux of inner time in which the musical content unfolds has been interrupted.

Such a close face-to-face relationship can be established in immediacy only among a small number of coperformers. Where a larger number of executants is required, one of them—a song leader, concert master, or continuo player—has to assume the leadership, that is, to establish with each of the performers the contact which they are unable to find with one another in immediacy. Or a nonexecutant, the conductor, has to assume this function. He does so by action in the outer world, and his evocative gestures into which he translates the musical events going on in inner time, replace for each performer the immediate grasping of the expressive activities of all his coperformers.

Our analysis of making music together has been restricted to what Halbwachs calls the musician's music. Yet there is in principle no difference between the performance of a modern orchestra or chorus and people sitting around a campfire and singing to the strumming of a guitar or a congregation singing hymns under the leadership of the organ. And there is no difference in principle between the performance of a string quartet and the improvisations at a jam session of accomplished jazz players. These examples simply give additional support to our thesis that the system of musical notation is merely a technical device and accidental to the social relationship prevailing among the performers. This social relationship is founded upon the partaking in common of different dimensions of time simultaneously lived through by the participants. On the one hand, there is the inner time in which the flux of the musical events unfolds, a dimension in which each performer re-creates in polythetic steps the musical thought of the (eventually anonymous) composer and by which he is also connected with the listener. On the other, making music together is an event in outer time, presupposing also a face-to-face relationship, that is, a community of space, and it is this dimension which unifies the fluxes of inner time and warrants their synchronization into a vivid present.

Tuning In

It appears that all possible communication presupposes a mutual tuning-in relationship between the communicator and the addressee of the communication. This relationship is established by the reciprocal sharing of the other's flux of experiences in inner time, by living through a vivid present together, by experiencing this togetherness as a "We." Only within this experience does the other's conduct become meaningful to the partner tuned in on him —that is, the other's body and its movements can be and are interpreted as a field of expression of events within his inner life. Yet not everything that is interpreted by the partner as an expression of an event in the other's inner life is meant by the other to express— that is, to communicate to the partner—such an event. Facial expressions, gait, posture, ways of handling tools and instruments, without communicative intent, are examples of such a situation. The process of communication proper is bound to an occurrence in the outer world, which has the structure of a series of events polythetically built up in outer time. This series of events is intended by the communicator as a scheme of expression open to adequate interpretation by the addressee. Its very polythetic character warrants the simultaneity of the ongoing flux of the communicator's experiences in inner time with the occurrences in the outer world, as well as the simultaneity of these polythetic occurrences in the outer world with the addressee's interpreting experiences in inner time. Communicating with one another presupposes, therefore, the simultaneous partaking of the partners in various dimensions of outer and inner time—in short in growing older together. This seems to be valid for all kinds of communication, the *essentially* polythetic ones as well as those conveying meaning in conceptual terms—that is, those in which the result of the communicative process can be grasped monothetically.

It is hardly necessary to point out that the remarks in the preceding paragraph refer to communication within the face-to-face relationship. It can, however, be shown that all the other forms of possible communication can be explained as derived from this paramount situation.

10

INDIRECT SOCIAL

RELATIONSHIPS

I. *Mediate Relationships: Contemporaries*

DERIVED RELATIONSHIPS   In none of them does the self of the other become accessible to the partner as a unity. The other appears merely as a partial self, as originator of these and those acts, which I do not share in a vivid present. The shared vivid present of the We-relation presupposes co-presence of the partners. To each type of derived social relationship belongs a particular type of time perspective which is derived from the vivid present. There is a particular quasi-present in which I interpret the mere outcome of the other's communicating—the written letter, the printed book—without having participated in the ongoing process of communicating acts. There are other time dimensions in which I am connected with contemporaries I never met, or with predecessors or with successors; another, the historical time, in which I experience the actual present as the outcome of past events; and many more. All of these time perspectives can be referred to a vivid present: my own actual or former one, or the actual or former vivid present of my fellow-man with whom, in turn, I am connected in an originary or derived vivid present and all this in the different modes of potentiality or quasi-actuality, each type having its own forms of temporal diminution and augmentation and its appurtenant style of skipping them in a direct move or "knight's move." There are furthermore the different forms of overlapping and interpenetrating of these different perspectives, their being put into and

---

Reprinted from the following items in the Bibliography: 1945*c*, 544–45; 1967, 176–78, 180–81, 181–83, 183–84, 184–85, 194–95, 202–4, 208–11, 214.

out of operation by a shift from one to the other and a transformation of one into the other, and the different types of synthesizing and combining or isolating and disentangling them. Manifold as these different time perspectives and their mutual relations are, they all originate in an intersection of *durée* and cosmic time.

In and by our social life with the natural attitude they are apprehended as integrated into one single supposedly homogeneous dimension of time which embraces not only the individual time perspectives of each of us during his wide-awake life but which is common to all of us. We shall call it the civic or *standard time*.

FROM DIRECT TO INDIRECT SOCIAL EXPERIENCE   In the face-to-face situation, directness of experience is essential, regardless of whether our apprehension of the Other is central or peripheral and regardless of how adequate our grasp of him is. I am still "Thou-oriented" even to the man standing next to me in the subway. When we speak of "pure" Thou-orientation of "pure" We-relationship, we are ordinarily using these as limiting concepts referring to the simple givenness of the Other in abstraction from any specification of the degree of concreteness involved. But we can also use these terms for the lower limits of experience obtainable in the face-to-face relationship, in other words, for the most peripheral and fleeting kind of awareness of the other person.

We make the transition from direct to indirect social experience simply by following this spectrum of decreasing vividness. The first steps beyond the realm of immediacy are marked by a decrease in the number of perceptions I have of the other person and a narrowing of the perspectives within which I view him. At one moment I am exchanging smiles with my friend, shaking hands with him, and bidding him farewell. At the next moment he is walking away. Then from the far distance I hear a faint good-by, a moment later I see a vanishing figure give a last wave, and then he is gone. It is quite impossible to fix the exact instant at which my friend left the world of my direct experience and entered the shadowy realm of those who are merely my contemporaries. As another example, imagine a face-to-face conversation, followed by a telephone call, followed by an exchange of letters, and finally messages exchanged through a third party. Here too we have a gradual progression from the world of immediately experienced social reality to the world of contemporaries. In both examples the total number of the other person's reactions open to my observation is progressively diminished until it reaches a minimum point. It is clear, then, that the world of contemporaries is itself a variant function of the face-to-face situation. They may even be spoken of as two poles between which stretches a continuous series of experiences. . . .

In everyday life there seems to be no practical problem of where the one situation breaks off and the other begins. This is because we interpret both our own behavior and that of others within contexts of meaning that far transcend the immediate here and now. For this reason, the question whether a social relationship we participate in or observe is direct or indirect seems to be an academic one. But there is a yet deeper reason for our customary indifference to this question. Even after the face-to-face situation has receded into the past and is present only in memory, it still retains its essential characteristics, modified only by an aura of pastness. Normally we do not notice that our just-departed friend, with whom we have a moment ago been interacting, perhaps affectionately or perhaps in an annoyed way, now appears to us in a quite different perspective. Far from seeming obvious, it actually seems absurd that someone we are close to has somehow become "different" now that he is out of sight, except in the trite sense that our experiences of him bear the mark of pastness. However, we must still sharply distinguish between such memories of face-to-face situations, on the one hand, and an intentional Act directed toward a mere contemporary, on the other. The recollections we have of another bear all the marks of direct experience. When I have a recollection of you, for instance, I remember you as you were in the concrete We-relationship with me. I remember you as a unique person in a concrete situation, as one who interacted with me in the mode of "mutual mirroring" described above. I remember you as a person vividly present to me with a maximum of symptoms of inner life, as one whose experiences I witnessed in the actual process of formation. I remember you as one whom I was for a time coming to know better and better. I remember you as one whose conscious life flowed in one stream with my own. I remember you as one whose consciousness was continuously changing in content. However, now that you are out of my direct experience, you are no more than my contemporary, someone who merely inhabits the same planet that I do. I am no longer in contact with the living you, but with the you of yesterday. You, indeed, have not ceased to be a living self, but you have a "new self" now; and, although I am contemporaneous with it, I am cut off from vital contact with it. Since the time we were last together, you have met with new experiences and have looked at them from new points of view. With each change of experience and outlook you have become a slightly different person. But somehow I fail to keep this in mind as I go about my daily round. I carry your image with me, and it remains the same. But then, perhaps, I hear that you have changed. I then begin to look upon you as a contemporary—not any contemporary, to be sure, but one whom I once knew intimately.

REGIONS OF ANONYMITY   We have been describing the intermediate zone between the face-to-face situation and the situation involving mere contemporaries. Let us continue our journey. As we approach the outlying world of contemporaries, our experience of others becomes more and more remote and anonymous. Entering the world of contemporaries itself, we pass through one region after another: (1) the region of those whom I once encountered face to face and could encounter again (for instance, my absent friend); then (2) comes the region of those once encountered by the person I am now talking to (for instance, your friend, whom you are promising to introduce to me); next (3) the region of those who are as yet *pure* contemporaries but whom I will soon meet (such as the colleague whose books I have read and whom I am now on my way to visit); then (4) those contemporaries of whose existence I know, not as concrete individuals, but as points in social space as defined by a certain function (for instance, the postal employee who will process my letter); then (5) those collective entities whose function and organization I know while not being able to name any of their members, such as the Canadian Parliament; then (6) collective entities which are by their very nature anonymous and of which I could never in principle have direct experience, such as "state" and "nation"; then (7) objective configurations of meaning which have been instituted in the world of my contemporaries and which live a kind of anonymous life of their own, such as the interstate commerce clause and the rules of French grammar; and finally (8) artifacts of any kind which bear witness to the subjective meaning-context of some unknown person. The farther out we get into the world of contemporaries, the more anonymous its inhabitants become, starting with the innermost region, where they can almost be seen, and ending with the region where they are by definition forever inaccessible to experience.

MEDIATE EXPERIENCE OF CONTEMPORARIES   My mere contemporary (or "contemporary") . . . is one who I know coexists with me in time but whom I do not experience immediately. This kind of knowledge is, accordingly, always indirect and impersonal. I cannot call my contemporary "Thou" in the rich sense that this term has within the We-relationship. Of course, my contemporary may once have been my consociate or may yet become one, but this in no way alters his present status.

Let us now examine the ways in which the world of contemporaries is constituted and the modifications which the concepts "Other-orientation" and "social relationship" undergo in that world. These modifications are necessitated by the fact that the contemporary is only indirectly accessible and that his subjective experiences can only be known in the form of *general types* of subjective experience.

That this should be the case is easy to understand if we consider the difference between the two modes of social experience. When I encounter you face to face I know you as a person in one unique moment of experience. While this We-relationship remains unbroken, we are open and accessible to each other's intentional Acts. For a little while we grow older together, experiencing each other's flow of consciousness in a kind of intimate mutual possession.

It is quite otherwise when I experience you as my contemporary. Here you are not prepredicatively given to me at all. I do not even directly apprehend your existence (*Dasein*). My whole knowledge of you is mediate and descriptive. In this kind of knowledge your "characteristics" are established for me by inference. From such knowledge results the indirect We-relationship.

To become clear about this concept of "mediacy," let us examine two different ways in which I come to know a contemporary. The first way we have already mentioned: my knowledge is derived from a previous face-to-face encounter with the person in question. But this knowledge has since become mediate or indirect because he has moved outside the range of my direct observation. For I make inferences as to what is going on in his mind under the assumption that he remains much the same since I saw him last, although, in another sense, I know very well that he must have changed through absorbing new experiences or merely by virtue of having grown older. But, as to how he has changed, my knowledge is either indirect or nonexistent.

A second way in which I come to know a contemporary is to construct a picture of him from the past direct experience of someone with whom I am now speaking (for example, when my friend describes his brother, whom I do not know). This is a variant of the first case. Here too I apprehend the contemporary by means of a fixed concept, or type, derived ultimately from direct experience but now held invariant. But there are differences. First, I have no concrete vivid picture of my own with which to start: I must depend on what my friend tells me. Second, I have to depend on my friend's assumption, not my own, that the contemporary he is describing has not changed.

These are the modes of constitution of all the knowledge we have of our contemporaries derived from our own past experience, direct or indirect, and of all the knowledge we have acquired from others, whether through conversation or through reading. It is clear, then, that indirect social experiences derive their original validity from the direct mode of apprehension. But the instances cited above do not exhaust all the ways by which I can come to know my contemporaries. There is the whole world of cultural objects, for instance, including everything from artifacts to institutions and conventional ways of doing things. These, too, contain within themselves implicit references to my contemporaries. I can "read" in these cultural objects the subjective experiences of others whom I do not know. Even here, however, I am making inferences on the basis of my previous direct experience of others. Let us say that the object before me is a finished product. Once, perhaps, I stood by the side of a man who was manufacturing something just like this. As I watched him work, I knew exactly what was going on in his mind. If it were not for this experience I would not know what to make of the finished product of the same kind that I now see. I might even fail to recognize it as an artifact at all and would treat it as just another natural object, like a stone or a tree. For what we have called the general thesis of the alter ego, namely, that the Thou coexists with me and grows older with me, can only be discovered in the We-relationship. Even in this instance, therefore, I have only an indirect experience of the other self, based on past direct experiences either of a Thou as such or of a particular Thou. My face-to-face encounters with others have given me a deep prepredicative knowledge of the Thou as a self. But the Thou who is *merely* my contemporary is never experienced personally as a self and never prepredicatively. On the contrary, all experience (*Erfahrung*) of contemporaries is predicative in nature. It is formed by means of interpretive judgments involving all my knowledge of the social world, although with varying degrees of explicitness.

Now this is real Other-orientation, however indirect it may be.

THEY-ORIENTATION   Under this indirect Other-orientation we will find the usual forms of simple Other-orientation, social behavior and social interaction. Let us call all such intentional Acts directed toward contemporaries cases of "They-orientation," in contrast to the "Thou-orientation" of the intentional Acts of direct social experience.

The term "They-orientation" serves to call attention to the peculiar way in which I apprehend the conscious experiences of my contemporaries. For I apprehend them as anonymous processes. Consider the contrast to the Thou-orientation. When I am Thou-oriented, I apprehend the other person's experiences within their setting in his stream of consciousness. I apprehend them as existing within a subjective context of meaning, as being the unique experiences of a particular person. All this is absent in the indirect social experience of the They-orientation. Here I am not aware of the ongoing flow of the Other's consciousness. My orientation is not toward the existence (*Dasein*) of a concrete individual Thou. It is not toward any subjective experiences now being constituted in all their uniqueness in another's mind nor toward the subjective configuration of meaning in which they are taking place. Rather, the object of my They-orientation is my own experience (*Erfahrung*) of social reality in general, of human beings and their conscious processes as such, in abstraction from any individual setting in which they may occur. My knowledge of my contemporaries is, therefore, inferential and discursive. It stands, by its essential nature, in an objective context of meaning and only in such. It has within it no intrinsic reference to persons nor to the subjective matrix within which the experiences in question were constituted. However, it is due to this very abstraction from subjective context of meaning that they exhibit the property which we have called their "again and again" character. They are treated as typical conscious experiences of "someone" and, as such, as basically homogeneous and repeatable. The unity of the contemporary is not constituted originally in his own stream of consciousness. . . . Rather, the contemporary's unity is constituted in my own stream of consciousness, being built up out of a synthesis of my own interpretations of his experiences. This synthesis is a synthesis of recognition in which I monothetically bring within one view of my own conscious experiences of someone else. Indeed, these experiences of mine may have been of more than one person. And they may have been of definite individuals or of anonymous "people." It is in this synthesis of recognition that the *personal ideal type* is constituted.

PERSONAL IDEAL TYPES We must be quite clear as to what is happening here. The subjective meaning-context has been abandoned as a tool of interpretation. It has been replaced by a series of highly complex and systematically interrelated objective meaning-contexts. The result is that the contemporary is anonymized in direct proportion to the number and complexity of these meaning-contexts. Furthermore, the synthesis of recognition does not apprehend the unique person as he exists within his living present. Instead it pictures him as always the same and homogeneous, leaving out of account all the changes and rough edges that go along with individuality. Therefore, no matter how many people are subsumed under the ideal type, it corresponds to no one in particular. It is just this fact that justified Weber in calling it "ideal."

Let us give a few examples to clarify this point. When I mail a letter, I assume that certain contemporaries of mine, namely, postal employees, will read the address and speed the letter on its way. I am not thinking of these postal employees as individuals. I do not know them personally and never expect to. Again, as Max Weber pointed out, whenever I accept money I do so without any doubt that others, who remain quite anonymous, will accept it in turn from me. To use yet another Weberian example, if I behave in such a way as to avoid the sudden arrival of certain gentlemen with uniforms and badges, in other words, to the extent that I orient myself to the laws and to the apparatus which enforces them, here, too, I am relating myself socially to my contemporaries conceived under ideal types.

On occasions like these I am always expecting others to behave in a definite way, whether it be postal employees, someone I am paying, or the police. My social relationship to them consists in the fact that I interact with them, or perhaps merely that, in planning my actions, I keep them in mind. But they, on their part, never turn up as real people, merely as anonymous entities defined exhaustively by their functions. Only as bearers of these functions do they have any relevance for my social behavior. How they happen to feel as they cancel my letter, process my check, or examine my income-tax return—these are considerations that never even enter into my mind. I just assume that there are "some people" who "do these things." Their behavior in the conduct of their duty is from my point of view defined purely through an objective context of meaning. In other words, when I am They-oriented, I have "types" for partners.

ANONYMITY OF THE CONTEMPORARY   The They-orientation is the pure form of understanding the contemporary in a predicative fashion, that is, in terms of his typical characteristics. Acts of They-orientation are, therefore, intentionally directed toward another person imagined as existing at the same time as oneself but conceived in terms of an ideal type. And just as in the cases of the Thou-orientation and the We-relationship, so also with the They-orientation can we speak of different *stages of concretization* and *actualization.*

In order to distinguish from one another the various stages of concretization of the We-relationship, we established as our criterion the degree of closeness to direct experience. We cannot use this criterion within the They-orientation. The reason is that the latter possesses by definition a high degree of remoteness from direct experience, and the other self which is its object possesses a corresponding higher degree of anonymity.

It is precisely this degree of anonymity which we now offer as the criterion for distinguishing between the different levels of concretization and actualization that occur in the They-orientation. The more anonymous the personal ideal type applied in the They-orientation, the greater is the use made of objective meaning-contexts instead of subjective ones, and likewise, we shall find, the more are lower-level personal ideal types and objective meaning-contexts pregiven. (The latter have in turn been derived from other stages of concretization of the They-orientation.)

Let us get clear as to just what we mean by the anonymity of the ideal type in the world of contemporaries. The pure Thou-orientation consists of mere awareness of the existence of the other person, leaving aside all questions concerning the characteristics of that person. On the other hand, the pure They-orientation is based on the presupposition of such characteristics in the form of a type. Since these characteristics are genuinely typical, they can in principle be presupposed again and again. Of course, whenever

I posit such typical characteristics, I assume that they now exist or did once exist. However, this does not mean that I am thinking of them as existing in a particular person in a particular time and place. The contemporary alter ego is therefore anonymous in the sense that its existence is only the individuation of a type, an individuation which is merely supposable or possible. Now since the very existence of my contemporary is always less than certain, any attempt on my part to reach out to him or influence him may fall short of its mark, and, of course, I am aware of this fact.

The concept which we have been analyzing is the concept of the anonymity of the partner in the world of contemporaries. It is crucial to the understanding of the nature of the indirect social relationship.

RELATIONSHIPS BETWEEN CONTEMPORARIES   As social relationships in the face-to-face situation are based on the pure Thou-orientation, so social relationships between contemporaries are based on the pure They-orientation. But the situation has now changed. In the face-to-face situation the partners look into each other and are mutually sensitive to each other's responses. This is not the case in relationships between contemporaries. Here each partner has to be content with the probability that the other, to whom he is oriented by means of an anonymous type, will respond with the same kind of orientation. And so an element of doubt enters into every such relationship.

When I board a train, for instance, I orient myself to the fact that the engineer in charge can be trusted to get me to my destination. My relationship to him is a They-relationship at this time, merely because my ideal type "railroad engineer" means by definition "one who gets passengers like myself to their destination." It is therefore characteristic of my social relationships with my contemporaries that the orientation by means of ideal types is mutual. Corresponding to my ideal type "engineer" there is the engineer's ideal type "passenger." Taking up mutual They-orientations, we think of each other as "one of them."

I am not therefore apprehended by my partner in the They-relationship as a real living person. From this it follows that I can expect from him only a typical understanding of my behavior.

A social relationship between contemporaries, therefore, consists in this: Each of the partners apprehends the other by means of an ideal type; each of the partners is aware of this mutual apprehension; and each expects that the other's interpretive scheme will be congruent with his own. The They-relationship here stands in sharp contrast to the face-to-face situation. In the face-to-face situation my partner and I are sensitively aware of the nuances of each other's subjective experiences. But in the They-relationship this is replaced by the assumption of a shared interpretive scheme. Now, even though I, on my side, make this assumption, I cannot verify it. I do, however, have more reason to expect an adequate response from my partner, the more standardized is the scheme which I impute to him. This is the case with schemes derived from law, state, tradition, and systems of order of all kinds, and especially with schemes based on the means-end relation, in short, with what Weber calls "rational" interpretive schemes.

These properties of social relationships between contemporaries have important consequences.

First of all, because of the element of chance that is always present, I cannot even be sure that the relationship exists until it has already been tried out, so to speak. Only retrospectively can I know whether my ideal type of my partner was adequate to him, either in the sense of meaning-adequacy or causal adequacy. This again differs from the face-to-face situation, where I can constantly correct my own responses to my partner. Another consequence is that the only in-order-to and because-motives of my partner that I can take into account in making my own plans of action are the motives I have already postulated for him in constructing my ideal type of him. To be sure, in the They-orientation, as in the face-to-face situation, I set up my project of action in such a way that my partner's because-motives are included in my own in-order-to motives; and I proceed in the expectation that his interpretive scheme of me as ideal type is adequate to mine of him as ideal type. If the partner in question is a postal clerk, for instance, the mere fact that my stamped letter lies before him will ordinarily become a genuine because-motive for his proceeding to forward it. Yet I cannot be sure of this. It may happen that there is a slip-up and that he will misdirect the letter before him, thereby causing it to be lost; to this extent he will fall short, of course, of my personal ideal type of a postal clerk. And this, in turn, of course, may have happened because he misinterpreted the address I put on the letter. All this results from the fact that we are not in direct touch with each other, as in the face-to-face situation.

In the face-to-face situation the partners are constantly revising and enlarging their knowledge of each other. This is not true in the same sense of the They-relationship. Certainly it is true that my knowledge of the world of my contemporaries is constantly being enlarged and replenished through every new experience from whatever part of the social world the latter may come. Furthermore, my ideal-typical schemes will always be changing in accordance with every shift in my situation. But all such modifications will be within a very narrow range so long as the original situation and my interest in it remain fairly even.

In the We-relationship I assume that your environment is identical with my own in all its variations. If I have any doubt about it, I can check on my assumption simply by pointing and asking you if that is what you mean. Such an identification is out of the question in the They-relationship. Nevertheless I assume, if you are my contemporary, that your environment can be understood by means of principles of comprehension drawn from my own. But even here the assumption is much less probable than it would be if we were face to face.

However, my environment also includes sign systems, and in the They-relationship also I use these as both expressive and interpretive schemes. Here again the degree of anonymity is of major importance. The more anonymous my partner is, the more "objectively" must I use the signs. I cannot assume, for instance, that my partner in a They-relationship will necessarily grasp the particular significance I am attaching to my words, or the broader context of what I am saying, unless I explicitly clue him in. As a result, I do not know, during the process of choosing my words, whether I am being understood or not. This explains why I cannot immediately be questioned as to what I mean and possibly correct any misunderstandings. In indirect social experience there is only one way to "question a partner as to what he means," and that is to use a dictionary—unless, of course, I decide to go to see him or call him up; but in this case I have left the They-relationship behind and have initiated a face-to-face situation. As a matter of fact, any They-relationship characterized by a relatively low degree of anonymity can be transformed into a face-to-face situation by means of passing through various intermediate stages.

II. *Predecessors and Successors*

WORLD OF PREDECESSORS I can define a predecessor as a person in the past not one of whose experiences overlaps in time with one of mine. The *pure* world of predecessors I can then define as entirely made up of such persons. The world of predecessors is what existed before I was born. It is this which determines its very nature. The world of predecessors is by definition over and done with. It has no open horizon toward the future. In the behavior of my predecessors there is nothing as yet undecided, uncertain, or awaiting fulfillment. I do not await the behavior of a predecessor. His behavior is essentially without any dimension of freedom and thus stands in contrast to the behavior of those with whom I am in immediate contact and even, to a certain extent, with the behavior of those who are merely my contemporaries. Relations between predecessors, since they are already past and hence fixed in themselves, require no further postulation of fixed ideal types in order to be understood.[1] I can, therefore, take up any kind of orientation toward my predecessors except one: I can never set out to influence them. Even the word "orientation" has a different meaning here: it is always passive. To say that an action of mine is oriented toward the action of one of my predecessors is to say that my action is in-

---

[1] To be sure, the world of predecessors can by its nature be known only through ideal types, but since past events are already completely fixed, the historical types in terms of which they are understood do not require a further act of fixing.

fluenced by his. Or, to put it another way, his action conceived in the pluperfect tense is the genuine because-motive of my own. I never influence my predecessors, they only influence me. These remarks, of course, apply also to Weber's concept of traditional action.

In the world of predecessors, therefore, the distinction between social relationship and social observation does not apply. What at first glance may appear to be a social relationship between myself and one of my predecessors will always turn out to be a case of one-sided Other-orientation on my part. The cult of ancestor worship is a good example of such orientation toward the world of predecessors. But there is only one kind of situation in which I can meaningfully speak of a reciprocal interaction between myself and one of my predecessors. This is the situation in which he acts upon me and I respond by behaving in such a way that my conduct can only be explained as oriented to his act, having the latter as its because-motive. This would be the case, for instance, if he bequeathed some property to me.

There are corresponding peculiarities in the way in which we experience our predecessors. I can know a predecessor only if someone tells me about him or writes about him. Of course, this go-between can be either a fellow man or a contemporary. For instance, my father may tell me about people now long dead and gone whom he remembers from his youth. The transition from the immediate present to the world of contemporaries is thus a continuous one. For my father is sitting across from me now, as he reminisces. His experiences, even though they are colored by pastness, are still the experiences of a person with whom I am now face to face. But for me those experiences are past beyond recall, because no moment of my life was contemporary with them; it is this which makes them truly part of the world of my predecessors. Even the past social experiences, direct or indirect, of another person are for me part of the world of predecessors, yet I apprehend them as if they were my own past social experience. For I apprehend them as the present subjective meaning-context of the person who is now telling me about them.

Second, I come to know the world of my predecessors through

records and monuments. These have the status of signs, regardless of whether my predecessors intended them as signs for posterity or merely for their own contemporaries.

It is hardly necessary to remark that my orientation toward the world of my predecessors can be more or less concrete, more or less actualized. This follows from the structure of my experience (*Erfahrung*) of that world. Insofar as it derives from what my fellow men or contemporaries have told me, it will be determined in the first instance by the degree of concreteness that their original lived experience had. But it will then be further conditioned by the degree of concreteness of my own orientation toward them as narrators.

Since my knowledge of the world of predecessors comes to me through signs, what these signs signify is anonymous and detached from any stream of consciousness. However, I know that every sign has its author and that every author has his own thoughts and subjective experiences as he expresses himself through signs. It is therefore perfectly proper for me to ask myself what a given predecessor meant by expressing himself in such and such a way. Of course, in order to do this, I must project myself backward in time and imagine myself present while he spoke or wrote. Now, historical research does not take as its primary object the subjective experiences of the authors of source materials. Yet these sources refer throughout to the direct and indirect social experience of their authors. As a result, the objective content communicated by the sign has a greater or lesser concreteness. The procedure of historical research is at this point the same as that used in interpreting the words of someone who is speaking to me. In the latter case I gain through communication an indirect experience of what the speaker has experienced directly. In the same way, when I am reading a historical document, I can imagine myself face to face with its author and learning from him about his contemporaries; one by one his contemporaries take their places within my world of predecessors.

My world of predecessors is, throughout, the world of other people and not my world. Of course it contains within itself many levels of social experience of varying degrees of concreteness, and in this respect it is like my world of contemporaries. It also resembles my world of contemporaries in the sense that the people in it are known to me through ideal types. But this knowledge is in one important respect different.

My predecessor lived in an environment radically different not only from my own but from the environment which I ascribe to my contemporaries. When I apprehend a fellow man or a contemporary, I can always assume the presence of a common core of knowledge. The ideal types of the We- and They-relationships themselves presuppose this kernel of shared experience. That highly anonymous ideal type, "my contemporary," shares by definition with me in that equally anonymous ideal type, "contemporary civilization." Naturally this is lacking to my predecessor. The same experience would seem to him quite different in the context of the culture of his time. Strictly speaking, it is meaningless even to speak of it as "the same" experience. I can, however, identify it as "human experience": any experience of my predecessor is open to my interpretation in terms of the characteristics of human experience in *general.* . . .

The schemes we use to interpret the world of our predecessors are necessarily different from the ones they used to interpret that world. If I wish to interpret the behavior of a contemporary, I can proceed with confidence on the assumption that his experiences will be pretty much like my own. But when it comes to understanding a predecessor, my chances of falling short of the mark are greatly increased. My interpretations cannot be other than vague and tentative. This is true even of the language and other symbols of a past age.

WORLD OF SUCCESSORS   In order to round out our picture of the social world, let us dwell for a moment on the world of successors. If the world of predecessors is completely fixed and determined, the world of consociates free, and the world of contemporaries probable, the world of successors is completely indeterminable. Our orientation toward our successors cannot amount to more than this: that we are going to have some. No key will open the door of this realm, not even that of ideal types. For the latter method is based on our experience of predecessors, consociates, and contemporaries, and there is no principle which permits us to extend it to the world of our successors. Of course, some of our consociates and contemporaries will outlive us, and we can assume that they will continue to act then as we know them to act now. In this way a kind of transitional zone can be set up between the two worlds. But the further removed the world of predecessors is from the Here and Now, the less reliable will such interpretations be.

This very point shows how erroneous in principle are all so-called "laws" of history. The whole world of successors is by definition nonhistorical and absolutely free. It can be anticipated in an abstract way, but it cannot be pictured in specific detail. It cannot be projected or planned for, for I have no control over the unknown factors intervening between the time of my death and the possible fulfillment of the plan.

11

DISTRIBUTION OF KNOWLEDGE

Incomplete and Piecemeal Knowledge

THE OUTSTANDING feature of a man's life in the modern world is his conviction that his life-world as a whole is neither fully understood by himself nor fully understandable to any of his fellow-men. There is a stock of knowledge theoretically available to everyone, built up by practical experience, science, and technology as warranted insights. But this stock of knowledge is not integrated. It consists of a mere juxtaposition of more or less coherent systems of knowledge which themselves are neither coherent nor even compatible with one another. On the contrary, the abysses between the various attitudes involved in the approach to the specialized systems are themselves a condition of the success of the specialized inquiry.

If this is true for the various fields of scientific inquiry it is for even better reasons valid for the various fields of practical activity. Where our practical interests predominate we are satisfied with our knowledge that certain means and procedures achieve certain desired or undesired results. The fact that we do not understand the Why and the How of their working and that we do not know anything of their origin does not hinder us from dealing undisturbed with situations, things, and persons. We use the most complicated gadgets prepared by a very advanced technology without knowing how the contrivances work. No car driver is supposed to be familiar with the laws of mechanics, no radio listener with those of electronics. One may even be a successful businessman without

Reprinted from the following items in the Bibliography: 1946, 463–64, 471–72, 472–73, 465–67, 473–75.

an insight into the functioning of the market, or a banker without a smattering of monetary theory. The same holds good for the social world we live in. We rely upon the fact that our fellowmen will react as we anticipate if we act upon them in a specific way, that institutions such as governments, schools, courts, or public utilities will function, that an order of laws and mores, of religious and political beliefs, will govern the behavior of our fellowmen as it governs our own.

. . . It is clear that all the members of an in-group do not accept the same sector of the world as granted beyond question and that each of them selects different elements of it as an object of further inquiry. Knowledge is socially distributed.

World within Common Reach

Our outline of the various zones of relevance revealed the world within my reach as the core of primary relevance. This world within my own reach is first of all that sector of the world within my actual reach; then, that sector which formerly was in my actual reach and is now within my potential reach because it can be brought back again within my actual reach; and finally, there is within my attainable reach what is within the actual reach of you, my fellowman, and would be within my actual reach if I were not here and where I am but there where you are—briefly, if I were in your place. Thus, actually or potentially, one sector of the world is within my and my fellowman's common reach; it is within *our* reach, provided—and this restriction is highly important—that my fellowman has a definite place within the world of my reach as I have in his. We have, then, a common surrounding to be defined by our common interests, his and mine. To be sure, he and I will have a different system of relevances and a different knowledge of the common surrounding if for no other reason than that he sees from "there" everything that I am seeing from "here." Nevertheless, I may within this common surrounding and within the zone of common interests establish social relationships with the individualized other; each may act upon the other and react to the other's action. In short, the other is partially within my control as I am within his, and he and I not only know of this fact but even know of our mutual knowledge which itself is a means for exercising control. Spontaneously turning to each other, spontaneously "tuning in" ourselves to each other, we have at least *some* intrinsic relevances in common.

But only *some*. In any social interaction there remains a portion of each partner's system of intrinsic relevances not shared by the other. This has two important consequences. In the first place, let Peter and Paul be partners in a social interaction of any kind whatever. In so far as Peter is the object of Paul's action and has to take into account Paul's specific goals which he, Peter, does not share, Paul's intrinsic relevances are to Peter imposed relevances and vice versa. (The concept of imposed relevances applied to social relationships does not contain any reference to the problem whether or not the imposition involved is accepted by the partner. It seems that the degree of readiness to accept or not to accept, to give place to, or to resist, the imposition of the other's intrinsic relevances could be used advantageously for a classification of the various social relationships.) In the second place, Peter has full knowledge only of his own system of intrinsic relevances. Paul's system of intrinsic relevances, as a whole, is not fully accessible to Peter. In so far as Peter has a partial knowledge of it—at least he will know what Paul imposes upon him—this knowledge will never have that degree of precision that would be sufficient if what is merely relevant to Peter by imposition were an element of his, Peter's, system of intrinsic relevances. Imposed relevances remain empty, unfulfilled anticipations.

Such is the distribution of knowledge in the social relationship between individuals if each has his definite place in the world of the other, if each is under the other's control. To a certain extent the same holds good for the relationship between in-groups and out-groups if each of them is known to the other in its specificity. But the more the other becomes anonymous and the less his place in the social cosmos is ascertainable to the partner, the more the zone of common intrinsic relevances decreases and that of imposed ones increases.

Social Distribution of Knowledge

Extending reciprocal anonymity of partners is . . . characteristic of our modern civilization. We are less and less determined in our social situation by relationships with individual partners within our immediate or mediate reach, and more and more by highly anonymous types which have no fixed place in the social cosmos. We are less and less able to choose our partners in the social world and to share our social life with them. We are, so to speak, potentially subject to everybody's remote control. No spot of this globe is more distant from the place where we live than sixty airplane hours; electric waves carry messages in a fraction of a second from one end of the earth to the other; and very soon every place in this world will be the potential target of destructive weapons released at any other place. Or own social surrounding is within the reach of everyone, everywhere; an anonymous other, whose goals are unknown to us because of his anonymity, may bring us together with our system of interests and relevances within his control. We are less and less masters in our own right to define what is, and what is not, relevant to us. Politically, economically, and socially imposed relevances beyond our control have to be taken into account by us as they are. Therefore, we have to know them. But to what extent?

Expert, Man in the Street, Well-Informed Citizen

For the purpose of our study let us construct three ideal types which shall be called the expert, the man on the street, and the well-informed citizen.

The expert's knowledge is restricted to a limited field but therein it is clear and distinct. His opinions are based upon warranted assertions; his judgments are not mere guesswork or loose suppositions.

The man on the street has a working knowledge of many fields which are not necessarily coherent with one another. His is a knowledge of recipes indicating how to bring forth in typical situations typical results by typical means. The recipes indicate procedures which can be trusted even though they are not clearly understood. By following the prescription as if it were a ritual, the desired result can be attained without questioning why the single procedural steps have to be taken and taken exactly in the sequence prescribed. This knowledge in all its vagueness is still *sufficiently* precise for the practical purpose at hand. In all matters not connected with such practical purposes of immediate concern the man on the street accepts his sentiments and passions as guides. Under their influence, he establishes a set of convictions and unclarified views which he simply relies upon as long as they do not interfere with his pursuit of happiness.

The ideal type that we propose to call the well-informed citizen (thus shortening the more correct expression: the citizen who aims at being well informed) stands between the ideal type of the expert and that of the man on the street. On the one hand, he neither is, nor aims at being, possessed of expert knowledge; on the other, he does not acquiesce in the fundamental vagueness of a mere recipe knowledge or in the irrationality of his unclarified passions and sentiments. To be well informed means to him to arrive at *reasonably founded* opinions in fields which as he knows are at least mediately of concern to him although not bearing upon his purpose at hand.

All three types thus roughly outlined are, of course, mere constructs. . . . As a matter of fact, each of us in daily life is at any moment simultaneously expert, well-informed citizen, and man on the street, but in each case with respect to different provinces of knowledge. Moreover, each of us knows that the same holds good for each of his fellowmen and this very fact codetermines the specific type of knowledge employed. For example, for the man on the street it is sufficient to know that there are experts available for consultation should he need their advice in achieving his practical purpose in hand. His recipes tell him when to see a doctor or a lawyer, where to get needed information and the like. The expert, on the other hand, knows very well that only a fellow expert will understand all the technicalities and implications of a problem in his field, and he will never accept a layman or dilettante as a competent judge of his performances. But it is the well-informed citizen who considers himself perfectly qualified to decide who *is* a competent expert and even to make up his mind after having listened to opposing expert opinions.

Many phenomena of social life can be fully understood only if they are referred to the underlying general structure of the social distribution of knowledge thus outlined. This resource alone makes possible a sociological theory of professions, of prestige and competence, of charisma and authority, and leads to the understanding of such complicated social relationships as those existing among the performing artist, his public, and his critics, or among manufacturer, retailer, advertising agent, and consumer, or among the government executive, his technical adviser, and public opinion.

. . . The man on the street . . . lives, in a manner of speaking, naïvely in his own and his in-group's intrinsic relevances. Imposed relevances he takes into account merely as elements of the situation to be defined or as data or conditions for his course of action. They are simply given and it does not pay to try to understand their origin and structure. Why some things are more relevant than others, why zones of seemingly intrinsic irrelevancy may conceal elements which might be imposed upon him tomorrow as matters of highest relevance is not his concern; these questions do not influence his acting and thinking. He will not cross the bridge before he reaches it and he takes it for granted that he will find a bridge when he needs it and that it will be strong enough to carry him. That is one of the reasons why in forming his opinions he is much more governed by sentiment than by information, why he prefers, as statistics have amply shown, the comic pages of the newspapers to the foreign news, the radio quizzes to news commentators.

The expert, as we understand this term, is at home only in a system of imposed relevances—imposed, that is, by the problems pre-established within his field. Or to be more precise, by his decision to become an expert he has accepted the relevances imposed within his field as the intrinsic, and the only intrinsic, relevances of his acting and thinking. But this field is rigidly limited. To be sure, there are marginal problems and even problems outside his specific field, but the expert is inclined to assign them to another expert whose concern they are supposed to be. The expert starts from the assumption not only that the system of problems established within his field is relevant but that it is the only relevant system. All his knowledge is referred to this frame of reference which has been established once and for all. He who does not accept it as the monopolized system of his intrinsic relevances does not share with the expert a universe of discourse. He can expect from the expert's advice merely the indication of suitable means for attaining pregiven ends, but not the determination of the ends themselves. Clemenceau's famous statement that war is too important a business to be left exclusively to generals illustrates the way in which a man oriented toward more comprehensive ends reacts to expert advice.

The well-informed citizen finds himself placed in a domain which belongs to an infinite number of possible frames of reference. There are no pregiven ready-made ends, no fixed border lines within which he can look for shelter. He has to choose the frame of reference by choosing his interest; he has to investigate the zones of relevances adhering to it; and he has to gather as much knowledge as possible of the origin and sources of the relevances actually or potentially imposed upon him. In terms of the classification previously used, the well-informed citizen will restrict, in so far as is possible, the zone of the irrelevant, mindful that what is today relatively irrelevant may be imposed tomorrow as a primary relevance and that the province of the so-called absolutely irrelevant may reveal itself as the home of the anonymous powers which may overtake him. Thus, his is an attitude as different from that of the expert whose knowledge is delimited by a single system of relevances as from that of the man on the street which is indifferent to the structure of relevance itself. For this very reason he has to form a reasonable opinion and to look for information.

V. Realms of Experience

12

TRANSCENDENCES AND MULTIPLE REALITIES

The Experience of Transcendence

I find myself in my everyday life within a world not of my own making. I know this fact, and this knowledge itself belongs to my biographical situation. There is, first, my knowledge that nature transcends the reality of my everyday life both in time and in space. In time, the world of Nature existed before my birth and will continue to exist after my death. It existed before man appeared on earth and will probably survive mankind. In space, the world within my actual reach carries along the open infinite horizons of my world in potential reach, but to my experiences of these horizons belongs the conviction that each world within potential reach, once transformed into actual reach, will again be surrounded by new horizons, and so on. Within the world in my reach there are, moreover, certain objects, such as the heavenly bodies, which I cannot bring within my manipulatory sphere, and there are events within my manipulatory area, such as the tides, which I cannot bring within my control.

I know, furthermore, that in a similar way the social world transcends the reality of my everyday life. I was born into a preorganized social world which will survive me, a world shared from the outset with fellow men who are organized in groups, a world which has its particular open horizons in time, in space, and also in what sociologists call social distance. In time, there is the infinite chain of generations which overlap one another; my clan refers to

Reprinted from the following items in the Bibliography: 1955*b*, 175–77, 177–78, 184, 178–82, 186–87, 187; 1945*c*, 552, 552–53, 553–54, 555–56, 564–68.

other clans, my tribe to other tribes, and they are enemies or
friends, speaking the same or another language, but they are always organized in their particular social form and living their particular way of life. My actual social environment refers always to a
horizon of potential social environments, and we may speak of a
transcendent infinity of the social world as we speak of a transcendent infinity of the natural one.

I experience both of these transcendences, that of Nature and
that of Society, as being imposed upon me in a double sense: on the
one hand, I find myself at any moment of my existence as being
within nature and within society; both are permanently coconstitu-
tive elements of my biographical situation and are, therefore, experienced as inescapably belonging to it. On the other hand, they
constitute the framework within which alone I have the freedom
of my potentialities, and this means they prescribe the scope of all
possibilities for defining my situation. In this sense, they are not
elements of my situation, but determinations of it. In the first sense,
I may—even more, I have to—take them for granted. In the second
sense, I have to come to terms with them. But in either sense, I have
to understand the natural and the social world in spite of their
transcendences, in terms of an order of things and events.

From the outset I know also that any human being experiences
the same imposed transcendences of Nature and of Society, although he experiences them in individual perspectives and with
individual adumbrations. But the order of Nature and of Society
is common to all mankind. It furnishes to everyone the setting of
the cycle of his individual life, of birth, aging, death, health and
sickness, hopes and fears. Each of us participates in the recurrent
rhythm of nature; to each of us the movements of sun and moon and
stars, the change between day and night, and the cycle of the seasons are elements of his situation. Each of us is a member of the
group into which he was born or which he has joined and which
continues to exist if some of its members die and others enter into
it. Everywhere there will be systems of kinship, age groups and sex
groups, differentiations according to occupations, and an organization of power and command which leads to the categories of social status and prestige. But in the commonsense thinking of

everyday life we simply know that Nature and Society represent some kind of order; yet the essence of this order as such is unknowable to us. It reveals itself merely in images by analogical apprehending. But the images, once constituted, are taken for granted, and so are the transcendences to which they refer.

How is this possible? "The miracle of all miracles is that the genuine miracles become to us an everyday occurrence," says Lessing's Nathan. This is so because we find in our sociocultural environment itself socially approved systems offering answers for our quest for the unknowable transcendences. Devices are developed to apprehend the disquieting phenomena transcending the world of everyday life in a way analogous to the familiar phenomena within it. This is done by the creation of appresentational references of a higher order, which shall be called *symbols* in contradistinction to the terms "marks," "indications," "signs," used so far.

Symbol

A symbol can be defined in first approximation as an appresentational reference of a higher order in which the appresenting member of the pair is an object, fact, or event within the reality of our daily life, whereas the other appresented member of the pair refers to an idea which transcends our experience of everyday life.

This definition corresponds substantially to the notion of symbol as developed by Karl Jaspers in the third volume of his *Philosophie*,[1] from which we give the following freely translated quotation, omitting certain references to Jasper's particular philosophical position:

We speak of meaning in the sense of sign and image, of simile, allegory, and metaphor. The main difference between meaning within the world and of metaphysical meaning consists in the criterion of whether in the relationship between the image and that which it represents the latter itself could be apprehended as an objectivity, or whether the image is an image for something that is not accessible in any other way; that is to say, whether that which is expressed in the image could also be stated or demonstrated in a direct way, or

[1] (Berlin, 1932), vol. 3, *Metaphysik*, chap. 1, p. 16.

whether it exists for us merely in so far as it exists in the image. Only in the latter case should we speak of a symbol. . . . The symbol cannot be interpreted except by other symbols. The understanding of a symbol does not, therefore, consist in grasping its significance in a rational way but in experiencing it existentially in the symbolic intention as this unique reference to something transcendent that vanishes at the limiting point.

. . . Symbolization is an appresentational reference of a higher order, that is, based on preformed appresentational references, such as marks, indications, signs, or even symbols. Jacob, awakened from his dream of the ladder in which God revealed Himself to him (Genesis, 28, 10–25), took the stone that he had put for his pillow and set it up for a pillar and poured oil upon the top of it, vowing that this stone shall be God's house. "Surely," he said, "the Lord is in this place; and I know it not." The irruption of the transcendent experience into the world of everyday life, which transforms it and gives each element of it an appresentational significance ("the Lord is in this Place"), which it did not have before ("I knew it not"), has hardly been told in a more dramatic way. The stone becomes the pillow, the pillow a pillar, the pillar God's house.

The Roots of Symbolism

We have now to study the problem of the constitution of the appresentational pairing which might function as a symbol. How is it possible that an object, event, or fact within the reality of our daily life is coupled with an idea which transcends our experience of our everyday life? This problem can be approached on two different levels. There are first sets of appresentational references which are universal and can be used for symbolization because they are rooted in the human condition. It is a problem of philosophical anthropology to study these sets of appresentational references. Secondly, the particular forms of symbolic systems as developed by the various cultures in different periods might be investigated. This is the problem of cultural anthropology and of the history of ideas. We have to restrict ourselves here to fugitive remarks describing some items of the first group, illustrating them by example, belonging to the second.

As to the latter, we prefer for reasons we shall mention briefly, not to take our examples from the world of our present Western culture. The latter has developed several systems of symbols such as science, art, religion, politics, and philosophy, some of which will be characterized in the next section. We have, however, to consider that the coexistence of several symbolic systems which are merely loosely, if at all, connected one with another, is the special feature of our own historical situation and the result of our attempt to develop an interpretation of the cosmos in terms of the positive methods of the natural sciences. We take the world as defined by the mathematical natural sciences as the archetype of an ideal order of symbolic references and are inclined to explain all the other symbolic systems as derivations from it or at least as subordinated to it. Whitehead in his book *Science and the Modern World*[2] has rightly stated that Galileo's discoveries and Newton's laws of motion established the fundamental concept of the *"ideally isolated system"* which is essential to scientific theory so that science would be impossible without it. Whitehead explains that

the isolated system is not a solipsistic system, apart from which there would be nonentity. It is isolated as within the universe. This means that there are truths respecting this system, which require reference only to the remainder of things by way of a uniform systematic scheme of relationships.

On the other hand, many investigations of modern anthropologists, sociologists, mythologists, philologists, political scientists, and historians[3] have shown that in other cultures and even in earlier periods of our own culture man experienced nature, society, and himself as equally participating in and determined by the order of the cosmos. . . .

[2]   New York, 1925. Also available as Pelican-Mentor Book (New American Library). See p. 47 of the latter edition.

[3]   We refer to the writings of Emile Durkheim, Lucien Lévy-Bruhl, Marcel Mauss, Marcel Granet, Bronislaw Malinowski, Ernst Cassirer, Bruno Snell, Alois Dempf, Arnold J. Toynbee, and Eric Voegelin.

An example of the full integration of the symbolic interrelation called by Cassirer the society of life can be found in classic Chinese thought. According to the French Sinologue Marcel Granet,[4] there is in classical Chinese literature a unity of structure between the microcosm—man—and the macrocosm—the universe—and the structure of the universe is explained by the structure of society. All these structures are dominated by two fundamental principles: first, the position of the Male and the Female, the positive and the negative, the *Yang* and the *Yin*; and second, the opposition between the chief and the vassal in the hierarchical structure of society. Based on these principles, etiquette prescribes and regulates meticulously all details of the everyday life world.

We shall try now to show by a few examples how universal symbols originate in the general human condition. As stated before, man considers himself as a center O of a system of coordinates under which he groups the objects of his environment in terms of "above and underneath," "before and behind," "right and left." Now, for every man an element of the underneath is the earth and of the above the sky. The earth is common to men and animals; it is the procreator of vegetative life, the provider of food. The sky is the place where the celestial bodies appear and disappear, but also the place from which rain comes, without which no fertility of the earth is possible. The head, the carrier of the main sense organs and the organ of breathing and speech, is on the upper part of the human body, and the digestive organs and that of procreation in the lower part. The connection of all these phenomena makes the spatial dimension "above and below" the starting point of a set of symbolic appresentations. In Chinese thought, for example, the head symbolizes the sky (and so does the roof of the house) whereas the feet (the floor) symbolize earth. But since the sky has to send rain in order to fertilize the earth, the sky is also to Chinese thought the male principle, the positive principle, *Yang*, and earth the negative, female *Yin*. And this symbolism of higher-lower has its correlate in Chinese medicine, music, dance, social

---

[4]   Granet, *Etudes sociologiques sur la Chine* (Paris, 1953), p. 268; see also Granet, *La pensée chinoise* (Paris, 1934), passim.

hierarchy, etiquette, all of which are correlated and can be brought into symbolic appresentational reference one with the other.[5] There is also a symbolism of the directions before-behind, things which are faced or have to be faced and are thus visible, and those which are not and therefore possibly dangerous, and also of right and left.[6]

Sun, moon, and stars rise and set for all men in opposite directions which are to everyone "marks" for finding his bearings. But the four cardinal points of the compass so ascertained have also their symbolic connotations, because they are connected with the change between day and night, light and darkness, being awake and asleep, the visible and the invisible, the coming-to-be and the passing-away. The life cycle of men—birth, childhood, adolescence, manhood, old age, death—has its analogy in the cycle of the seasons and the cycle of vegetative and animal life which is equally important for farming, fishing, and animal husbandry, and is in turn correlated to the motions of the heavenly bodies. Again a set of correlations is established which permits the appresentational pairing of its elements in the form of symbols. The social organization with its hierarchies of rulers and subordinates, chiefs and vassals, has its correlate in the hierarchy of the heavenly bodies. Thus, the cosmos, the individual, and the community form a unit and are equally subject to the universal forces which govern all events. Man has to understand these forces and, because he cannot dominate them, to conjure them or to appease them. To do so is, however, not the business of the isolated individual, it is the concern of the whole community and its organization.

The symbolic forms in which the forces of the universe of nature as well as of society are appresented (*mana, orenda, manitu, Yin* and *Yang*, deities of various kinds and hierarchies, etc.) are as manifold as the symbols appresenting them (expressive, purposive, or mimetic gestures, linguistics or pictorial presentations, charms, spells, magical or religious rites, ceremonies). The symbols of

5　　Ibid.
6　　See the highly interesting article by Granet, "La droite et la gauche en Chine," in *Etudes sociologiques*, pp. 261–78.

myths have the particular function of justifying and vouching for the truth and validity of the order established by the other symbolic systems (Malinowski).[7]

At this level the world of the sacred and that of the profane are closely interrelated.

Provinces of Meaning

In a famous chapter of his *Principles of Psychology*[8] William James shows that there are several, probably an infinite number of orders of realities, each with its special and separate style of existence. James calls them "subuniverses," and mentions as examples the world of senses or physical things (as the paramount reality), the world of science, the world of ideal relations, the worlds of mythology and religion, the world of "idols of the tribe," the various worlds of individual opinions, and the world of sheer madness and vagary. "Each world *whilst it is attended to* is real after its own fashion; only the reality lapses with the attention." Reality means simply relation to our emotional and active life; whatever excites and stimulates our interest is real. Our primitive impulse is to affirm immediately the reality of all that is conceived, as long as it remains uncontradicted. ". . . All propositions, whether attributive or existential, are believed through the very fact of being conceived, unless they clash with other propositions believed at the same time, by affirming that their terms are the same with the terms of these other propositions."[9]

The ingenious theory of William James has, of course, to be detached from its psychological setting and analyzed for its many implications. . . . We prefer to speak of finite provinces of meaning upon which we bestow the accent of reality, instead of subuniverses as does William James. By this change of terminology we emphasize that it is the meaning of our experiences, and not the ontological structure of the objects, which constitutes reality. Each

[7]   Bronislaw Malinowski, *Magic, Science, and Religion* (New York, 1954), pp. 100 ff.
[8]   Vol. 2, chap. 21.
[9]   Ibid., pp. 293, 290.

province of meaning—the paramount world of real objects and events into which we can gear by our actions, the world of imaginings and fantasms, such as the play world of the child, the world of the insane, but also the world of art, the world of dreams, the world of scientific contemplation—has its particular cognitive style. It is this particular style of a set of our experiences which constitutes them as a finite province of meaning. All experiences within each of these worlds are, with respect to this cognitive style, consistent in themselves and compatible with one another (although not compatible with the meaning of everyday life). Moreover, each of these finite provinces of meaning is, among other things, characterized by a specific tension of consciousness (from full awakeness in the reality of everyday life to sleep in the world of dreams), by a specific time-perspective, by a specific form of experiencing oneself, and, finally, by a specific form of sociality.

Paramount Reality

William James rightly calls the subuniverse of senses, of physical things, the paramount reality. But we prefer to take as a paramount reality the finite province of meaning which we have called the reality of our everyday life. . . . The reality of our everyday life which our commonsense thinking takes for granted includes not only the physical objects, facts, and events within our actual and potential reach perceived as such in the mere apperceptual scheme, but also appresentational references of a lower order by which the physical objects of nature are transformed into sociocultural objects. But since these appresentations of a lower order also have objects, facts, or events of the outer world as their appresenting member, we believe that our definition is compatible with that of James.

The Cognitive Style of the Paramount Reality

(1) A specific tension of consciousness, namely wide-awakeness, originating in full attention to life;

(2) A specific *epoché,* namely suspension of doubt;

(3) A prevalent form of spontaneity, namely working (a meaningful spontaneity based upon a project and characterized by the intention bring about the projected state of affairs by bodily movements gearing into the outer world);

(4) A specific form of experiencing one's self (the working self as the total self);

(5) A specific form of sociality (the common intersubjective world of communication and social action);

(6) A specific time-perspective (the standard time originating in an intersection between *durée* and cosmic time as the universal temporal structure of the intersubjective world).

These are at least some of the features of the cognitive style belonging to this particular province of meaning. As long as our experiences of this world—the valid as well as the invalidated ones —partake of this style we may consider this province of meaning as real, we may bestow upon it the accent of reality. And with respect to the paramount reality of everyday life we, with the natural attitude, are induced to do so because our practical experiences prove the unity and congruity of the world of working as valid and the hypothesis of its reality as irrefutable. Even more, this reality seems to us to be the natural one, and we are not ready to abandon our attitude toward it without having experienced a specific *shock* which compels us to break through the limits of this "finite" province of meaning and to shift the accent of reality to another one

Transitions

To be sure those experiences of shock befall me frequently amidst my daily life; they themselves pertain to its reality. They show me that the world of working in standard time is not the sole finite province of meaning but only one of many others accessible to my intentional life.

There are as many innumerable kinds of different shock experiences as there are different finite provinces of meaning upon which I may bestow the accent of reality. Some instances are: the shock of falling asleep as the leap into the world of dreams; the inner transformation we endure if the curtain in the theater rises as the transition into the world of the stage-play; the radical change in our attitude if, before a painting, we permit our visual field to be limited by what is within the frame as the passage into the pictorial world; our quandary, relaxing into laughter, if, in listening to a joke, we are for a short time ready to accept the fictitious world of the jest as a reality in relation to which the world of our daily life takes on the character of foolishness; the child's turning toward his toy as the transition into the play-world; and so on. But also the religious experiences in all their varieties—for instance, Kierkegaard's experience of the "instant" as the leap into the religious sphere—is such a shock as well as the decision of the scientist to replace all passionate participation in the affairs of "this world" by a disinterested contemplative attitude.

Nonparamount Realities

(1) All these worlds—the world of dreams, of imageries and phantasms, especially the world of art, the world of religious experience, the world of scientific contemplation, the play world of the child, and the world of the insane—are finite provinces of meaning. This means that (a) all of them have a peculiar cognitive style (although not that of the world of working with the natural attitude); (b) all experiences within each of these worlds are, with respect to this cognitive style, consistent in themselves and compatible with one another (although not compatible with the meaning of everyday life); (c) each of these finite provinces of meaning may receive a specific accent of reality (although not the reality accent of the world of working).

(2) Consistency and compatibility of experiences with respect to their peculiar cognitive style subsists merely *within* the borders of the particular province of meaning to which those experiences belong. By no means will that which is compatible within the province of meaning P be also compatible within the province of meaning Q. On the contrary, seen from P, supposed to be real, Q and all the experiences belonging to it would appear as merely fictitious, inconsistent and incompatible and vice versa.

(3) For this very reason we are entitled to talk of *finite* provinces of meaning. This finiteness implies that there is no possibility of referring one of these provinces to the other by introducing a formula of transformation. The passing from one to the other can only be performed by a "leap," as Kierkegaard calls it, which manifests itself in the subjective experience of a shock.

(4) What has just been called a "leap" or a "shock" is nothing else than a radical modification in the tension of our consciousness, founded in a different *attention à la vie*.

(5) To the cognitive style peculiar to each of these different provinces of meaning belongs, thus, a specific tension of consciousness and, consequently, also a specific *epoché*, a prevalent form of spontaneity, a specific form of self experience, a specific form of sociality, and a specific time perspective.

(6) The world of working in daily life is the archetype of our experience of reality. All the other provinces of meaning may be considered as its modifications.[10]

Worlds of Phantasy

Under this heading we shall discuss some general characteristics of the cognitive style peculiar to a group of otherwise most heterogeneous finite provinces of meaning, none of them reducible to the other. This group is commonly known as that of fancies or

---

[10]   A word of caution seems to be needed here. The concept of finite provinces of meaning does not involve any static connotation such as if we had to select one of these provinces as our home to live in, to start from or to return to. That is by no means the case. Within a single day, even within a single hour our consciousness may run through most different tensions and adopt most different attentional attitudes to life. There is, furthermore, the problem of "enclaves," that is of regions belonging to one province of meaning enclosed by another, a problem which, important as it is, cannot be handled within the frame of the present paper, which admittedly restricts itself to the outlining of a few principles of analysis. To give an example of this disregarded group of problems: Any projecting within the world of working is itself, as we have seen, a phantasying and involves in addition a kind of theoretical contemplation, although not necessarily that of the scientific attitude.

imageries and embraces among many others the realms of day-dreams, of play, of fiction, of fairy-tales, of myths, of jokes. So far philosophy has not worked upon the problem of the specific constitution of each of these innumerable provinces of our imaginative life. Each of them originates in a specific modification, which the paramount reality of our daily life undergoes, because our mind, turning away in decreasing tensions of consciousness from the world of working and its tasks, withdraws from certain of its layers the accent of reality in order to replace it by a context of supposedly quasi-real phantasms. For the problem in hand a fugitive survey of what all these worlds have in common has to be sufficient.

Living in one of the many worlds of phantasy we have no longer to master the outer world and to overcome the resistance of its objects. We are free from the pragmatic motive which governs our natural attitude toward the world of daily life, free also from the bondage of "interobjective" space and intersubjective standard time. No longer are we confined within the limits of our actual, restorable, or attainable reach. What occurs in the outer world no longer imposes upon us issues between which we have to choose nor does it put a limit on our possible accomplishments.

However, there are no "possible accomplishments" in the world of phantasms if we take this term as a synonym of "performable." The imagining self neither works nor performs within the meaning of the aforegiven definitions. Imagining may be projected inasmuch as it may be conceived in advance and may be included in a hierarchy of plans. But this meaning of the term "project" is not exactly the same in which we used it when we defined action as projected conduct. Strictly speaking the opposite holds good, namely, that the projected action is always the imagined performed act, imagined in the future-perfect tense. Here we are not particularly interested in investigating whether all or merely some or no form of our imaginative life may be qualified as "action" or whether fancying belongs exclusively to the category of mere thinking. Yet it is of highest importance to understand that imagining as such always lacks the intention to realize the phantasm; it lacks in other words the purposive "fiat." Using the language of Husserl's *Ideas* we may say that all imagining is "neutral," it lacks the specific positionality of the thetic consciousness.

However we have to distinguish sharply between imagining as a manifestation of our spontaneous life and the imageries imagined. Acting may be imagined as a true acting and even working within the meaning of our previous definitions; it may be imagined as referring to a preconceived project; as having its specific in-order-to and because motives; as originating in choice and decision; as having its place within a hierarchy of plans. Even more: it may be imagined as endowed with an intention to realize the project, to carry it through, and may be fancied as gearing into the outer world. All this, however, belongs to the imageries produced in and by the imagining act. The "performances" and "working acts" are merely imagined *as* performances and working acts, and they and the correlated categories bear, to borrow Husserl's term, "quotation-marks." Imagining itself is, however, necessarily inefficient and stays under all circumstances outside the hierarchies of plans and purposes valid within the world of working. The imagining self does not transform the outer world.

Province of Scientific Reasoning

Scientific theorizing—and in the following the terms theory, theorizing, etc., shall be exclusively used in this restricted sense—does not serve any practical purpose. Its aim is not to master the world but to observe and possibly to understand it. . . .

All theoretical cogitations are "actions" and even "performances" within the meaning of the definitions given hereinbefore. They are actions, because they are emanations of our spontaneous life carried out according to a project and they are performances because the intention to carry through the project, to bring about the projected result supervenes. Thus, scientific theorizing has its own in-order-to and because motives, it is planned, and planned within a hierarchy of plans established by the decision to pursue and carry on scientific activities. (This "action-character" of theorizing alone would suffice to distinguish it from dreaming.) It is, furthermore, purposive thinking (and this purposiveness alone would suffice to distinguish it from mere fancying!) the purpose being the intention to realize the solution of the problem at hand. Yet, theoretical cogitations are not acts of working, that is they do not gear into the outer world. To be sure, they are based upon working acts (such as measuring, handling instruments, making experiments); they can be communicated only by working acts (such as writing a paper, delivering a lecture); and so on. All these activities performed within and pertaining to the world of working are either conditions or consequences of the theorizing but do not belong to the theoretical attitude itself, from which they can be easily separated. Likewise we have to distinguish between the scientist *qua* human being who acts and lives among his fellow-men his everyday life and the theoretical thinker who is, we repeat it, not interested in the mastery of the world but in obtaining knowledge by observing it.

This attitude of the "disinterested observer" is based upon a peculiar *attention à la vie* as the prerequisite of all theorizing. It consists in the abandoning of the system of relevances which prevails within the practical sphere of the natural attitude. The whole universe of life, that which Husserl calls the *Lebenswelt*, is pregiven to both the man in the world of working and to the theorizing thinker. But to the former other sections and other elements of this world are more relevant than to the latter.

The theoretical thinker . . . has anticipations which, on the one hand, refer back to his stock of sedimented experiences and, on the other hand, to its special system of relevances. . . . However, unlike man in daily life, he is not passionately interested in the question, whether his anticipations, if fulfilled, will prove helpful for the solution of his practical problems, but merely whether or not they will stand the test of verification by supervening experiences. This involves—in the well-understood meaning of the aforegiven definition—a certain detachment of interest in life and a turning away from what we called the state of wide-awakeness.

Since theoretical thought does not gear into the outer world it is revocable within the meaning of this term defined hereinbefore. That means it is subject to permanent revision, it can be undone, "struck out," "cancelled," modified, and so on, without creating

any change in the outer world. In the process of theoretical thinking I may come back again and again to my premises, revoke my
conclusions, annihilate my judgments, enlarge or restrict the scope
of the problem under scrutiny, etc.

. . . The theoretical thinker is interested in problems and solutions valid in their own right for everyone, at any place, and at any
time, wherever and whenever certain conditions, from the assumption of which he starts, prevail. The "leap" into the province of
theoretical thought involves the resolution of the individual to
suspend his subjective point of view. And this fact alone shows that
not the undivided self but only a partial self, a taker of a rôle, a
"Me," namely, the theoretician, "acts" within the province of scientific thought. This partial self lacks all "essentially actual" experiences connected with his own body, its movements, and its
limits.

We may now sum up some of the features of the *epoché*
peculiar to the scientific attitude. In this *epoché* there is "bracketed" (suspended): (1) the subjectivity of the thinker as man
among fellow-men, including his bodily existence as psycho-
physical human being within the world;[11] (2) the system of orientation by which the world of everyday life is grouped in zones
within actual, restorable, attainable reach etc.; (3) the fundamental anxiety and the system of pragmatic relevances originating
therein. But within this modified sphere the life-world of all of us
continues to subsist as reality, namely as the reality of theoretical
contemplation, although not as one of practical interest. With the
shift of the system of relevances from the practical to the theoretical field all terms referring to action and performance within
the world of working, such as "plan," "motive," "projects" change
their meaning and receive "quotation marks."

We have now to characterize with a few words the system of

[11]   Needless to say, this form of *epoché* must not be confused with the
epoché leading to the phenomenological reduction by which not only the
subjectivity of the thinker but the whole world is bracketed. The theoretical thinking has to be characterized as belonging to the "natural attitude," this term *here* (otherwise than in the text) being used in contradistinction to "phenomenological reduction."

relevances prevailing within the province of scientific contemplation. This system originates in a voluntary act of the scientist by
which he selects the object of his further inquiry, in other words,
by the *stating of the problem at hand.* Therewith the more or less
emptily anticipated solution of this problem becomes the supreme
goal of the scientific activity. On the other hand by the mere stating
of the problem the sections or elements of the world which actually
are or potentially may become related to it as relevant, as bearing
upon the matter in hand, are at once defined. Henceforth, this cir-
cumscription of the relevant field will guide the process of inquiry.
It determines, first of all, the so-called "level" of the research. As
a matter of fact the term level is just another expression for the
demarcation line between all that does and does not pertain to the
problem under consideration, the former being the topics to be
investigated, explicated, clarified; the latter the other elements of
the scientist's knowledge which, because they are irrelevant to his
problem, he decides to accept in their givenness without questioning as mere "data." In other words, the demarcation line is the
locus of the points actually interesting the scientist and at which
he has decided to stop further research and analysis. Secondly, the
stating of the problem at once reveals its open horizons, the outer
horizon of connected problems which will have to be stated afterwards, as well as the inner horizon of all the implications hidden
within the problem itself which have to be made visible and explicated in order to solve it

All this, however, does not mean that the decision of the scientist in stating the problem is an arbitrary one or that he has the
same "freedom of discretion" in choosing and solving his problems
which the phantasying self has in filling out its anticipations. This
is by no means the case. Of course, the theoretical thinker may
choose at his discretion, only determined by his inclination, which
is rooted in his intimate personality, the scientific field in which
he wants to take interest and possibly also the level (in general)
upon which he wants to carry on his investigations. But as soon as
he has made up his mind in this respect, the scientist enters a pre-
constituted world of scientific contemplation handed down to him
by the historical tradition of his science. Henceforth he will partici-

pate in a universe of discourse embracing the results obtained by others, problems stated by others, solutions suggested by others, methods worked out by others. This theoretical universe of the special science is itself a finite province of meaning, having its peculiar cognitive style with peculiar implications of problems and horizons to be explicated. The regulative principle of constitution of such a province of meaning, called a special branch of science, can be formulated as follows: Any problem emerging within the scientific field has to partake of the universal style of this field and has to be compatible with the preconstituted problems and their solution by either accepting or refuting them. Thus, the latitude for the discretion of the scientist in stating the problem is in fact a very small one.

VI. The Province of Sociology

13

INTERPRETATIVE SOCIOLOGY

I. *Basic Considerations*

LIMITS OF THE BEHAVIORIST POSITION   At first sight it is not easily understandable why the subjective point of view should be preferred in the social sciences. Why address ourselves always to this mysterious and not too interesting tyrant of the social sciences, called the subjectivity of the actor? Why not honestly describe in honestly objective terms what really happens, and that means speaking our own language, the language of qualified and scientifically trained observers of the social world? And if it be objected that these terms are but artificial conventions created by our "will and pleasure," and that therefore we cannot utilize them for real insight into the meaning which social acts have for those who act, but only for our interpretation, we could answer that it is precisely this building up of a system of conventions and an honest description of the world which *is* and is alone the task of scientific thought; that we scientists are no less sovereign in our system of interpretation than the actor is free in setting up his system of goals and plans; that we social scientists in particular have but to follow the pattern of natural sciences, which have performed with the very methods we should abandon the most wonderful work of all time; and, finally, that it is the essence of science to be objective, valid not only for me, or for me and you and a few others, but for everyone, and that scientific propositions do not refer to my private world but to the one and unitary life-world common to us all.

Reprinted from the following items in the Bibliography: 1960, 203–5, 205–9; 1954, 272–73, 265–67, 264–65, 269–70; 1953*c*, 28–30, 30–31; 1943, 145; 1953*c*, 33–34, 34–36; 1943, 146; 1967, 186–88, 188–90; 1943, 144–45; 1967, 196–98, 198–200, 200–201, 228.

The last part of this thesis is incontestably true; but doubtless even a fundamental point of view can be imagined, according to which social sciences have to follow the pattern of natural sciences and to adopt their methods. Pushed to its logical conclusion it leads to the method of behaviorism. To criticize this principle is not within the scope of the present study. We restrict ourselves to the remark that radical behaviorism stands and falls with the basic assumption that there is no possibility of proving the intelligence of "the fellowman." It is highly probable that he is an intelligent human being, but that is a "weak fact" not capable of verification (Russell, similarly Carnap).

Yet, it is not then quite understandable why an intelligent individual should write books for others or even meet others in congresses where it is reciprocally proved that the intelligence of the other is a questionable fact. It is even less understandable that the same authors who are convinced that no verification is possible for the intelligence of other human beings have such confidence in the principle of verifiability itself, which can be realized only through cooperation with others by mutual control. Furthermore they feel no inhibition about starting all their deliberations with the dogma that language exists, that speech reactions and verbal reports are legitimate methods of behavioristic psychology, that propositions in a given language are able to make sense, without considering that language, speech, verbal report, proposition, and sense already presuppose intelligent alter egos, capable of understanding the language, of interpreting the proposition, and of verifying the sense. But the phenomena of understanding and interpreting themselves cannot be explained as pure behavior, provided we do not recur to the subterfuge of a "covert behavior" which evades a description in behavioristic terms.

These few critical remarks, however, do not hit the center of our problem. Behaviorism as well as every other objective scheme of reference in the social sciences has, of course, as its chief purpose, to explain with scientifically correct methods what really happens in the social world of our everyday life. It is, of course, neither the goal nor the meaning of any scientific theory to design and to describe a fictitious world having no reference whatsoever to our common sense experience and being therefore without any practical interest for us. The fathers of behaviorism had no other purpose than that of describing and explaining real human acts within a real human world. But the fallacy of this theory consists in the substitution of a fictional world for social reality by promulgating methodological principles as appropriate for the social sciences which, though proved true in other fields, prove a failure in the realm of intersubjectivity.

THE OBJECTIVE AND THE SUBJECTIVE APPROACH   But behaviorism is only one form of objectivism in the social sciences, though the most radical one. The student of the social world does not find himself placed before the inexorable alternative either of accepting the strictest subjective point of view, and, therefore, of studying the motives and thoughts in the mind of the actor; or of restricting himself to the description of the overt behavior and of admitting the behavioristic tenet of the inaccessibility of the other's mind and even of the unverifiability of the other's intelligence. There is rather a basic attitude conceivable—and, in fact, several of the most successful social scientists have adopted it— which accepts naively the social world with all the alter egos and institutions in it as a meaningful universe, meaningful namely for the observer whose only scientific task consists in describing and explaining his and his co-observers' experiences of it.

To be sure, those scientists admit that phenomena like nation, government, market, price, religion, art, science refer to activities of other intelligent human beings for whom they constitute the world of their social life; they admit furthermore that alter egos have created this world by their activities and that they orient their further activities to its existence. Nevertheless, so they pretend, we are not obliged to go back to the subjective activities of those alter egos and to their correlates in their minds in order to give a description and explanation of the facts of this social world. Social scientists, they contend, may and should restrict themselves to telling what this world means to them, neglecting what it means to the actors within this social world. Let us collect the facts of this social world, as our scientific experience may present them in a reliable form, let us describe and analyze these facts, let us group them under pertinent categories and study the regularities in their shape and development which then will emerge, and we shall arrive at a system of the social sciences, discovering the basic principles and the analytical laws of the social world. Having once reached this point the social sciences may confidently leave the subjective analyses to psychologists, philosophers, metaphysicists, or however else you like to call idle people bothering with such problems. And, the defender of such a position may add, is it not this scientific ideal which the most advanced social sciences are about to realize? Look at modern economics! The great progress of this science dates exactly from the decision of some advanced spirits to study curves of demand and supply and to discuss equations of prices and costs instead of striving hard and in vain to penetrate the mystery of subjective wants and subjective values.

Doubtless such a position is not only possible but even accepted by the majority of social scientists. Doubtless on a certain level real scientific work may be performed and has been performed without entering into the problems of subjectivity. We can go far ahead in the study of social phenomena, like social institutions of all kinds, social relations, and even social groups, without leaving the basic frame of reference, which can be formulated as follows: what does all this mean for us, the scientific observer? We can develop and apply a refined system of abstraction for this purpose which intentionally eliminates the actor in the social world, with all his subjective points of view, and we can even do so without coming into conflict with the experiences derived from social reality. Masters in this technique—and there are many of them in all fields of social research—will always guard against leaving the consistent level within this technique may be adopted and they will therefore confine their problems adequately.

All this does not alter the fact that this type of social science does not deal directly and immediately with the social life-world, common to us all, but with skillfully and expediently chosen idealizations and formalizations of the social world which are not repugnant to its facts. Nor does it make the less indispensable reference to the subjective point of view on other levels of abstraction if the original problem under consideration is modified. But then—and that is an important point—this reference to the subjective point of view always *can* be performed and should be performed. As the social world under any aspect whatsoever remains a very complicated cosmos of human activities, we can always go back to the "forgotten man" of the social sciences, to the actor in the social world whose doing and feeling lies at the bottom of the whole system. We, then, try to understand him in that doing and feeling and the state of mind which induced him to adopt specific attitudes towards his social environment.

In such a case the answer to the question "what does this social world mean for me the observer?" requires as a prerequisite the answering of the quite other questions "what does this social world mean for the observed actor within this world and what did he mean by his acting within it?" In putting our questions thus we no longer naïvely accept the social world and its current idealizations and formalizations as ready-made and meaningful beyond all question, but we undertake to study the process of idealizing and formalizing as such, the genesis of the meaning which social phenomena have for us as well as for the actors, the mechanism of the activity by which human beings understand one another and themselves. We are always free, and sometimes obliged, to do so.

This possibility of studying the social world under different points of view reveals the fundamental importance of the formula of Professor Znaniecki, [that all social phenomena can be described under one of the following four schemes of reference: social personality; social act; social group; social relations.] Each social phenomenon may be studied under the scheme of reference of social relationship or social groups (or may we be allowed to add social institutions) but with equal legitimacy under the scheme of social acts or social persons. The first group of schemes of reference is the objective one; such a scheme will do good service if applied exclusively to problems belonging to the sphere of objective phenomena for whose explanation its specific idealizations and formalizations have been designed, provided, however, that they do not contain any inconsistent element or elements incompatible with the other schemes (the subjective) and with our common-sense experience of the social world in general. Mutatis mutandis the same thesis is valid for the subjective schemes.[1]

In other words, the scientific observer's decision to study the social world under an objective or subjective frame of reference circumscribes from the beginning the section of the social world (or, at least, the aspect of such a section) which is capable of being studied under the scheme chosen once and for all. The basic postulate of the methodology of social science, therefore, must be the following: choose the scheme of reference adequate to the problem you are interested in, consider its limits and possibilities, make its terms compatible and consistent with one another, and having once accepted it, stick to it! If, on the other hand, the ramifications of your problem lead you in the progress of your work to the acceptance of other schemes of reference and interpretation, do not forget that with the change in the scheme all terms in the formerly used scheme necessarily undergo a shift of meaning. To preserve the consistency of your thought you have to see to it that the "subscript" of all the terms and concepts you use is the same!

This is the real meaning of the so often misunderstood postulate of "purity of method." It is harder than it seems to comply with it. Most of the fallacies in the social sciences can be reduced to a mergence of subjective and objective points of view which, unnoticed by the scientist, arose in the process of transgressing from one level to the other in the continuation of the scientific work. These are the dangers that the mixing up of subjective and objective points of view would involve in the concrete work of social scientists. But for a theory of action the subjective point of view

[1]   To be as precise as possible: on the level of what we have just called objective schemes the dichotomy of subjective and objective points of view does not even become visible. It emerges at all within the basic assumption that the social world *may* be referred to activities of individual human beings and to the meaning those individuals bestow on their social life-world. But precisely this basic assumption which alone makes the problem of subjectivity in the social sciences accessible is that of modern sociology.

must be retained in its fullest strength, in default of which such a theory loses its basic foundations, namely its reference to the social world of everyday life and experience. The safeguarding of the subjective point of view is the only but sufficient guarantee that the world of social reality will not be replaced by a fictional non-existing world constructed by the scientific observer.

ON THE UNITY OF THE SCIENCES   A word on the problem of the methodological unity of the empirical sciences. It seems to me that the social scientist can agree with the statement that the principal differences between the social and the natural sciences have not to be looked for in a different logic governing each branch of knowledge. But this does not involve the admittance that the social sciences have to abandon the particular devices they use for exploring social reality for the sake of an ideal unity of methods which is founded on the entirely unwarranted assumption that only methods used by the natural sciences, and especially by physics, are scientific ones. So far as I know no serious attempt has ever been made by the proponents of the "unity of science" movement to answer or even to ask the question whether the methodological problem of the natural sciences in their present state is not merely a special case of the more general, still unexplored, problem how scientific knowledge is possible at all and what its logical and methodological presuppositions are. It is my personal conviction that phenomenological philosophy has prepared the ground for such an investigation. Its outcome might quite possibly show that the particular methodological devices developed by the social sciences in order to grasp social reality, are better suited than those of the natural sciences to lead to the discovery of the general principles which govern all human knowledge.

THE BASIC SUBJECT MATTER OF SOCIOLOGY   Philosophers as different as James, Bergson, Dewey, Husserl, and Whitehead agree that the common-sense knowledge of everyday life is the unquestioned but always questionable background within which inquiry starts and within which alone it can be carried out. It is this *Lebenswelt,* as Husserl calls it, within which, according to him, all scientific and even logical concepts originate; it is the social matrix within which, according to Dewey, unclarified situations emerge, which have to be transformed by the process of inquiry into warranted assertibility; and Whitehead has pointed out that it is the aim of science to produce a theory which agrees with experience by explaining the thought-objects constructed by common sense through the mental constructs or thought objects of science. For all these thinkers agree that any knowledge of the world, in common-sense thinking as well as in science, involves mental constructs, syntheses, generalizations, formalizations, idealizations specific to the respective level of thought organization. The concept of Nature, for instance, with which the natural sciences have to deal is, as Husserl has shown, an idealizing abstraction from the *Lebenswelt*, an abstraction which, on principle and of course legitimately, excludes persons with their personal life and all objects of culture which originate as such in practical human activity. Exactly this layer of the *Lebenswelt*, however, from which the natural sciences have to abstract, is the social reality which the social sciences have to investigate.

. . . A theory which aims at explaining social reality has to develop particular devices foreign to the natural sciences in order to agree with the common-sense experience of the social world. This is indeed what all theoretical sciences of human affairs—economics, sociology, the sciences of law, linguistics, cultural anthropology, etc.—have done.

This state of affairs is founded on the fact that there is an essential difference in the structure of the thought objects or mental constructs formed by the social sciences and those formed by the natural sciences. It is up to the natural scientist and to him alone to define, in accordance with the procedural rules of his science, his observational field, and to determine the facts, data, and events within it which are relevant for his problem or scientific purpose at hand. Neither are those facts and events pre-selected, nor is the observational field pre-interpreted. The world of nature, as explored by the natural scientist, does not "mean" anything to the molecules, atoms, and electrons therein. The observational field of the social scientist, however, namely the social reality, has a specific meaning and relevance structure for the human beings living, acting, and thinking therein. By a series of common-sense constructs they have pre-selected and pre-interpreted this world which they experience as the reality of their daily lives. It is these thought objects of theirs which determine their behavior by motivating it. The thought objects constructed by the social scientist, in order to grasp this social reality, have to be founded upon the thought objects constructed by the common-sense thinking of men, living their daily life within their social world. Thus, the constructs of the social sciences are, so to speak, constructs of the second degree, namely constructs of the constructs made by the actors on the social scene, whose behavior the social scientist has to observe and to explain in accordance with the procedural rules of his science.

Thus, the exploration of the general principles according to which man in daily life organizes his experiences, and especially those of the social world, is the first task of the methodology of the social sciences.

SOCIOLOGY OF UNDERSTANDING   The fact that in common-sense thinking we take for granted our actual or potential knowledge of the meaning of human actions and their products, is, so I submit, precisely what social scientists want to express if they speak of understanding or *Verstehen* as a technique of dealing with human affairs. *Verstehen* is, thus, primarily not a method used by the social scientist, but the particular experiential form in which common-sense thinking takes cognizance of the social cultural world. It has nothing to do with introspection, it is a result of processes of learning or acculturation in the same way as the common-sense experience of the so-called natural world. *Verstehen* is, moreover, by no means a private affair of the observer which cannot be controlled by the experiences of other observers. It is controllable at least to the same extent to which the private sensory perceptions of an individual are controllable by any other individual under certain conditions. You have just to think of the discussion by a trial-jury whether the defendant has shown "premeditated malice" or "intent" in killing a person, whether he was capable of knowing the consequences of his deed, etc. Here we even have certain "rules of procedure" furnished by the "rules of evidence" in the juridical sense and a kind of verification of the findings resulting from processes of *Verstehen* by the Appellate Court, etc. Moreover, predictions based on *Verstehen* are continuously and with high success made in common-sense thinking. There is more than a fair chance that a duly stamped and addressed letter put in a New York mailbox will reach the addressee in Chicago.

Nevertheless, both defenders and critics of the process of *Verstehen* maintain, and with good reason, that *Verstehen* is "subjective." Unfortunately, however, this term is used by each party in a different sense. The critics of understanding call it subjective, because they hold that understanding the motives of another man's action depends upon the private, uncontrollable, and unverifiable intuition of the observer or refers to his private value system. The social scientists, such as Max Weber, however, call *Verstehen* subjective because its goal is to find out what the actor "means" in his action, in contrast to the meaning which this action has for the actor's partner or a neutral observer. This is the origin of Max Weber's famous postulate of subjective interpretation. . . . The whole discussion suffers from the failure to distinguish clearly between *Verstehen* (1) as the experiential form of common-sense knowledge of human affairs, (2) as an epistemological problem, and (3) as a method peculiar to the social sciences.

SUBJECTIVE INTERPRETATION　The constructs involved in common-sense experience of the intersubjective world in daily life, which is called *Verstehen* . . . are the first-level constructs upon which the second-level constructs of the social sciences have to be erected. . . . It has been shown that the constructs on the first level, the common-sense constructs, refer to subjective elements, namely the *Verstehen* of the actor's action from his, the actor's, point of view. Consequently, if the social sciences aim indeed at explaining social reality, then the scientific constructs on the second level, too, must include a reference to the subjective meaning an action has for the actor. This is, I think, what Max Weber understood by his famous postulate of subjective interpretation, which has, indeed, been observed so far in the theory-formation of all social sciences. The postulate of subjective interpretation has to be understood in the sense that all scientific explanations of the social world *can*, and for certain purposes *must*, refer to the subjective meaning of the actions of human beings from which the social reality originates. . . .

How is it possible to form objective concepts and an objectively verifiable theory of subjective meaning-structures? The basic insight that the concepts formed by the social scientist are constructs of the constructs formed in common-sense thinking by the actors on the social scene offers an answer. The scientific constructs formed on the second level, in accordance with the procedural rules valid for all empirical sciences, are objective ideal typical constructs and, as such, of a different kind from those developed on the first level of common-sense thinking which they have to supersede. They are theoretical systems embodying testable general hypotheses.

II. *Observation, Conceptualization, Ideal Types*

THE STANCE OF THE SOCIOLOGICAL OBSERVER It is . . . the particular problem of the social sciences to develop methodological devices for attaining objective and verifiable knowledge of a subjective meaning structure. In order to make this clear we have to consider very briefly the particular attitude of the scientist to the social world.

This attitude of the social scientist is that of a mere disinterested observer of the social world. He is not involved in the observed situation, which is to him not of practical but merely of cognitive interest. It is not the theater of his activities but merely the object of his contemplation. He does not act within it, vitally interested in the outcome of his actions, hoping or fearing what their consequences might be but he looks at it with the same detached equanimity with which the natural scientist looks at the occurrences in his laboratory. . . . By resolving to adopt the disinterested attitude of a scientific observer—in our language: by establishing the life-plan for scientific work—the social scientist detaches himself from his biographical situation within the social world. What is taken for granted in the biographical situation of daily life may become questionable for the scientist and vice versa; what seems to be of highest relevance on one level may become entirely irrelevant on the other. The center of orientation has been radically shifted and so has the hierarchy of plans and projects. By making up his mind to carry out a plan for scientific work governed by the disinterested quest for truth in accordance with pre-established rules, called the scientific method, the scientist has entered a field of pre-organized knowledge, called the corpus of his science. He has either to accept what is considered by his fellow-scientist as established knowledge or to "show cause" why he cannot do so. Merely within this frame he may select his particular scientific problem and make his scientific decisions. This frame constitutes his "being in a scientific situation" which supersedes his biographical situation as a human being within the world. It is henceforth the scientific problem once established which determines alone what is and what is not relevant to its solution, therewith what has to be investigated and what can be taken for granted as a "datum," and, finally, the level of research in the broadest sense, that is, the abstractions, generalizations, formalizations, idealizations, briefly: the constructs required and admissible for considering the problem as being solved. In other words, the scientific problem is the "locus" of all possible constructs relevant to its solution, and each construct carries along—to borrow a mathematical term—a subscript referring to the problem for the sake of which it has been established. It follows that any shifting of the problem under scrutiny and the level of research involves a modification of the structures of relevance and of the constructs formed for the solution of another problem or on another level; a great many misunderstandings and controversies especially in the social sciences originate from disregarding this fact.

FORMATION OF SOCIOLOGICAL CONSTRUCTS   The social scientist has no "Here" within the social world or, more precisely, he considers his position within it and the system of relevances attached thereto as irrelevant for his scientific undertaking. His stock of knowledge at hand is the corpus of his science and he has to take it for granted—which means in this context: as scientifically ascertained—unless he makes explicit why he cannot do so. To this corpus of science belong also the rules of procedure which have stood the test, namely, the methods of his science, including the methods of forming constructs in a scientifically sound way. This stock of knowledge is of quite another structure than that which man in everyday life has at hand. To be sure, it will also show manifold degrees of clarity and distinctness. But this structurization will depend upon knowledge of problems solved, of their still hidden implications and open horizons of other still not formulated problems. The scientist takes for granted what he defines to be a datum, and this is independent of the beliefs accepted by any in-group in the world of everyday life. The scientific problem, once established, determines alone the structure of relevances.

Having no "Here" within the social world the social scientist does not organize this world in layers around himself as the center. He can never enter as a consociate in an interaction pattern with one of the actors on the social scene without abandoning, at least temporarily, his scientific attitude. The participant observer or field worker establishes contact with the group studied as a man among fellowmen; only his system of relevances which serves as the scheme of his selection and interpretation is determined by the scientific attitude, temporarily dropped in order to be resumed again.

Thus, adopting the scientific attitude, the social scientist observes human interaction patterns or their results insofar as they are accessible to his observation and open to his interpretation. These interaction patterns, however, he has to interpret in terms of their subjective meaning structure lest he abandon any hope of grasping "social reality."

In order to comply with this postulate the scientific observer proceeds in a similar way as the observer of a social interaction pattern in the world of everyday life, although guided by an entirely different system of relevances.

SOCIOLOGICAL RELEVANCE   In a scientific system the problem has exactly the same significance for the scientific activity as the practical interests have for activities in every-day work. The scientific problem as formulated has a two-fold function:

(*a*) It determines the limits within which possible propositions become relevant to the inquiry. It thus creates the realm of the scientific subject matter within which all concepts must be compatible.

(*b*) The simple fact that a problem is raised creates a scheme of reference for the construction of all ideal types which may be utilised as relevant.

For the better understanding of the last remark we have to consider that the concept "type" is not an independent one but always needs a supplement. We cannot speak simply of an "ideal type" as such; we must indicate the reference scheme within which this ideal type may be utilised, that is, the problem for the sake of which the type has been constructed.

POSTULATES FOR THE CONSTRUCTION OF CONCEPTS OF HUMAN ACTION   It is the main problem of the social sciences to develop a method in order to deal in an objective way with the subjective meaning of human action and that the thought of the social sciences have to remain consistent with the thought objects of common sense, formed by men in everyday life in order to come to terms with the social reality. The model constructs as described before fulfill these requirements if they are formed in accordance with the following postulates:

(1) *The postulate of logical consistency.* The system of typical constructs designed by the scientist has to be established with the highest degree of clarity and distinctness of the conceptual framework implied and must be fully compatible with the principles of formal logic. Fulfillment of this postulate warrants the objective validity of the thought objects constructed by the social scientist and their strictly logical character is one of the most important features by which scientific thought objects are distinguished from the thought objects constructed by common-sense thinking in daily life which they have to supersede.

(2) *The postulate of subjective interpretation.* In order to explain human actions the scientist has to ask what model of an individual mind can be constructed and what typical contents must be attributed to it in order to explain the observed facts as the result of the activity of such a mind in an understandable relation. The compliance with this postulate warrants the possibility of referring all kinds of human action or their result to the subjective meaning such action or result of an action had for the actor.

(3) *The postulate of adequacy.* Each term in a scientific model of human action must be constructed in such a way that a human act performed within the life world by an individual actor in the way indicated by the typical construct would be understandable for the actor himself as well as for his fellow-men in terms of common-sense interpretation of everyday life. Compliance with this postulate warrants the consistency of the constructs of the social scientist with the constructs of common-sense experience of the social reality.

MODELS OF RATIONAL ACTION   All model constructs of the social world in order to be scientific have to fulfill the requirements of these three postulates. But is not any construct complying with the postulate of logical consistency, is not any scientific activity by definition a rational one?

This is certainly true but here we have to avoid a dangerous misunderstanding. We have to distinguish between rational constructs of models of human actions on the one hand, and constructs of models of rational human actions on the other. Science may construct rational models of irrational behavior, as a glance in any textbook of psychiatry shows. On the other hand, common-sense thinking frequently constructs irrational models of highly rational behavior, for example, in explaining economic, political, military and even scientific decisions by referring them to sentiments or ideologies presupposed to govern the behavior of the participants. The rationality of the construction of the model is one thing and in this sense all properly constructed models of the sciences—not merely of the social sciences—are rational; the construction of models of rational behavior is quite another thing. It would be a serious misunderstanding to believe that it is the purpose of model constructs in the social sciences or a criterion for their scientific character that irrational behavior patterns be interpreted as if they were rational.

In the following we are mainly interested in the usefulness of scientific—therefore rational—models of rational behavior patterns. It can easily be understood that the scientific construct of a perfect rational course-of-action type, of its corresponding personal type and also of rational interaction patterns is, as a matter of principle, possible. This is so because in constructing a model of a fictitious consciousness the scientist may select as relevant for his problem merely those elements which make rational actions or reactions of his homunculi possible. The postulate of rationality which such a construct would have to meet can be formulated as follows:

The rational course-of-action and personal types have to be constructed in such a way that an actor in the life world would perform the typified action if he had a perfectly clear and distinct knowledge of all the elements, and only of the elements, assumed by the social scientist as being relevant to this action and the constant tendency to use the most appropriate means assumed to be at his disposal for achieving the ends defined by the construct itself.

The advantages of the use of such models of rational behavior in the social sciences can be characterized as follows:

(1) The possibility of constructing patterns of social interaction under the assumption that all participants in such interaction act rationally within a set of conditions, means, ends, motives defined by the social scientist and supposed to be either common to all participants or distributed among them in a specific manner. By this arrangement standardized behavior such as so-called social roles, institutional behavior, etc. can be studied in isolation.

(2) Whereas the behavior of individuals in the social life world is not predictable unless in empty anticipations, the rational behavior of a constructed personal type is by definition supposed to be predictable, namely, within the limits of the elements typified in the construct. The model of rational action can, therefore, be used as a device for ascertaining deviating behavior in the real so-

cial world and for referring it to "problem-transcending data," namely, to non-typified elements.

(3) By appropriate variations of some of the elements several models or even sets of models of rational actions can be constructed for solving the same scientific problem and compared with one another.

The last point, however, seems to require some comment. Did we not state earlier that all constructs carry along a "subscript" referring to the problem under scrutiny and have to be revised if a shift in the problem occurs? Is there not a certain contradiction between this insight and the possibility of constructing several competing models for the solution of one and the same scientific problem?

The contradiction disappears if we consider that any problem is merely a locus of implications which can be made explicit or, to use a term of Husserl's, that it carries along its inner horizon of unquestioned but questionable elements.

In order to make the inner horizon of the problem explicit we may vary the conditions within which the fictitious actors are supposed to act, the elements of the world of which they are supposed to have knowledge, their assumed interlocked motives, the degree of familiarity or anonymity in which they are assumed to be interrelated, etc. I may, for example, construct as an economist concerned with the theory of oligopoly,[2] models of a single firm or of an industry or of the economic system as a whole. If restricting myself to the theory of the individual firm (say, if analyzing the effects of a cartel agreement on the output of the commodity concerned), I may construct a model of a producer acting under conditions of unregulated competition, another of a producer with the same cost-conditions acting under the cartel restrictions imposed upon him and with the knowledge of similar restrictions imposed on the other suppliers of the "same" commodity. We can then compare the output of "the" firm in the two models.

[2]   I gratefully acknowledge the permission of my friend, Professor Fritz Machlup, to borrow the following examples from his book *The Economics of Seller's Competition Model Analysis of Seller's Conduct* (Baltimore, 1952), pp. 4 ff.

All these models are models of rational actions but not of actions performed by living human beings in situations defined by them. They are assumed to be performable by the personal types constructed by the economist within the artificial environment in which he has placed his homunculi.

WHY IDEAL TYPES OF SUBJECTIVE CONDUCT?   Why form personal ideal types at all? Why not simply collect empirical facts? Or, if the technique of typological interpretation may be applied successfully, why not restrict oneself to forming types of impersonal events, or types of the behaviour of groups? . . . Why go back to the scheme of social action and to the individual actor?

The answer is this: It is true that a very great part of social science can be performed and has been performed at a level which legitimately abstracts from all that happens in the individual actor. But this operating with generalisations and idealisations on a high level of abstraction is in any case nothing but a kind of intellectual shorthand. Whenever the problem under inquiry makes it necessary, the social scientist must have the possibility of shifting the level of his research to that of individual human activity, and where real scientific work is done this shift will always become possible.

The real reason for this is that we cannot deal with phenomena in the social world as we do with phenomena belonging to the natural sphere. In the latter, we collect facts and regularities which are not understandable to us, but which we can refer only to certain fundamental assumptions about the world. We shall never understand why the mercury in the thermometer rises if the sun shines on it. We can only interpret this phenomenon as compatible with the laws we have deduced from some basic assumption about the physical world. Social phenomena, on the contrary, we want to understand and we cannot understand them otherwise than within the scheme of human motives, human means and ends, human planning—in short—within the categories of human action.

The social scientist must therefore ask, or he must, at least, always be in a position to ask, what happens in the mind of an individual actor whose act has led to the phenomenon in question.

KINDS OF IDEAL TYPES   We understand the behavior of others in terms of ideal types. . . . The process consist[s] essentially of taking a cross-section of our experience of another person and, so to speak, "freezing it into a slide." . . . This is done by means of a synthesis of recognition. However, there is something ambiguous about this concept of an ideal type of human behavior. It denotes at one and the same time ideal types covering (1) pre-given objective meaning-contexts, (2) products, (3) courses of action, and (4) real and ideal objects, whenever any of the above are the result of human behavior. Included also would be interpretations of the products of ideal-typical behavior. The latter are the interpretations to which we resort when we know nothing of the individual experiences of those who created these products. Whenever we come upon any ordering of past experience under interpretive schmes, any act of abstraction, generalization, formalization, or idealization, whatever the object involved, there we shall find this process in which a moment of living experience is lifted out of its setting and then, through a synthesis of recognition, frozen into a hard and fast "ideal type." Insofar as the term "ideal type" can be applied to any interpretive scheme under which experience is subsumed—as in Max Weber's early writings—it raises no special problem for the social scientist. We could speak in exactly the same sense of ideal types of physical objects and processes, of meteorological patterns, of evolutionary series in biology, and so forth. How useful the concept of ideal types would be in these fields is not for us to say, since we are concerned here with a specific group of problems in the social sciences.

The concept "ideal type of human behavior" can be taken in two ways. It can mean first of all the ideal type of another person who is expressing himself or has expressed himself in a certain way. Or it may mean, second, the ideal type of the expressive process itself, or even of the outward results which we interpret as the signs of the expressive process. Let us call the first the "personal ideal type"* and the second the "material" or "course-of-action

---

*   EDITOR'S NOTE: The elementary aspects of this type have been discussed under the subheading "Personal Ideal Types" in chapter 10.

type." Certainly an inner relation exists between these two. I cannot, for instance, define the ideal type of a postal clerk without first having in mind a definition of his job. The latter is a course-of-action type, which is, of course, an objective context of meaning. Once I am clear as to the course-of-action type, I can construct the personal ideal type, that is "the person who performs this job." And, in doing so, I imagine the corresponding subjective meaning-contexts which would be in his mind, the subjective contexts that would have to be adequate to the objective contexts already defined. The personal ideal type is therefore *derivative,* and the course-of-action type can be considered quite independently as a purely objective context of meaning.

PERSONAL TYPE AND COURSE-OF-ACTION TYPE   By looking at language we can see the personal ideal type in the very process of construction. I am referring to those nouns which are merely verbs erected into substantives. Thus every present participle is the personal typification of an act in progress, and every past participle is the ideal type of a completed act. Acting is that act may be. Consequently, when I seek to understand another's behavior in ideal-typical fashion, a twofold method is available to me. I can begin with the finished act, then determine the type of action that produced it, and finally settle upon the type of person who must have acted in this way. Or I can reverse the process and, knowing the personal ideal type, deduce the corresponding act. We have, therefore, to deal with two different problems. One problem concerns which aspects of a finished act[3] are selected as typical and how we deduce the personal type from the course-of-action type. The other problem concerns how we deduce specific actions from a given personal ideal type. The first question is a general question about the genesis of the typical. It has to do with the constitution of ideal types—whether course-of-action types or personal types—from given concrete acts. The second question has to do with the deduction of an action from a personal ideal type, and we shall

---

[3]   For the sake of convenience we are dealing here only with acts, but our remarks can be applied *pari passu* to products of all kinds and to their generation.

deal with it under the heading "the freedom of the personal ideal type."

Let us first clarify the point that the understanding of personal ideal types is based on the understanding of course-of-action types.

In the process of understanding a given performance via an ideal type, the interpreter must start with his own perceptions of someone else's manifest act. His goal is to discover the in-order-to or because-motives (whichever is convenient) behind that act. He does this by interpreting the act within an objective context of meaning in the sense that the same motive is assigned to any act that repeatedly achieves the same end through the same means. This motive is postulated as constant for the act regardless of who performs the act or what his subjective experiences are at the time. For a personal ideal type, therefore, there is one and only one typical motive for a typical act. Excluded from consideration when we think of the personal ideal type are such things as the individual's subjective experience of his act within his stream of consciousness, together with all the modifications of attention and all the influences from the background of his consciousness which such experiences may undergo. Ideal-typical understanding, then, characteristically deduces the in-order-to and because-motives of a manifest act by identifying the constantly achieved goal of that act. Since the act is by definition both repeatable and typical, so is the in-order-to motive. The next step is to postulate an agent behind the action, a person who, with a typical modification of attention, typically intends this typical act—in short, a personal ideal type.

The conscious processes of the personal ideal types are, therefore, logical constructions. They are deduced from the manifest act and are pictured as temporally prior to that act, in other words, in the pluperfect tense. The manifest act is then seen as the regular and repeatable result of these inferred conscious processes. It should be noted that the conscious processes themselves are conceived in a simplified and tailored form. They are lacking all the empty protentions and expectations that accompany real conscious experiences. It is not an open question as to whether the typical action will succeed in being a finished act. Such success has been built into it by definition. The ideal-typical actor never has the

The action is thoroughly rational

based on

its accomplishment.

experience of choosing or of preferring one thing to another. Never does he hesitate or try to make up his mind whether to perform a typical or an atypical action. His motive is always perfectly straightforward and definite: the in-order-to motive of the action is the completed act on whose definition the whole typification is based. This completed act is at the same time the *major* goal of the actor's typical state of mind at that time. For if the act were merely a means to another goal, then it would be necessary for the inter-preter to construct for his ideal actor another typical state of mind capable of planning out that wider goal. This would mean that the wider goal would have to become the objective meaning-context of primary importance from the interpreter's point of view. In other words, the wider goal would be the one in terms of which the act would be defined. Finally, all this will hold true for the construc-tion of the genuine because-motive. This must be postulated in some typical experience or passage of experience that could have given rise to the in-order-to motive we have already constructed.

and defined ultimately by a because motive

The following, then, is the way in which a personal ideal type is constructed: The existence of a person is postulated whose actual living motive could be the object context of meaning already chosen to define a typical action. This person must be one in whose consciousness the action in question could have been constructed step by step in polythetic Acts. He must be the person whose own lived experiences provide the subjective context of meaning which corresponds to the objective context, the action which corresponds to the act.

And now we see the basic reason why, in both the social sci-ences and the everyday understanding of another's behavior, we can ignore the "total action" in the sense that the latter concept includes the ultimate roots of the action in the person's conscious-ness. The technique of constructing personal ideal types consists in postulating persons who can be motivated by the already defined material ideal type. The manifest act or external course of action which the observer sees as a unity is changed back into a subjective context of meaning and is inserted into the consciousness of the personal ideal type. But the unity of this subjective context derives entirely from the original objective context of meaning, the context of meaning which is the very basis of the personal ideal type. And we cannot too strongly emphasize that this unity of "the other person's action" is only a cross-section which the observer lifts out of its total factual context. What is thus defined in abstraction as the unity of the other person's act will depend on the point of view of the observer, which will vary in turn with his interests and his problems. This point of view will determine both the meaning which the observer gives to his own perceptions of the act and the typical motive which he assigns to it. But for every such typical motive, for every such frozen cross-section of consciousness, there is a corresponding personal ideal type which could be subjectively motivated in the manner in question. Therefore, the personal ideal type is itself always determined by the interpreter's point of view. *It is a function of the very question it seeks to answer.* It is dependent upon the objective context of meaning, which it merely translates into subjective terms and then personifies.

THE IDEAL-TYPICAL PUPPET   The puppet called "personal ideal type" is . . . never a subject or a center of spontaneous activity. He does not have the task of mastering the world, and, strictly speaking, he has no world at all. His destiny is regulated and determined by his creator, the social scientist, and in such a perfect pre-established harmony as Leibnitz imagined the world created by God. By the grace of its constructor, he is endowed with just that kind of knowledge he needs to perform the job for the sake of which he was brought into the scientific world. The scientist distributes his own store of experience, and that means of scientific experience in clear and distinct terms, among the puppets with which he peoples the social world. But this social world, too, is organized in quite another way; it is not centered in the ideal type; it lacks the categories of intimacy and anonymity, of familiarity and strangeness: in short, it lacks the basic character of perspective appearance. What counts is the point of view from which the *scientist* envisages the social world. This point of view defines the general perspective framework in which the chosen sector of the social world presents itself to the scientific observer as well as to the fictitious consciousness of the puppet type. This central point of view of the scientist is called his "scientific problem under examination."

HABITUAL IDEAL TYPE* A "characterological" type . . . should be distinguished from a "habitual" type, which defines a contemporary solely in terms of his functions. The concept of a postal clerk, for instance, is a habitual type. The postal clerk is by definition "he who forwards the mail. . . . A habitual type is therefore less concrete than a characterological type. It is based on a course-of-action type which it presupposes and refers to. The characterological type, on the other hand, presupposes and refers to a real person whom I could meet face to face. Furthermore, the habitual type is more anonymous. As a matter of fact, when I drop the letter in the box, I don't even need to have in mind the personal type "postal clerk" in the sense of thinking of an individual who has certain specific subjective meaning-contexts in mind as he goes about his work, such as thinking of receiving payment. The only thing relevant for me in this situation is the *process* of forwarding, and I merely "hang" this on the abstract type "postal clerk." And I don't even have to think of a postal clerk as such as I mail the letter. It is enough for me to know that somehow it will reach its destination.

Under the heading of habitual types come those types which deal with the "behaving" or the "habit." The fixation in conceptual form of external modes of behavior or sequences of action, derived from either direct or indirect observation, leads to a catalogue of

---

* EDITOR'S NOTE: In the course of his initial discussion of ideal types, Schutz considered the construction of such types in conjunction with the formation of ideal types in everyday life. Being concerned with the degree of concreteness or abstractness involved in particular type concepts, he distinguished the relatively concrete, relatively close-to-life type concepts formed by a person of other persons with whom he is directly or indirectly acquainted, and type concepts oriented solely on an established social role, a standardized function, etc. The first type he called "characterological," thereby indicating that it referred back to the personality features, motivations, etc., of specific individuals. The second type he named "habitual." Both these types occur conspicuously in the world of everyday life. The second, however, is sociologically more significant.

material course-of-action types, to which corresponding personal types are then adjoined. But these course-of-action types can be of different degrees of generality: they can be more or less "standardized," that is, they can be derived from behavior of greater or lesser statistical frequency. The ideality of the personal ideal type based on such frequency types (in other words, the irreducibility of the kinds of behavior to the conscious experiences of real other people) is, however, in principle independent of the degree of generality of the behavior itself. On the other hand, the "standardization" of typified behavior can in turn refer back to a previously constructed personal ideal type. Let us take as an example Weber's "traditional behavior," "the great bulk of all everyday action to which people have become habitually accustomed," which is already based on the previously constructed personal ideal type of the man who acts according to custom; and, as an additional example, let us take all behavior oriented to the validity of an order. This latter means, in terms of the constitution of ideal types of contemporaries, that the valid order functions as an interpretive scheme for them. It establishes as required conduct definite patterns of action and definite personal ideal types, to the extent that the person accepting such standard types and orienting himself to them can be assured that his behavior will be adequately interpreted by contemporaries oriented to the same order. . . . The point of importance for us here is that even behavior that is oriented to the validity of an order is, in our sense of the term, habitual behavior. Our concept of the habitual is, therefore, broader than that found in ordinary usage.

IDEAL TYPES OF COLLECTIVES   There are other ideal types that are characterized by a still greater degree of anonymity than the habitual ideal types. The first group of these consists of the so-called "social collectives," all of which are constructs referring to the world of contemporaries.

This large class contains ideal types of quite different degrees of anonymity. The board of directors of a given corporation or the United States Senate are relatively concrete ideal types, and the number of other ideal types which they presuppose is quite limited.

But we frequently use sentences in which ideal types like "the state," "the press," "the economy," "the nation," "the people," or perhaps "the working class" appear as grammatical subjects. In doing this, we naturally tend to personify these abstractions, treating them as if they were real persons known in indirect social experience. But we are here indulging in an anthropomorphism. Actually these ideal types are absolutely anonymous. Any attribution of behavior we make to the type permits no inference whatever as to a corresponding subjective meaning-context in the mind of a contemporary actor. "For the subjective interpretation of action in sociological work," says Max Weber,

these collectivities must be treated as solely the resultants and modes of organization of the particular acts of individual persons, since these alone can be treated as agents in a course of subjectively understandable action. . . . For sociological purposes . . . there is no such thing as a collective personality which "acts." When reference is made in a sociological context to a "state," a "nation," a "corporation," a "family" or an "army corps," or to similar collectivities, what is meant is, on the contrary, *only* a certain kind of development of actual or possible social actions of the individual persons.[4]

In fact, every "action" of the state can be reduced to the actions of its functionaries, whom we can apprehend by means of personal ideal types and toward whom we can assume a They-orientation, regarding them as our contemporaries. From the sociological point of view, therefore, the term "state" is merely an abbreviation for a highly complex network of interdependent personal ideal types. When we speak of any collectivity as "acting," we take this complex structural arrangement for granted. We then proceed to attribute the objective meaning-contexts, in terms of which we understand the anonymous acts of the functionaries, to the personal ideal type of the social collective. We do this in a manner that parallels our interpretation of individual actions by means of typical conscious experiences in the minds of typical actors. But when we proceed in this way, we forget that, whereas the conscious

[4]   Weber, *The Theory of Social and Economic Organization* (New York: Oxford University Press, 1947), pp. 101, 102.

experiences of typical individuals are quite conceivable, the conscious experiences of a collective are not. What is lacking, therefore, in the concept of the "action" of a collective is precisely this subjective meaning-context as something that is even conceivable. That people should ever have been led to take such a metaphor literally can only be explained psychologically, that is, attributed to the fact that certain value systems have been at work here.

Needless to say, our reduction of statements about social collectives to personal ideal typifications does not foreclose a sociological analysis of these constructs. On the contrary, such an analysis is one of the most important tasks of sociology. Only a sociological theory of construct formation can bring to completion our previously postulated theory of the forms of the social world. Such a theory will have as its primary task the description of the stratification of social collectivities in terms of their relative anonymity or concreteness. Here it will be crucial to determine whether a social collectivity is essentially based on a direct or an indirect social relationship, or possibly on a relationship of both kinds, existing between the component individuals. It will also be necessary to study the exact sense, if any, in which a subjective meaning-context can be ascribed to a social collectivity. This will involve determining whether, by the subjective meaning-contexts of a collectivity, we do not really mean those of its functionaries. This is the problem of the responsibility of officials, a question of major importance in the fields of constitutional and international law. Another question deserving investigation is whether and to what extent the concept of social collectivity can serve as a scheme of interpretation for the actions of contemporaries, since it is itself a function of certain objective standards common to a certain group. Such standards may be matters of habitual conduct, of traditional attitude, of belief in the validity of some order or norm, and they may be not only taken for granted but obeyed. Here, indeed, is one legitimate sense in which one can speak of the subjective meaning of a social collectivity.

IDEAL TYPES OF LANGUAGES AND CULTURAL OBJECTS What we have said about social collectivities holds true for languages as well. Here, too, a correlation can be set up between the product and that which produces it; we can hypostatize, for instance, an ideal anonymous "German speaker" corresponding to the German language. But here, as in the case we just discussed, we must beware of treating this typical speaker as a real individual with his own subjective contexts of meaning. It is quite illegitimate, for instance, to speak of an "objective language spirit,"[5] at least in the social sciences. Whether such concepts are permissible in other disciplines is not for us to say here.

These observations apply as well to all culture objects. To the ideal objectivity of a culture construct there corresponds no subjective meaning-context in the mind of a real individual whom we could meet face to face. Rather, corresponding to the objective meaning-context of the culture object we always find an abstract and anonymous personal ideal type of its producer toward which we characteristically assume a They-orientation.

Finally, this applies also to all artifacts such as tools and utensils. But to understand a tool, we need not only the ideal type of its producer but the ideal type of its user, and both will be absolutely anonymous. Whoever uses the tool will bring about typical results. A tool is a thing-in-order-to; it serves a purpose, and for the sake of this purpose it was produced. Tools are, therefore, results of past human acts and means toward the future realization of aims. One can, then, conceive the "meaning" of the tool in terms of the means-end relation. But from this objective meaning-context, that is, from the means-end relation in terms of which the tool is understood, one can deduce the ideal type of user or producer without thinking of them as real individual people. . . .

The artifact is the final member of the series of progressive anonymizations marking the typifying construction of the social world.

APPLICATION OF IDEAL TYPES   Let us remember the important distinction between the construction of the ideal type and

5   Cf. Vossler, *Geist und Kultur in der Sprache* (Heidelberg, 1925), pp. 153 f. [Translation by Oscar Oeser: *The Spirit of Language in Civilization* (London, 1932), p. 138.]

the application of this type as an interpretive scheme to real concrete actions. Let us take a case of interpreting a *future* action by
means of an ideal type. Our ideal type will be defined as having
definite and invariant motives, and from these motives we will be
able to deduce invariant acts and sequences of acts. Suppose that
our ideal type is that of a bureaucrat. Applying the type to a concrete person, I can say, "N is a typical bureaucrat; therefore we
may expect him to be visiting our office regularly." Or else, "N
has just performed action a; a corresponds to ideal type A; a' is
also characteristic of A; we may, therefore, expect N also to perform action a'." Now, how reliable are such judgments? Since
action a' is still in the future and therefore free, I cannot be certain
that N will perform it. The application of a personal ideal type to
a future action of another person is something that can only be
done with the assumption that it is *probably* correct. If the person
does not act as predicted, we must assume that we have applied the
wrong ideal type to the person in question. We will therefore look
around for *another* personal ideal type which *will* make his action
comprehensible. This principle will hold regardless of whether N
is immediately experienced or is himself known only as a type.
Now, the more freedom N has, the less anonymous he is, the closer
to the We-relationship he stands, the less likelihood will there be
that he will behave "according to ideal type." But if N himself is
no more than an ideal type, if his actions are controlled by his observer, then the ideal type must *always* receive positive verification,
must always "come out right" insofar as it was constructed according to a correct methodology, that is to say, in a manner that
is both adequate on the level of meaning and causally adequate.

14

SOCIOLOGICAL INQUIRIES

The Homecomer

The Phaeacian sailors deposited the sleeping Odysseus on the shore of Ithaca, his homeland, to reach which he had struggled for twenty years of unspeakable suffering. He stirred and woke from sleep in the land of his fathers, but he knew not his whereabouts. Ithaca showed to him an unaccustomed face; he did not recognize the pathways stretching far into the distance, the quiet bays, the crags and precipices. He rose to his feet and stood staring at what was his own land, crying mournfully: "Alas! and now where on earth am I? What do I here myself?" That he had been absent for so long was not the whole reason why he did not recognize his own country; in part it was because goddess Pallas Athene had thickened the air about him to keep him unknown "while she made him wise to things." Thus Homer tells the story of the most famous home-coming in the literature of the world.[1]

To the homecomer home shows—at least in the beginning—an unaccustomed face. He believes himself to be in a strange country, a stranger among strangers, until the goddess dissipates the veiling mist. But the homecomer's attitude differs from that of the stranger. The latter is about to join a group which is not and never has been his own. He knows that he will find himself in an unfamiliar world, differently organized than that from which he comes, full of pitfalls

---

Reprinted from the following items in the Bibliography: 1945*a*, 369–76; 1957*a*, 64, 72–78.

[1] The presentation follows the translation of Homer's *Odyssey* by T. E. Shaw ("Lawrence of Arabia") (New York: Oxford University Press, 1932).

and hard to master.[2] The homecomer, however, expects to return to an environment of which he always had and—so he thinks— still has intimate knowledge and which he has just to take for granted in order to find his bearings within it. The approaching stranger has to anticipate in a more or less empty way what he will find; the homecomer has just to recur to the memories of his past. So he feels; and because he feels, so he will suffer the typical shock described by Homer.

These typical experiences of the homecomer will be analyzed in the following *in general terms* of the social psychology. The returning veteran is, of course, an outstanding example of the situation under scrutiny. His special problems, however, have recently been widely discussed in many books and articles,[3] and it is not my aim to refer to them otherwise than as examples. We could refer also to the traveler who comes back from foreign countries, the emigrant who returns to his native land, the boy who "made good" abroad and now settles in his home town.[4] They all are instances of the "homecomer," defined as one who comes back for good to his home,—not as one returning for a temporary stay, such as the soldier on a thirty-day leave or the college boy spending the Christmas vacation with his family.

[2]   Cf. the present writer's paper "The Stranger," *American Journal of Sociology*, XLIX, No. 6 (May, 1944), 500–507.

[3]   We mention, in the first place, Professor Willard Waller's *Veteran Comes Back* (New York: Dryden Press, 1944), an excellent sociological analysis of the civilian made into a professional soldier and of the soldier-turned-veteran who comes back to an alien homeland; also—Professor Dixon Wecter, *When Johnny Comes Marching Home* (Cambridge, Mass.: Houghton, Mifflin, 1944), with valuable documents relating to the American soldier returning from four wars and very helpful bibliographical references; finally, the discussion of the veteran problem in the *New York Herald Tribune*, "Annual Forum on Current Problems," October 22, 1944 (Sec. VIII), especially the contributions of Mrs. Anna Rosenberg, Lieutenant Charles G. Bolte, and Sergeant William J. Caldwell. See also the very interesting collection of servicemen's *Letters Home*, arranged and edited by Mina Curtiss (Boston: Little, Brown, 1944).

[4]   Cf. the fine analysis of this situation in Thomas Wolfe's short story, "The Return of the Prodigal," in *The Hills Beyond* (New York: Harper & Bros., 1941).

What, however, has to be understood by "home"? "Home is where one starts from," says the poet.[5] "The home is the place to which a man intends to return when he is away from it," says the jurist.[6] The home is starting-point as well as terminus. It is the null-point of the system of co-ordinates which we ascribe to the world in order to find our bearings in it. Geographically "home" means a certain spot on the surface of the earth. Where I happen to be is my "abode"; where I intend to stay is my "residence"; where I come from and whither I want to return is my "home." Yet home is not merely the homestead—my house, my room, my garden, my town—but everything it stands for. The symbolic character of the notion "home" is emotionally evocative and hard to describe. Home means different things to different people. It means, of course, father-house and mother-tongue, the family, the sweetheart, the friends; it means a beloved landscape, "songs my mother taught me," food prepared in a particular way, familiar things for daily use, folkways, and personal habits—briefly, a peculiar way of life composed of small and important elements, likewise cherished. *Chevron,* a Marine Corps newspaper, inquired what United States soldiers in the South Pacific miss most, outside of families and sweethearts. Here are some of the answers: " 'A fresh lettuce and tomato sandwich with ice-cold fresh milk to wash it down.' 'Fresh milk and the morning paper at the front-door.' 'The smell of a drugstore.' 'A train and the engine whistle.' "[7] All these things, badly missed if not available, were probably not particularly appreciated so long as they were accessible at any time. They had just their humble place among the collective value "homely things." Thus, home means one thing to the man who never has left it, another thing to the man who dwells far from it, and still another to him who returns.

---

5   T. S. Eliot, *Four Quartets* (New York: Harcourt, Brace, 1943), p. 17.
6   Joseph H. Beale, *A Treatise on the Conflict of Laws* (New York: Baker, Voorhis, 1935), I, 126.
7   Quoted from *Time,* June 5, 1944; other examples can be found in Wecter, *op. cit.,* pp. 495 ff.

"To feel at home" is an expression of the highest degree of familiarity and intimacy. Life at home follows an organized pattern of routine; it has its well-determined goals and well-proved means to bring them about, consisting of a set of traditions, habits, institutions, timetables for activities of all kinds, etc. Most of the problems of daily life can be mastered by following this pattern. There is no need to define or redefine situations which have occurred so many times or to look for new solutions of old problems hitherto handled satisfactorily. The way of life at home governs as a scheme of expression and interpretation not only my own acts but also those of the other members of the in-group. I may trust that, using this scheme, I shall understand what the other means and make myself understandable to him. The system of relevances[8] adopted by the members of the in-group shows a high degree of conformity. I have always a fair chance—subjectively and objectively—to predict the other's action toward me as well as the other's reaction to my own social acts. We not only may forecast what will happen tomorrow, but we also have a fair chance to plan correctly the more distant future. Things will in substance continue to be what they have been so far. Of course, there are new situations, unexpected events. But at home, even deviations from the daily routine life are mastered in a way defined by the general style in which people at home deal with extraordinary situations. There is a way—a proved way—for meeting a crisis in business life, for settling family problems, for determining the attitude to adopt toward illness and even death. Paradoxically formulated, there is even a routine way for handling the novel.

In terms of social relationships, it could be said that life at home is, for the most part, actually or at least potentially life in so-called primary groups. This term was coined by Cooley[9] to designate intimate face-to-face relationship and has become a cur-

---

[8]   This term has been discussed in the afore-mentioned paper on "The Stranger," *loc. cit.*, pp. 500 ff.

[9]   Charles H. Cooley, *Social Organization* (New York: Scribners, 1909), chaps. iii–v.

rent, although contested,[10] feature of sociological textbooks. It will be helpful for our purpose to analyze some of the implications hidden in this highly equivocal term.

First of all, we have to distinguish between face-to-face relationships and intimate relationships. A face-to-face relationship presupposes that those who participate in it have space and time in common as long as the relation lasts. Community of space means, on the one hand, that for each partner the other's body, his facial expressions, his gestures, etc., are immediately observable as symptoms of his thought. The field of the other's expressions is wide open for possible interpretation, and the actor may control immediately and directly the effect of his own social acts by the reaction of his fellow. On the other hand, community of space means that a certain sector of the outer world is equally accessible to all the partners in the face-to-face relationship. The same things are within reach, within sight, within hearing, and so on. Within this common horizon there are objects of common interest and common relevance; things to work with or upon, actually or potentially. Community of time does not refer so much to the extent of outer (objective) time shared by the partners but to the fact that each of them participates in the onrolling inner life of the other. In the face-to-face relation I can grasp the other's thoughts in a vivid present as they develop and build themselves up, and so can he with reference to my stream of thought; and both of us know and take into account this possibility. The other is to me, and I am to the other, not an abstraction, not a mere instance of typical behavior, but, by the very reason of our sharing a common vivid present, this unique individual personality in this unique particular situation. These are, very roughly outlined, some of the features of the face-to-face relation which we prefer to call the "pure we-relation." It is,

[10]   Cf. R. M. MacIver, *Society* (New York: Farrar & Rinehart, 1937), chapter on the "Primary Group and Large Scale Association" (esp. p. 236 n.) ; Edward C. Jandy, *Charles H. Cooley, His Life and Social Theory* (New York: Dryden Press, 1942) ; pp. 171–81; Ellsworth Faris, "Primary Group, Essence and Accident," *American Journal of Sociology*, XXX (July, 1932), 41–45; Frederick R. Clow, "Cooley's Doctrine of Primary Groups," *American Journal of Sociology*, XXV (November, 1919), 326–47.

indeed, of outstanding importance in its own right because it can be shown that all other social relationships can, and for certain purposes have to be, interpreted as derived from the pure we-relation.

Yet it is important to understand that the pure we-relation refers merely to the formal structure of social relationships based upon community of space and time. It may be filled with a great variety of contents showing manifold degrees of intimacy and anonymity. To share the vivid present of a woman we love or of the neighbor in the subway are certainly different kinds of face-to-face relations. Cooley's concept of primary groups, however, presupposes a particular content of such a relationship—namely, intimacy.[11] We have to forego here the analysis of this ill-defined term which could be made explicit only by embarking upon an investigation of the layers of personality involved, the schemes of expression and interpretation presupposed, and the common system of relevance referred to by the partners. It suffices that the category of intimacy is independent of that of the face-to-face relation.

However, the term "primary group," as generally used, implies a third notion, which itself is independent of either of the two mentioned above, namely, the recurrent character of certain social relationships. It is by no means restricted to pure we-relations and to intimate relations, although we are going to choose our examples from them. A marriage, a friendship, a family group, a kindergarten, does not consist of a permanent, a strictly continuous, primary face-to-face relationship but rather of a series of merely intermittent face-to-face relationships. More precisely, the so-called "primary groups" are institutionalized situations which make it possible to re-establish the interrupted we-relation and to continue where it was broken off last time. There is, of course, no certainty, but just a mere chance, that such a re-establishment and continuation will succeed. But it is characteristic in the primary group as conceived by Cooley that the existence of such a chance is taken for granted by all its members.

After these parenthetical and all too casual explications, we may, for the present purpose, stick to our previous statement that

[11]   We disregard here entirely Cooley's untenable theory of "primary ideals," such as loyalty, truth, service, kindness, etc.

life at home means, for the most part, life in actual or potential primary groups. The meaning of this statement has now become clear. It means to have in common with others a section of space and time, and therewith surrounding objects as possible ends and means, and interests based upon an underlying more or less homogeneous system of relevances; it means, furthermore, that the partners in a primary relationship experience one another as unique personalities in a vivid present, by following their unfolding thought as an ongoing occurrence and by sharing, therefore, their anticipations of the future as plans, as hopes or as anxieties; it means, finally, that each of them has the chance to re-establish the we-relation, if interrupted, and to continue it as if no intermittance had occurred. To each of the partners the other's life becomes, thus, a part of his own autobiography, an element of his personal history. What he is, what he grew to be, what he will become is codetermined by his taking part in the manifold actual or potential primary relationships which prevail within the home-group.

This is the aspect of the social structure of the home world for the man who lives in it. The aspect changes entirely for the man who has left home. To him life at home is no longer accessible in immediacy. He has stepped, so to speak, into another social dimension not covered by the system of coordinates used as the scheme of reference for life at home. No longer does he experience as a participant in a vivid present the many we-relations which form the texture of the home group. His leaving home has replaced these vivid experiences with memories, and these memories preserve merely what home life meant up to the moment he left it behind. The ongoing development has come to a standstill. What has been so far a series of *unique* constellations, formed by individual persons, relations, and groups, receives the character of mere *types*; and this typification entails, by necessity, a deformation of the underlying structure of relevances. To a certain degree the same holds good for those left behind. By cutting off the community of space and time, for example, the field within which the other's expressions manifest themselves and are open to interpretation has been narrowed. The other's personality is no longer accessible as a unit; it has been broken down into pieces. There is no longer the total experience of the beloved person, his gestures, his way of walking and of speaking, of listening and of doing things; what remains are recollections, a photograph, some hand-written lines. This situation of the separated persons is, to a certain degree, that of those in bereavement; "partir, c'est mourir un peu."

To be sure, there still are means of communication, such as the letter. But the letter-writer addresses himself to the type of ad-dressee as he knew him when they separated, and the addressee reads the letter as written by the person typically the same as the one he left behind.[12] Presupposing such a typicality (and any typicality) means assuming that what has been proved to be typical in the past will have a good chance to be typical in the future, or, in other words, that life will continue to be what it has been so far: the same things will remain relevant, the same degree of intimacy in personal relationships will prevail, etc. Yet by the mere change of surroundings, other things have become important for both, old experiences are re-evaluated; novel ones, inaccessible to the other, have emerged in each partner's life. Many a soldier in the combat line is astonished to find letters from home lacking any understand-ing of his situation, because they underscore the relevance of things which are of no importance to him in his actual situation, although they would be the subject of many deliberations if he were at home and had to handle them. This change of the system of rele-vance has its corollary in the changing degree of intimacy. The term "intimacy" designates *here* merely the degree of reliable knowledge we have of another person or of a social relationship, a group, a cultural pattern, or a thing. As far as a person is con-cerned, intimate knowledge enables us to interpret what he means and to forecast his actions and reactions. In the highest form of intimacy, we know, to quote Kipling, the other's "naked soul." But separation conceals the other behind a strange disguise, hard to re-move. From the point of view of the absent one the longing for re-establishing the old intimacy—not only with persons but also with things—is the main feature of what is called "homesickness." Yet,

12   Cf. Georg Simmel's excellent analysis of the sociology of the letter in his *Soziologie, Untersuchungen über die Formen der Vergesellschaftung* (Leipzig, 1922), pp. 379–82.

the change in the system of relevance and in the degree of intimacy just described is differently experienced by the absent one and by the home group. The latter continues its daily life within the customary pattern. Certainly, this pattern, too, will have changed and even in a more or less abrupt way. But those at home, although aware of this change, lived together through this changing world, experienced it as changing in immediacy, adapted their interpretative system, and adjusted themselves to the change. In other words, the system may have changed entirely, but it changed as a system; it was never disrupted and broken down; even in its modification it is still an appropriate device for mastering life. The in-group has now other goals and other means for attaining them, but still it remains an in-group.

The absent one has the advantage of knowing the general style of this pattern. He may from previous experiences conclude what attitude mother will take to the task of running the household under the rationing system, how sister will feel in the war plant, what a Sunday means without pleasure driving.[13] Those left at home have no immediate experience of how the soldier lives at the front. There are reports in the newspapers and over the radio, recitals from homecomers, movies in technicolor, official and unofficial propaganda, all of which build up a stereotype of the soldier's life "somewhere in France" or "somewhere in the Pacific." For the most part, these stereotypes are not spontaneously formed but are directed, censored for military or political reasons, and designed to build up morale at the home front or to increase the efficiency of war production or the subscription of war bonds. There is no warrant whatsoever that what is described as typical by all these sources of information is also relevant to the absent member of the in-group. Any soldier knows that his style of living depends upon the military group to which he belongs, the job allotted to him within this group, the attitude of his officers and comrades.

---

[13]   This, of course, does not hold in case of a violent destruction of the home by catastrophies or enemy action. Then, however, not only may the general style of the pattern of home life have changed entirely but even the home itself may have ceased to exist. The absent one is then "homeless" in the true sense and has no place to return to.

That is what counts, and not the bulletin "All quiet on the western front." But whatever occurs to him under these particular circumstances is his individual, personal, unique experience which he never will allow to be typified. When the soldier returns and starts to speak—if he starts to speak at all—he is bewildered to see that his listeners, even the sympathetic ones, do not understand the uniqueness of these individual experiences which have rendered him another man. They try to find familiar traits in what he reports by subsuming it under *their* preformed types of the soldier's life at the front. To them there are only small details in which his recital deviates from what every homecomer has told and what they have read in magazines and seen in the movies. So it may happen that many acts which seem to the people at home the highest expression of courage are to the soldier in battle merely the struggle for survival or the fulfilment of a duty, whereas many instances of real endurance, sacrifice, and heroism remain unnoticed or unappreciated by people at home.[14]

This discrepancy between the uniqueness and decisive importance that the absent one attributes to his experiences and their pseudo-typification by the people at home, who impute to them a pseudo-relevance, is one of the biggest obstacles to mutual reestablishment of the disrupted we-relations. Yet the success or failure of the homecoming will depend upon the chance of transforming these social relations into recurrent ones. But, even if such a discrepancy did not prevail, the complete solution of this problem would remain an unrealizable ideal.

What is here in question is nothing less than the irreversibility of inner time. It is the same problem which Heraclitus visualized with his statement that we cannot bathe twice in the same river; which Bergson analyzed in his philosophy of the *durée;* which Kierkegaard described as the problem of "repetition"; which Péguy had in mind in saying that the road which leads from Paris to Chartres has a different aspect from the road which leads from Chartres to Paris; and it is the same problem which, in a some-

14   "Without exception G.I.'s most dislike tin-horn war and home-front heroics" is the summary of a poll by *Time* correspondents: "What kind of movies do G.I.'s like?" (*Time,* August 14, 1944).

what distorted fashion, occupies G. H. Mead's *Philosophy of the Present*. The mere fact that we grow older, that novel experiences emerge continuously within our stream of thought, that previous experiences are permanently receiving additional interpretative meanings in the light of these supervenient experiences, which have, more or less, changed our state of mind—all these basic features of our mental life bar a recurrence of the same. Being recurrent, the recurrent is not the same any more. Repetition might be aimed at and longed for: what belongs to the past can never be reinstated in another present exactly as it was. When it emerged, it carried along empty anticipations, horizons of future developments, references to chances and possibilities; now, in hindsight, these anticipations prove to have been or not to have been fulfilled; the perspectives have changed; what was merely in the horizon has shifted toward the center of attention or disappeared entirely; former chances have turned into realities or proved to be impossibilities—briefly, the former experience has now another meaning.

This is certainly not the place to embark upon an analysis of the highly complicated philosophical problems of time, memory, and meaning here involved. They are just mentioned for two reasons: First, in the present state of the social sciences it seems always to be useful to show that the analysis of a concrete sociological problem, if only driven far enough, necessarily leads to certain basic philosophical questions which social scientists cannot dodge by using unclarified terms such as "environment," "adjustment," "adaptation," "cultural pattern," and so on. Second, this set of problems determines decisively the form, if not the content, of the attitude of the homecomer even if he does not find that substantial changes have occurred in the life of the home group or in its relations to him. Even then, the home to which he returns is by no means the home he left or the home which he recalled and longed for during his absence. And, for the same reason, the homecomer is not the same man who left. He is neither the same for himself nor for those who await his return.

This statement holds good for any kind of home-coming. Even if we return home after a short vacation, we find that the old accustomed surroundings have received an added meaning derived from and based upon our experiences during our absence. Whatever the accompanying evaluation may be, things and men will, at least in the beginning, have another face. It will need a certain effort to transform our activities again into routine work and to reactivate our recurrent relations with men and things. No wonder, since we intended our vacation to be an interruption of our daily routine.

Homer tells of the landing of Odysseus' comrades at the island of the lotus-eaters. The lotus-eaters devised not death for the intruders but gave them a dish of their lotus flowers; and as each tasted this honey-sweet plant, the wish to return grew faint in him: he preferred to dwell forever with the lotus-eating men, feeding upon lotus and letting fade from his mind all longing for home.

To a certain extent, each homecomer has tasted the magic fruit of strangeness, be it sweet or bitter. Even amid the overwhelming longing for home there remains the wish to transplant into the old pattern something of the novel goals, of the newly discovered means to realize them, of the skills and experiences acquired abroad. We cannot be astonished, therefore, that a United States War Department survey of June, 1944,[15] showed that 40 per cent of the discharged veterans being sent back to civilian life through eastern "separation centers" did not want their old jobs back and did not want even to return to their old communities. On the Pacific Coast the percentage of those men was even greater.

A small-town newspaper celebrated the home-coming of the local hero, giving a full account of his feats of extraordinary boldness, efficient leadership, steadfastness, and willingness to assume responsibility. The recital ends with the enumeration of the decorations justly awarded to him and with the statement that Lieutenant X. had always enjoyed the good will of his community, where he had served for years as cigar clerk in a prominent local store. This case seems to be a rather typical one. A young man lives for years in a small town, a regular fellow, liked by everybody, but in an occupation which, honorable as it is, does not give him any chance to prove his worth. Quite possibly, he himself was not aware of

15   According to *Time*, June 12, 1944.

what he could perform. The war gives him such an opportunity; he makes good and receives the reward he deserves. Can we expect, can we wish, that such a man should come home not only to family and sweetheart but also to his place behind the cigar counter? Have we not to hope that Lieutenant X. will avail himself of the facilities provided by Congress in the "G.I. Bill of Rights" to obtain a position in civil life more appropriate to his gifts?

But—and here we touch upon a chief problem of the home-comer—it is unfortunately an unwarranted assumption that social functions which stood the test within one system of social life will continue to do so if transplanted into another system. This general proposition is especially applicable to the problem of the returning veteran. From the sociological point of view, army life shows a strange ambivalence. Considered as an in-group, the army is characterized by an exceptionally high degree of constraint, of discipline imposed authoritatively upon the behavior of the individual by a controlling normative structure. The sense of duty, comradeship, the feeling of solidarity, and subordination are the outstanding features developed in the individual—all this, however, within a frame of means and ends imposed by the group and not open to his own choice. These features prevail in times of peace as well as in times of war. However, in times of war they do not regulate the behavior of the members of the in-group in relation to members of the out-group—that is, the enemy. The combatant's attitude toward the enemy in battle is, and is supposed to be, rather the opposite of disciplined constraint. War is the archetype of that social structure which Durkheim calls the state of *"anomie."* The specific valor of the fighting warrior consists in his will and adroitness in overcoming the other in a desperate struggle of power, and it cannot be easily used within that pattern of civilian life which has prevailed in Western democracies. Moreover, the homecoming soldier returns to an in-group, the homeworld in the postwar period, which itself is marked by a certain degree of *anomie*, of lack of control and discipline. He finds, then, that *anomie* is no longer to be the basic structure of his relations with the out-group but is a feature of the in-group itself, toward the members of which he cannot apply the techniques permitted and required within the *anomie* situation of battle. In this civil world he will have to choose his own goals and the means to attain them and can no longer depend upon authority and guidance. He will feel, as Professor Waller puts it, like a "motherless chile."

Another factor supervenes. In times of war the members of the armed forces have a privileged status within the community as a whole. "The best for our boys in the service" is more than a mere slogan. It is the expression of prestige deservedly accorded to those who might have to give their life for their country or at least to those who left family, studies, occupation, and the amenities of civil life for a highly valued interest of the community. The civilian looks at the man in uniform as an actual or future fighter; and so, indeed, the man in uniform looks at himself, even if he performs merely desk work in an army office somewhere in the United States. This humbler occupation does not matter; to him, too, the induction marked a turning-point in his life. But the discharged homecomer is deprived of his uniform and with it of his privileged status within the community. This does not mean that he will lose, by necessity, the prestige acquired as an actual or potential defender of the homeland, although history does not show that exaggerated longevity is accorded to the memory of glory. This is partly because of the disappointment at home that the returning veteran does not correspond to the pseudo-type of the man whom they have been expecting.

This leads to a practical conclusion. Much has been done and still more will be done to prepare the homecoming veteran for the necessary process of adjustment. However, it seems to be equally indispensable to prepare the home group accordingly. They have to learn through the press, the radio, the movies, that the man whom they await will be another and not the one they imagined him to be. It will be a hard task to use the propaganda machine in the opposite direction, namely, to destroy the pseudo-type of the combatant's life and the soldier's life in general and to replace it by the truth. But it is indispensable to undo the glorification of a questionable Hollywood-made heroism by bringing out the real picture of what these men endure, how they live, and what they think and feel—a picture no less meritorious and no less evocative.

In the beginning it is not only the homeland that shows to the homecomer an unaccustomed face. The homecomer appears equally strange to those who expect him, and the thick air about him will keep him unknown. Both the homecomer and the welcomer will need the help of a Mentor to "make them wise to things."

Equality and Opportunity

The fact that equality can prevail only within the same domain of relevances, explains why we can speak of separating political equality, equality before the law, equality in wealth, equality of opportunity, religious or moral equality, etc. . . . And from the very fact that domains of relevances are defined and ordered by each social group in a different way, it follows that the content of the concept of equality is also an element of the relative natural conception of the world taken for granted by the particular social group. (Here, as everywhere in this paper, we intentionally disregard concepts of equality based on philosophical or religious principles.) To give an example for our present culture: the Universal Declaration of Human Rights of the United Nations (art. 2) proclaims moral and juridical equality, that is to say, it is equality in dignity, formal equality in rights and equality of opportunity, but not necessarily material equality as to the extent and content of the rights of all individuals.

. . . It cannot be sufficient to refer equality just to the structure of relevances and the natural conception of the world prevailing in a particular group, because both of these terms are again equivocal. The natural conception of the world prevailing in a group may be interpreted on various levels (self-interpretation, interpretation by outsiders, by scientific, and by philosophical thinking). And the term "group" itself can be stated in subjective and in objective terms. Our present endeavor is to find the subjective and objective elements in the notion of equality. . . .

Equality, in any connotation, means something different to group *A* or its individual members aspiring to obtain a position equal to another group *B*, and to group *B* with which the first one,

A, aspires to become equal, or by which it desires to be treated on an equal footing.

It was Simmel who analyzed this problem in his remarkable studies on the development of the ideas of equality and freedom in the eighteenth and nineteenth centuries, and in the chapter of his sociology dealing with superordination and subordination. Typically speaking, says Simmel, nobody is satisfied with the position he occupies with respect to his fellow men, and everybody wishes to attain a position that is in some sense more favorable.[16] Equality with the superior is the first objective that offers itself to the impulse toward one's own elevation—and, characteristically enough, equality with the immediate superior. Yet this equality is merely a point of transition. Myriad experiences have shown that once the subordinate is equal to the superior this condition, which previously was the essential aim of his endeavor, is merely a starting point for a further effort, the first station on the unending road to the most favored position. Wherever an attempt is made at effecting equalization, the individual's striving to surpass others comes to the fore in all possible forms on the newly reached stage. But, says Simmel, it makes a characteristic difference whether this attempt at winning cherished values is to be obtained by means of abolishing what he calls the "sociological form" (and what we should call the prevailing system of relevances and their order) or whether it is to be obtained *within* this form, which is thereby preserved.

Doubtless the meaning of equality is a different one for those who are aspiring to an equal position with the superior, whether a superordinate individual or a "predominant" group, and for those in the privileged position who are required to grant equal treatment.

An example can be seen in the analysis of . . . two types of minorities. . . . To minority groups of the type (a), assimilation is the kind of equality aimed-at. To those of type (b), however, *real* equality is the kind aimed-at; that is, obtaining special rights such as the use of their national languages in schools, before the courts,

16   Kurt H. Wolff, ed., *The Sociology of Georg Simmel* (Glencoe, Ill.: The Free Press, 1950), p. 275.

etc. The history of the cultural struggle of national minorities in the old Austro-Hungarian monarchy is an excellent instance of the point in question. The predominant group may interpret equality-to-be-granted as *formal* equality, and may even be willing to concede full equality before the law and full political equality, and yet resist bitterly any claim to special rights. Another instance is the different interpretation of the rank order of discrimination by white man and by Negro.

Of particular significance for the twofold interpretation of equality under scrutiny is, however, Simmel's previously noted observation, that it makes a characteristic difference whether tensions of this kind can be solved by shifts within the prevailing common system of relevance, or whether this system itself must be abolished. The first attitude is characteristic of conservative thinking, the second, of revolutionary thinking. Those in the privileged position will interpret equality-to-be-granted in terms of the former, while those who aim at obtaining equality frequently interpret it in terms of the latter. . . .

The difficulty of analyzing the notion of equal opportunity consists in the fact that not only . . . does the term equality have different meaning in subjective and objective interpretation, but the term "opportunity" also permits of a twofold interpretation. We start with an analysis of the notion of opportunity in the objective sense. . . .

In the objective sense a social group is a structural-functional system formed by a web of interconnected interaction processes, social roles, positions, and statuses. Not the concrete individual or the concrete person, but the role, is the conceptual unit of the social system. Each role carries along a particular set of role expectations which any incumbent of the role is expected to fulfil.

In our terminology these role expectations are nothing but typifications of interaction patterns which are socially approved ways of solving typical problems, and are frequently institutionalized. Consequently, they are arranged in domains of relevances which in turn are ranked in a particular order originating in the group's relative natural conception of the world, its folkways, mores, morals, etc.

We may express the same idea in terms of institutionalization by interpreting the social system as an interlaced network of positions, each defined by a socially approved typification of particular interaction-patterns. These typifications also establish the requirements of the position, its authority and duty, to which any incumbent of this position, whoever he may be, has to live up. They also determine the abilities, skills, or fitness—in brief, the competence and qualifications—each incumbent is supposed to have in order adequately to fulfil his functions. The conclusions would naturally follow that only qualified persons should be eligible for such positions.

The postulate of equal opportunity in the objective sense is mostly stated in the form of the slogan, "The career open to the talents." In this form it means, however, something more: not only competent persons should be eligible, but *all* competent persons, regardless of any other criteria, should be equally eligible, it being understood that among all the *eligible* persons the best qualified should obtain the position. The French Declaration of Human Rights of 1789 postulates that

all are equally eligible for all honors, places, and employments, according to their different abilities without any distinction other than that created by their virtues and talents.

This postulate corresponds to Aristotle's notion of distributive justice, that award should be granted according to merit. But Aristotle had already stated that the concept of "merit" is different for each society. In our terminology we should say it is the relative natural conception of the world that determines, or at least codetermines, the competences and qualifications everyone eligible for a position has to possess. The reference of the definition of these qualifications to the natural conception of the world prevailing in the particular group leads frequently to the consequence that elements are included in the definition which have no, or merely a remote connection with the proper fulfilment of the particular position. It is, for instance, characteristic of the present American scene that the qualifications required for certain jobs exclude from eligibility, as they do not in other countries of the West, persons over thirty-five years of age. . . .

Consideration must next be given to the subjective meaning of opportunity, that is, the meaning this notion has for the individual who in objective terms would be eligible to avail himself of an opportunity. Such an individual experiences what we have defined in the objective sense as an opportunity, as a possibility for self-realization that stands to his choice, as a chance given to him, as a likelihood of attaining his goals in terms of his private definition of his situation within the group.

This subjective chance[17] exists, however, from the subjective viewpoint of the objectively qualified individual, only under several conditions: (1) the individual has to be aware of the existence of such a chance; (2) the chance has to be within his reach, compatible with his private system of relevances, and has to fit into his situation as defined by him; (3) the objectively defined typifications of role expectations have to be, if not congruent, then at least consistent with the individual's self-typification, in other words, he has to be convinced that he can live up to the requirements of his position; (4) the role for which the individual is eligible has to be compatible with all the other social roles in which he is involved with a part of his personality.

It can readily be seen that opportunities which are equal from the objective point of view may be, and in a strict sense must be, unequal in terms of the subjective chances of the particular individual, and *vice versa*. This is so because, merely from the *objective* viewpoint, social roles constitute the conceptual unit of the social system that can be typified and defined in terms of role expectations and competence. Moreover, merely from the objective viewpoint, everyone with equal qualifications can be deemed an equally eligible incumbent of the role.

From the *subjective* viewpoint, however, the individual does not look at himself as an eligible incumbent of a social role, but as a human being, who is involved in multiple social relations and

---

[17]   We prefer to keep this technical term coined by Max Weber despite the fact that the English translators (Weber, *The Theory of Social and Economic Organization*, tr. Talcott Parsons and M. Henderson (New York: Oxford University Press, 1947), have rendered it for reasons explained by them (p. 100, n. 21) by "probability" and sometimes by "likelihood."

group memberships, in each of which he participates with a part of his personality. Hence, even if it made sense to assume that equal subjective chances correspond to objectively equal opportunities, the individual human being would weigh the chances in terms of his personal hopes, anxieties, and passions, which are his alone.

Strictly speaking, therefore, equal opportunity exists merely from the objective point of view. The subjective chances are unequal and as we learned from Plato . . . to unequals equals become unequal.

Nevertheless, the ideal of equal opportunity in the objective sense is worthwhile fighting for. It should not, however, be so interpreted that the effect of its realization would be to provide "an equal start for everyone." Most of the authors dealing with this problem have referred to many factors that make an equal start impossible: differences of wealth, the pressure of mere material surroundings such as housing, sanitation, etc., economic conditions (such as the fact that only few men can devote their energies to education until manhood without being compelled to compete early for employment, or the inequality of access to information, particularly to financial information), are among them. Perhaps inequality of leisure time should be added to this catalogue. . . .

But the ideal of equality of opportunity may mean something else, although something far more modest. It should assure to the individual who finds himself in the human bondage of his various group memberships the right to the pursuit of happiness . . . and, therewith—in terms of his own definition—the maximum of self-realization which his situation in the social reality permits.

EPILOGUE: SOCIAL SCIENCE
MAKES SENSE

Where can the scientist find the guarantee that he is establishing a real unified system? Where are the scientific tools to perform that difficult task? The answer is that in every branch of the social sciences which has arrived at the theoretical stage of its development there is a fundamental hypothesis which both defines the fields of research and gives the regulative principle for building up the system of ideal types. Such a fundamental hypothesis, for instance, is in classical economics the utilitarian principle, and in modern economics the marginal principle. The sense of this postulate is the following: "Build your ideal types as if all actors had oriented their life plan and, therefore, all their activities to the chief end of realising the greatest utility with the minimum of costs; human activity which is oriented in such a way (and only this kind of human activity) is the subject matter of your science."

But at the back of all these statements arises a very disturbing question. If the social world as object of our scientific research is but a typical construction, why bother with this intellectual game? Our scientific activity and, particularly, that which deals with the social world, is also performed within a certain means-ends relation, namely, in order to acquire knowledge for mastering the world, the real world, not the one created by the grace of the scientist. We want to find out what happens in the real world and not in the fantasies of a few sophisticated eccentrics.

There are a few arguments for quieting such an interlocutor. First of all, the construction of the scientific world is not an arbitrary act of the scientist which he can perform at his own discretion:

Reprinted from the following item in the Bibliography: 1943, 148–49.

1. There are the historical boundaries of the realm of his science which each scientist has inherited from his ancestors as a stock of approved propositions.

2. The postulate of adequacy requires that the typical construction be compatible with the totality of both our daily life and our scientific experience. . . .

The social scientist, therefore, may continue his work in full confidence. His clarified methods, governed by the postulates mentioned, give him the assurance that he will never lose contact with the world of daily life. And as long as he uses with success methods which have stood this test and still do so, he is quite right in continuing without worrying about methodological problems. Methodology is not the preceptor or the tutor of the scientist. It is always his pupil, and there is no great master in his scientific field who could not teach the methodologists how to proceed. But the really great teacher always has to learn from his pupils. Arnold Schönberg, the famous composer, starts the preface to his masterly book on the theory of harmony with the sentence: "This book I have learned from my pupils." In this rôle, the methodologist has to ask intelligent questions about the technique of his teacher. And if those questions help others to think over what they really do, and perhaps to eliminate certain intrinsic difficulties hidden in the foundation of the scientific edifice where the scientists never set foot, methodology has performed its task.

Glossary of Selected Terms

Schutz's writings are interspersed with terms which are either germane to phenomenology or which have been redefined by phenomenologists. In order to help the reader who is not familiar with this terminology, such terms have been assembled and explained here.

Apperception. The spontaneous interpretation of sensory perception in terms of past experiences and previously acquired knowledge of the perceived object.

Apprehension. The mental grasp not only of perceptions but also of recollections and images of phantasy.

Appresentation. An actual experience which refers to another experience not perceptionally given. For example, when perceiving an object, we immediately add to our mental image of it aspects which are not within the range of our perception, such as the color and shape of its back.

Attention. Active attention rests in the full alertness and the sharpness of apperception connected with consciously turning toward an object, etc., combined with further considerations and anticipations, etc., of its characteristics and uses. An *act of attention* is a "free act" of willfully and selectively turning toward, or alertly paying attention to, certain features, objects, etc., in the actual given environment at a specific moment.

Attitude. A general posture or stance taken toward larger spheres of life and interest, including a particular "style" of thinking, for example: the common-sense attitude; the scientific attitude.

Bracketing. A methodological device of phenomenological inquiry consisting in a deliberate effort to set all ontological judgments about the "nature" and "essence" of things, events, etc., aside. Thereby, the "reality" of things and events is not denied but "put into brackets." This procedure makes the mental processes of experiencing into the central subject matter of phenomenology.

Cogitation. The term is used in the broadest sense, including volitions, feelings, and emotions as well as rational thought.

Cognitive style. The style governing conduct and experiencing when being involved in a particular realm of experience, such as everyday life, poetry, science. It involves different degrees of alertness and inattention, focusing and diffuseness, critical scrutiny and blind acceptance, etc., and it influences one's perception of himself and of others, but also his experience of time.

Constitution. The term refers to the constitution of thought objects *(cogitata)* and indicates the processes of clarification of meaning, establishment of meaning context, and mobilization of prior knowledge concerning specific objects of the ongoing conscious life. It is a cumulative process in which the cognitive results of repeated experiences of the "same object" are deposited ("sedimented") in the mind.

Deliberation. The "experience of doubt, of questioning, of choosing and deciding" (Schutz). Deliberation may lead to the constitution and revision of thought objects or to decisions on a specific course of action.

Doubt. A situation of doubt arises when a person can no longer take a situation for granted because certain if not all elements in it defy explanation in terms of his knowledge at hand. Doubt may lead to resignation, to inquiry, to a redefinition of the situation, or to replanning of action.

Eidetic approach. The main level of phenomenological inquiry. It serves the establishment of the "essential" features and characteristics of concrete objects of apperception. Eidetic features of thought objects consist of general meanings as constituted by cognitive processes.

Eidos. The "essential" or general characteristics of any perceivable object, in contrast to its varying empirical features. Eidos belongs to the sphere of meanings in which objects of perception and cogitation are constituted.

Epoché. - The suspension of belief in the ontological characteristics of experienced objects, etc. Each basic realm of human experience (everyday life, science, etc.) has its particular epoché.

Evidence. That which, in the light of a person's accumulated experiences and knowledge, appears as unquestionably true.

Experience. The basic starting point of all phenomenological considerations is the *essential actual,* or *immediately vivid,* experience, that is, the subjective, spontaneously flowing *stream of experience* in which the individual lives and which, as a stream of consciousness, carries with it spontaneous linkages, memory traces, etc., of other, prior, experiences. Experience becomes *subjectively meaningful experience* only by an act of reflection in which an essentially actual experience, in retrospect, is consciously apprehended and cognitively constituted. In the course of his life, a person compiles a *stock of experience,* which enables him to define the situations in which he finds himself and to guide his conduct in them.

Founded objects. Objects in the environment of a person upon which he bestows a specific intentional meaning.

Gearing into the world. Said of all human action which affects the objects, persons, and events of the "outer world" of a person's environment.

Horizon. A phenomenon characteristic of all mental experiences and cognitive efforts. There is a core, or "kernel," of each apperception, recollection, problem, etc., which is surrounded by a "fringe" of related, at the moment not central, impressions, factors, memories, considerations, expectations, etc. Together, they form the horizon of the given phase of mental awareness. The fringe areas may be structured (e.g.: foreground, middleground, background) and thus form several horizons around the same core of conscious experience.

Idealization. A general principle issuing from many kinds of past experiences and expressing confident expectations concerning future experiences. For example, with the idealization of "I can do it again," the conviction of the reliability and basic stability of the world of everyday life is expressed.

Immediacy. The fundamental characteristic of all actual experience, of experiencing. Immediacy is spatial and temporal: here and now.

Intentionality. The most basic characteristic of consciousness: it is always the consciousness of something; it is directed toward something, and in turn is "determined by the intentional object *whereof* it is a consciousness" (Schutz). The *intentional object,* then, is the object intended and meant by the individual, and singled out by him for apperceptional and cognitive attention. An *intentional act* is any act in and through which a person experiences an object, whether physical or ideal. Through it, the object itself is cognitively constituted.

Interest. The specific motivational focus which determines, in a specific situation, a person's definition of the situation and his particular objective, purpose, or other guideline of conduct. The situationally concrete interest is called *interest at hand.*

Intersubjectivity. A category which, in general, refers to what is (especially cognitively) common to various individuals. In daily life, a person takes the existence of others for granted. He reasons and acts on the self-understood assumption that these others are basically persons like himself, endowed with consciousness and will, desires and emotions. The bulk of one's ongoing life experiences confirms and reinforces the conviction that, in principle and under "normal" circumstances, persons in contact with one another "understand" each other at least to the degree to which they are able to deal successfully with one another. Phenomenologists have posed the *problem of intersubjectivity.* In terms of phenomenological psychology, this problem may be subdivided into two questions: (1) How is the "other Self" constituted in my mind as a Self of basically the same (eidetic) characteristics as my own Self? (2) How is the experience of a successful intercourse with another Self possible, or: how is the experience of my "understanding" the other, and his "understanding" me, constituted?

Knowledge. For a person in everyday life, knowledge is whatever he thinks is the case. Essentially, it concerns practical matters and, frequently, consists of recipes for all kinds of conduct and activity. Common-sense knowledge may range from near-expertness to extreme vagueness. What a person knows, in toto, is his *stock of knowledge.* As a whole, this stock is incoherent, inconsistent, and only partially clear. It serves its purposes adequately as long as its recipes yields satisfactory results in acting, and its tenets satisfactory explanations. By contrast, philosophical and scientific knowledge serves purely intellectual interests and is subject to controls, principles of coherence and consistency, etc.

Life Plan. The "supreme system" of overall objectives and guidelines for an individual's life as a whole, in contrast to plans for limited periods and objectives. Such a plan does not have to be deliberate; it may be imposed; and it may change in the course of a person's life.

Life-World; also: *World of everyday life.* The total sphere of experiences of an individual which is cicumscribed by the objects, persons, and events encountered in the pursuit of the pragmatic objectives of living. It is a "world" in which a person is "wide-awake," and which asserts itself as the "paramount reality" of his life.

Meaning. The meaning of an experience is established, in retrospect, through interpretation. *Subjective meaning* is that meaning which a person ascribes to his own experiences and actions. *Objective meaning* is the meaning imputed to the conduct of another person by an observer. All human conduct appears in a *subjective meaning context.* The meaningful self-interpretation of conduct consists in relating specific experiences to other experiences in the light of one's interests and motives involved. By contrast, interpretation of the conduct of another person consists in relating the observed conduct to an *objective meaning context,* consisting of preestablished generalized and typified conceptions.

Monothetic—polythetic—synthetic. Modes of apperception, apprehension, comprehension, etc. Any object of experience may be seen "in one single ray" or *monothetically.* This may be so even though the object itself can only be grasped *polythetically,* that is, in a sequence of steps following each other in time, like the presentation of an idea in the unfolding speech of a person. The communicative action of the speaker, on its part, constitutes a *polythetic act.* The successive statements of his speech become *synthetic* because its polythetic elements are posited together and, eventually, form a complex unit. In retrospect, the synthetic unit of polythetic elements may blend into a single idea, and become a *monothetic object.*

Natural Attitude. The mental stance a person takes in the spontaneous and routine pursuits of his daily affairs, and the basis of his interpretation of the life world as a whole and in its various aspects. The life world is the *world of the natural attitude.* In it, things are taken for granted.

Noema and Noesis. The *noema* is the intentional object, the thing apperceived and experienced. *Noesis* is the process of experiencing.

Objectivity. The mental stance of the disinterested onlooker. Basically, the *objective point of view* is the point of view of the detached observer.

Outer World. That sphere of apperceived objects, persons, and events to which the experiencing individual ascribes "real existence" outside of his own mind.

Pairing. A crucial feature of appresentation. It occurs whenever we, from cognitive necessity, appresent characteristics with a perceived phenomenon which do not perceptionally appear but without which we are unable to think the perceived object. For example, we directly perceive the moving body of another person, and we necessarily pair it with our general notion of an alter ego.

Phenomenological reduction. The basic procedure of phenomenological method. Through "bracketing" of all judgments about the ontological nature of the perceived objects, etc., and by disregarding their uniqueness, that which is given in cognitive experience is reduced to the "essentials" of its form.

Predicative experience. Indirect experience of objects, etc. It is based on interpretative judgments, made under utilization of one's preexisting store of knowledge, and it consists in predicating certain characteristics to objects, etc., outside one's realm of personal acquaintance.

Prepredicative experience. The direct experience of objects, persons, etc. It establishes the prepredicative, or directly given, knowledge of them.

Protention—Retention. Protention designates an experience expected to follow immediately after the present experience. *Retention* refers to the remembrance of an experience which has just passed.

Reach. The range of a person's cognitive or manipulative grasp of his environment. Objects, etc., in his environmental "world" are either within his *actual reach*, or in his *potential* or *attainable reach*, or have been in his actual and are now in *restorable reach*; finally, they may be situated in a "world beyond his reach" and control.

Relevance. The importance ascribed by an individual to selected aspects, etc., of specific situations and of his activities and plans. In accordance with a person's multifarious interests and involvements, there exist various *domains of relevance* for him. Together, they form his *system of relevances* with its own priorities and preferences, not necessarily always clearly distinguished and not necessarily stable for longer periods. At any particular time, however, this system falls into specific *zones* of primary or minor relevances and of relative irrelevance. Insofar as relevances spring from a person's own interests and motivations, they are *volitional*. If they are urged upon him either by situational conditions or by social imposition, they are *imposed*. Thus, *social systems of relevance* are imposed. *Common relevances* occur in direct interpersonal involvement (We-relations).

Sedimentation. The process by which elements of knowledge, their interpretations and implications are integrated into the layers of previously acquired knowledge. The sedimented items are fused with existing typifications, etc., or form the core of new ones. Either way they become a person's "habitual possessions." The "experiencing activities" of the human consciousness, then, constitute a person's stock of knowledge by way of sedimentation.

Spontaneity. The basic mode of immediate, essentially active, experience. It means being immersed in ongoing experience and excludes self-awareness.

Subjectivity. In the immediate sense, the term refers exclusively to the experiences, cogitations, motives, etc., of a concrete individual. Strictly speaking, the *subjective meaning* inherent in conduct is always the meaning which the acting person ascribes to his own conduct: it consists of his motives, that is, both his reasons for acting and his objectives, his immediate or long-range plans, his definition of the situation and of other persons, his conception of his own role in the given situation, etc. Genuine subjectivity must be distinguished from the *subjective point of view* of sociological observers who hold that subjective meanings are crucial factors in all interactional relationships under study. Dealing with them, they use specific frames of reference, that is, sets of objective concepts which refer to the subjectivity of human conduct. Methodologically, these concepts differ in no way from those of an objective point of view. The difference is one of subject matter and the procedure by which sociological information is obtained. The only direct source of subjective information is the observed individual himself. The application of an objective frame of reference honoring the subjective point of view leads to the sociological analysis of the gathered subjective information and leads to the *subjective interpretation* of social phenomena.

Tension of consciousness. The attentive state of consciousness which varies in different realms of experience, ranging from "full awakeness in the reality of everyday life to sleep in the world of dreams" (Schutz).

They orientation. The orientation upon others with whom we have no direct dealings and of whose existence we have but vague general notions. For example, entrusting a letter to the mail with the expectation that "someone" (mailmen as general type) will see to it that it reaches its destination.

Thou orientation. The orientation upon another person with whom one is in direct, that is, face-to-face contact and of whom one conceives as a specific person.

Understanding—Verstehen. To understand, in general, means to comprehend the meaning of something. What is understood is meaningful. Understanding is the basis of all interactive intersubjectivity. Persons deal with one another successfully only to the degree to which they reciprocally understand each other's motives, intentions, etc., at least to the degree to which this is relevant to their purposes on hand. Understanding is "the experiential form of common-sense knowledge of human affairs" (Schutz). *Sociological understanding* is the result of a sociologist's subjective interpretation of the phenomena of human conduct which he studies. As such, it belongs to the objective realm of sociological method and interpretative theory.

We-relationship. The relationship which ensues when two persons, dealing with one another in a face-to-face situation, consider each other reciprocally in a Thou orientation. It is consumed in a period of participation in each other's life, however short. No emotional attachment is presupposed.

World. The term refers to subjective experience and comprehension. It is, first, a world of somebody, namely the concretely experiencing individual, and second, the world of a more or less specific sphere of experience. In the directly subjective sense, a world is the totality of a specific sphere of experience as seen and understood by a specific individual at a particular time and under specific circumstances. Any individual may live successively, alternatively, or occasionally, in an indetermined number of worlds: the life world, the world of play and pretention, the world of dreams, etc. The application of the term *world* to these multiple spheres of experience is subjectively justified in that, for the experiencing individual, the sphere in which he finds himself at the moment is indeed the whole world. Objectively, for the phenomenological sociologist, each sphere is limited and of mere relative relevance. Therefore, he prefers to call it a "finite province of meaning."

Bibliography of the
Writings of Alfred Schutz

I. Books

1932   *Der Sinnhafte Aufbau der sozialen Welt.* Vienna: Springer, 1932. 2d ed., unchanged, Vienna: Springer, 1960.

1967   *The Phenomenology of the Social World.* Translated by George Walsh and Frederick Lehnert. Evanston, Ill.: Northwestern University Press, 1967.

1970   *Reflections on the Problem of Relevance.* Edited, Annotated, and with an Introduction by Richard M. Zahner. New Haven, Conn.: Yale University Press, 1970.

CP I   *Collected Papers I: The Problem of Social Reality.* Edited and Introduced by Maurice Natanson. With a Preface by H. L. Van Breda. The Hague: Nijhoff, 1962.

CP II   *Collected Papers II: Studies in Social Theory.* Edited and Introduced by Arvid Brodersen. The Hague: Nijhoff, 1964.

CP III *Collected Papers III: Studies in Phenomenological Philosophy.* Edited by Ilse Schutz. With an Introduction by Aron Gurwitsch. The Hague: Nijhoff, 1966.

II. Papers and Essays

1940a "Phenomenology and the Social Sciences." In Marvin Farber (ed.), *Philosophical Essays in Memory of Edmund Husserl.* Cambridge, Mass.: Harvard University Press, 1940; 164–86. CP I, 118–39.

1940b "Editor's Preface" to "Edmund Husserl: Notizen zur Raumkonstitution." *Philosophy and Phenomenological Research* 1,1 (1940):21–23.

1941   "William James' Concept of the Stream of Thought Phenomenologically Interpreted." *Philosophy and Phenomenological Research* 1,4 (1941):442–52. CP III, 1–14.

1942 "Scheler's Theory of Intersubjectivity and the General Thesis of the Alter Ego." *Philosophy and Phenomenological Research* 2,3 (1942):323–47. CP I, 150–79.

1943 "The Problem of Rationality in the Social World." *Economica* 23d Year: New Series 10,38 (1943):130–49. CP II, 64–88.

1944 "The Stranger: An Essay in Social Psychology." *American Journal of Sociology* 49,6 (1944):499–507. CP II, 91–105.

1945a "The Homecomer." *American Journal of Sociology* 50,5 (1945): 369–76. CP II, 106–19.

1945b "Some Leading Concepts of Phenomenology." *Social Research* 12,1 (1945):77–97. CP I, 99–117.

1945c "On Multiple Realities." *Philosophy and Phenomenological Research* 5,4 (1945):533–76. CP I, 207–59.

1946 "The Well-Informed Citizen: An Essay on the Social Distribution of Knowledge." *Social Research* 13,4 (1946):463–78. CP II, 120–34.

1948 "Sartre's Theory of the Alter Ego." *Philosophy and Phenomenological Research* 9,2 (1948):181–99. CP I, 180–203.

1950a "Language, Language Disturbances, and the Texture of Consciousness." *Social Research* 17,3 (1950):365–94. CP I, 260–86.

1950b "Felix Kaufmann: 1895–1949." *Social Research* 17,1 (1950):1–7.

1951a "Choosing Among Projects of Action." *Philosophy and Phenomenological Research* 12,2 (1951):161–84. CP I, 67–96.

1951b "Making Music Together: A Study in Social Relationships." *Social Research* 18,1 (1951):76–97. CP II, 159–78.

1952 "Santayana on Society and Government." *Social Research* 19,2 (1952):220–46. CP II, 201–25.

1953a "Discussion: Edmund Husserl's Ideas, Volume II." *Philosophy and Phenomenological Research* 13,3 (1953):394–413. CP III, 15–39.

1953b "Discussion: Die Phänomenologie und die Fundamente der Wissenschaften (Ideas III. By Edmund Husserl)." *Philosophy and Phenomenological Research* 13,4 (1953):506–14. CP III, 40–50.

1953c "Common Sense and Scientific Interpretation of Human Action." *Philosophy and Phenomenological Research* 14,1 (1953):1–37. CP I, 3–47.

1954 "Concept and Theory Formation in the Social Sciences." *The Journal of Philosophy* 51,9 (1954):257–74. CP I, 48–66.

1955a "Don Quijote y el problema de la realidad." translated by Professor and Mrs. Luis Recasens-Siches. *Dianoia,* Anuario de Filosofia, 1,1 (1955) :312–30. English under the title, "Don Quixote and the Problem of Reality." In CP II, 135–58.

1955b "Symbol, Reality and Society." Chapter 7 of Lyman Bryson, Louis Finkelstein, Hudson Hoagland, and R. M. MacIver, *Symbols and Society:* Fourteenth Symposium on Science, Philosophy, and Religion. New York: Conference on Science, Philosophy, and Religion, 1955. Distributed by Harper and Brothers. CP I, 287–356.

1956a "Mozart and the Philosophers." *Social Research* 23,2 (1956): 219–42. CP II, 179–200.

1956b "Max Scheler: 1874–1928." French Translation in Maurice Merleau-Ponty (ed.), *Les philosophes célèbres.* Paris: Lucien Mazenod, 1956; 330–35.

"Max Scheler's Philosophy." Original English text published in CP III, 133–44.

1957a "Equality and the Meaning Structure of the Social World." in Lyman Bryson, Clarence H. Faust, and Louis Finkelstein (eds.), *Aspects of Human Equality.* New York: Conference on Science, Philosophy and Religion in their Relation to the Democratic Way of Life, Inc. 1956. Distributed by Harper and Brothers, New York. CP II, 226–73.

1957b "Das Problem der transzendentalen Intersubjectivität by Husserl." *Philosophische Rundschau:* Eine Vierteljahresschrift für Philosophische Kritik, 5 (1957) :81 ff.

"The Problem of Transcendental Intersubjectivity in Husserl." CP III, 51–84.

"Le problème de l'intersubjectivité transcendentale chez Husserl." *Husserl,* Cahiers de Royaumont, Philosophie No. 3. Paris: Les Editions de Minuit, 1959.

1957c "Answer to Comments Made in the Discussion of 'The Problem of Transcendental Intersubjectivity in Husserl' (Royaumont; April 28, 1957.)" Translation from the German original in CP III, 87–91.

1957d "Max Scheler's Epistemology and Ethics, I." *Review of Metaphysics* 11, 2 (December 1957) :304–14. CP III, 144–54.

1958a "Max Scheler's Epistemology and Ethics: II." *Review of Metaphysics* 11, 3 (March 1958) :486–501. CP III, 163–78.

1958b "Some Equivocations of the Notion of Responsibility." In Sidney

Hook (ed.), *Determinism and Freedom*. New York: New York University Press, 1958; 206–8. CP II, 274–76.

1959a   "Tiresias, or Our Knowledge of Future Events." *Social Research* 26,1 (1959) :71–89. CP II, 277–93.

1959b   "Type and Eidos in Husserl's Late Philosophy." *Philosophy and Phenomenological Research* 20,2 (1959) :147–65. CP III, 92–115.

1959c   "Husserl's Importance for the Social Sciences." In H. L. van Breda et al. (eds.), *Edmund Husserl, 1859–1959*. Recueil commémoratif publié à l'occasion du centenaire de la naissance du philosophe. Vol. 4 of the series, *Phaenomenologica*. The Hague; Nijhoff, 1959; 86–98. CP I, 140–49.

1960   "The Social World and the Theory of Social Action." *Social Research* 27,2 (1960) :203–21. CP II, 3–19.

1966a   "Some Structures of the Life World." CP III, 116–32.

1966b   "Scheler's Criticism of Kant's Philosophy." CP III, 155–63.

III. *Unpublished Works*

"Parsons' Theory of Social Action." Essay written in 1940.

"Die Strukturen der Lebenswelt." Outlines for a book-length manuscript. The work on the completion of this manuscript is being carried out by Professor Thomas Luckmann of the University of Frankfurt a.M. An English translation is also in preparation.